CURUCUCU

THE ADVENTURES OF A
BRITISH EX-PAT IN COLOMBIA

Ben Curry

Foreword by Louis de Bernières

HELLGATE PRESS   ASHLAND, OREGON

CURUCUCÚ

©2010 Ben Curry

Published by Hellgate Press (An imprint of L&R Publishing, LLC)

Hellgate Press
PO Box 3531
Ashland, OR 97520

email: info@hellgatepress.com

Editor: Harley B. Patrick
Cover design: L.I. Redding
Front and back cover photos: Brian Moser

Library of Congress Cataloging-in-Publication Data

Curry, Ben, 1950-
  Curucucú : the adventures of a British ex-pat in Colombia / Ben Curry ; foreword by Louis de Bernières
      p. cm.
    ISBN 978-1-55571-675-2
  1. Curry, Ben, 1950---Travel--Colombia. 2. Colombia--Description and travel. 3. Colombia--Social life and customs. 4. British--Colombia--Biography. I. Title.
    F2264.2.C87 2010
    918.6104'63092--dc22
                        2010034168

Printed and bound in the United States of America
First edition 10 9 8 7 6 5 4 3 2 1

To the memory of my wife, Jill,
and for our family who helped to make Curucucú a home,
and for their children's children

CURUCUCÚ

THE ADVENTURES OF A
BRITISH EX-PAT IN COLOMBIA

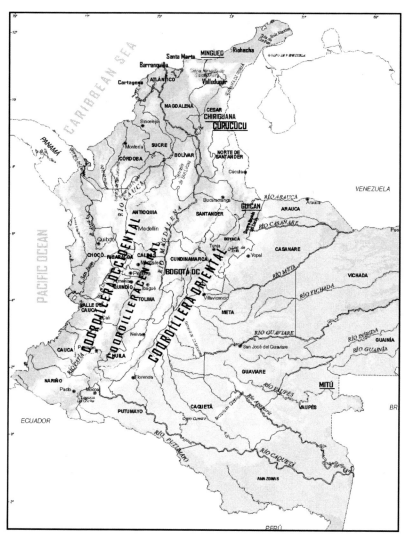

Map of Colombia.

Contents

The Road Not Taken
A Poem by Robert Frost

Two roads diverged in a yellow wood,
And sorry I could not travel both
And be one traveller, long I stood
And looked down one as far as I could
To where it bent in the undergrowth;

Then took the other, as just as fair,
And having perhaps the better claim,
Because it was grassy and wanted wear;
Though as for that the passing there
Had worn them really about the same.

And both that morning equally lay
In leaves no step had trodden black.
Oh, I kept the first for another day!
Yet knowing how way leads on to way,
I doubted if I should ever come back.

I shall be telling this with a sigh
Somewhere ages and ages hence:
Two roads diverged in a wood, and I—
I took the one less travelled by,
And that has made all the difference.

Acknowledgments

In gratitude to the following:

My grandfather, the Rev. A.A.Isherwood, who made me aware of reverence.

My father, W.B.Curry, Headmaster of Dartington Hall School, who gave me an understanding of intellectual integrity.

My mother, Ena Isherwood Curry, who first made me aware of love.

My aunt, Margaret Isherwood, who shared her joy of poetry.

My aunt, Helen Isherwood, who demonstrated the truth of spirituality.

Dorothy and Leonard Elmhirst, whose concern for humanity created a community at Dartington Hall where art, music and beauty were more important than worldly success.

G.W.Taylor, English master at Fountain Valley School, Colorado, U.S.A., who introduced me to the art of writing.

My sister, Anne, and her husband, Lin Wyant, who provided me with a home while I struggled with the first draft of this book.

Joan Brady for advice in organising its contents.

Matthew Leighton, Brian Moser and Roger Perry for permission to illustrate the text with their photographs.

E.J.H. Corner F.R.S., Emeritus Professor of Tropical Botany at Cambridge, whose inspiration, humanity and humour helped me make decisions.

Ishbel Campbell whose astonishing generosity once saved my life.

Nan Plummer whose patient devotion, encouragement and editing helped prepare the manuscript.

Edgar Castro of Migueo, Guajira, for his courteous patience in teaching me how to use a lap-top without losing my temper.

The host of Colombians who helped me with their advice, support and companionship.

In particular, I say "thank you" to Adriano Palomino Barasa, Lucho Olfidio Hernandez and Sofanor Molina Perez.

Without the contributions, suggestions, inspiration and help of these and many other friends, this book would never have been attempted and certainly never finished.

Foreword

There are in anyone's life a few people who have an extraordinary and disproportionate influence upon it, sometimes quite unintentionally. In my own case Ben Curry stepped out of the shadows as if by fate pre-ordained.

I had been expected by my family to make a military career, and I had myself expected to do so until it was almost too late. I managed to complete four months of officer training at Sandhurst before realising that if I became any more desperate I would either go mad or have to kill myself. Although I enjoyed rushing about on assault courses and having ludicrous mock-battles with Ghurkas, I did not like being told what to do, and neither did I have any interest in telling anyone else what to do. Furthermore, those were the times when almost everyone of my background and generation just wanted to learn the guitar, grow our hair, pretend to be pacifists, and be the next Bob Dylan. In the army I felt as if I had been abducted by aliens, and I was convinced that the warrant officers who yelled insults in my face were actually psychopaths. A friend of my grandmother's died, and left me just enough money to buy myself out.

The atmosphere at home was exceedingly bad, as my parents were deeply disappointed in me, but I worked for some time as a garden stoneworker's assistant, and wondered if I had completely messed up my life before I had even started it. I was not remotely suited to any career that required me to wear a tie or be obedient.

Providence intervened in the form of a friend who had an uncle who was an anthropologist who knew a farmer in South America who needed a tutor for his wife's children. Don Ben was that farmer, and he came over to England to interview me. I motorcycled on a single-cylinder machine from Surrey to the West Country to see him. In order to determine whether I was tough enough for Colombia, Ben suggested we go skinny-dipping in a wild, rocky, and freezing sea on a blustery and sunless day. I passed the test, and have been puzzling ever since as to how it demonstrated my suitability for the tropics.

The next time I saw Ben it was at the base camp of an RAF mountaineering expedition in the Sierra Nevada de Santa Marta. It is a miracle to me that I ever found him. I had landed at Barranquilla airport, where I was instantly stupefied by the heat. Getting out of the aeroplane was like having a hot wet blanket suddenly popped over my head by kidnappers. From a phone box I rang up somebody with a Welsh name who worked for a farm machinery company called the Casa Inglesa. He was definitely not Welsh, but he came to the airport anyway, picked me up, and let me sleep the night at his house. The next morning he alerted the Casa Inglesa in Valledupar, and put me on a plane. It was a Dakota painted cheerfully in red, and it was too tired to go very high. We wove past hills and mountains, whilst air hostesses in red skirts and high heels tottered about heroically amid the turbulence with trays of orange juice. In Valledupar I was again given hospitality by a complete stranger, whose family spent its spare time watching a television that displayed only parallel black and white lines that travelled successively from the bottom of the screen to the top. The following morning I was put on a taxi to Atanquez. The taxi was a Russian jeep with dozens of people hanging off it at every possible angle, the road was a ruin, and Atanquez was a sad little town where everyone slept in hammocks and lived off yams and salted fish. I waited there until a mule-train of Kogi Indians arrived to collect supplies for the mountaineers. I once saw a television programme that maintained that the Kogi were a hidden race which had had no contact with the outside world for hundreds of years. That was rubbish of course, but it is true that not one of them spoke a word to me for three days. They were impressive people dressed in heavy white linen robes with domed hats of the same material. They carried antique muskets, and constantly pounded coca leaves with snail shells in a small gourd, which they then sucked off the pestle. They had sandals made of car tyres, and their calf muscles were as developed as a rugby player's thighs. On the three day climb I saw hummingbirds and condors, and the most fantastic vegetation that became more and more weird as the altitude increased. I was wide-eyed with wonder, and didn't feel like talking anyway.

When I arrived at the base camp Ben greeted me as if I had just stepped off a bus. The children were playing with a crashed Colombian army helicopter, wondering if any parts of it were worth detaching, the RAF expedition were splashing in a freezing lake in order to remove their dingleberries, and

Ben's wife Jill, looking very like the madonna, was nursing her new baby, Diccon. Jill was a sweet-natured, pretty, sensitive and artistic woman, who was probably a good influence on Ben, whose natural inclination is to be mischievous. The eldest child was Rachel, who was self-assured and as sweet-natured and pretty as her mother, but in entirely different ways. Marcus was the oldest boy, with a mop of blonde hair, a love of odd figures of speech, and an interest in teaching me all the more important obscenities and names for body parts in Castilian. Barnaby was a wonderful horseman, who rode a grey stallion called "Hippy," and Felix was a delightful, grinning little boy of about six. What I particularly remember about them all is their joie de vivre, their knowledge of the local fauna and flora, and their deftness with such things as machetes and lassoes. They were completely accomplished cowhands.

Up in the mountains the condensation froze on my sleeping bag at night. Ben, Barnaby and I climbed one of the mountains, from the top of which Ben guaranteed us a fantastic view over the Caribbean. When we finally reached the summit, a heavy cloud enveloped us, and all we could see was a stone cairn with a cross on the top, presumably erected to commemorate the mountain's dead.

Back at the hacienda I had a stomach upset for two weeks, and Ben showed me how to use a revolver in case the terrorists turned up and tried to drive the family away, or attempt a kidnapping. I settled into the life of the farm, which Ben very accurately evokes in the pages that follow, and which I therefore do not need to describe, and when I got home to England in order to go to Manchester University, I suffered the most terrible culture shock. I had stopped being British and had almost nothing in common with my fellow students. Britain and the British suddenly struck me as utterly incomprehensible and peculiar. I have still not properly adapted, and can hardly imagine what it might be like to try and set a novel in England.

That Ben is a remarkable man who has led a remarkable life is evident in his account of it. Like many people he has contradictory qualities that emerge at different times, except that in Ben's case his personality is several times larger than the European average. Sometimes Ben is reflective and philosophical, taking stoical pleasure in the wisdom he has accumulated over a long life, and sometimes gleefully badly behaved. I remember him warning me in very picturesque and graphic terms not to get too attached to Rachel, but in general Ben also enjoys other peoples' misbehaviour, relating their stupidities or accidents with considerable relish.

Ben is the Don Quijxote of Colombia. He loves adventures, and when in adventurous mode, is not at all interested in being sensible. He is quite prepared to spend all day beneath an implacable sun with a metal detector, looking for treasure in some godforsaken savannah, just because somebody dreamed it was there and sold him the right to dream. He enjoys parlous situations, and would probably throw himself into the path of an axe-murderer in order to see what happens. He enjoys trekking off to meet terrorists, and might even be pleased when his Land Rover breaks down in the middle of a raging torrent, because then he will have all the fun of finding an ingenious wheeze for getting himself out of the mess.

Ben has a kind of blunt and provocative humour which consists partly of saying the uncomfortable truth with a sweet smile, and partly of making outrageous suggestions whose seriousness or levity it is impossible for an outsider to judge. Everyone who knows Ben becomes rapidly very fond of him, but it is necessary first to learn how to cope with this particular quirk of his nature. People who have read my South American trilogy will realise that in order to create the character of Don Emanuel, I greatly exaggerated Ben's characteristics, and then put him into situations that were purely invented. It is very much to his credit (and my relief) that he has never sued me for defamation, and does not bear me a grudge.

Most importantly, Ben is someone who loves. He loved his wife, and he loves his children and stepchildren. This much is ordinary, but Ben also loves Colombia. He loves the mountains, the plants, the weather, even the nastier animals. Ben loved his hacienda, which he carved out of the wilderness, and loved his cattle for making his dream a reality. He loved his workers, and had the reputation of being the best employer in the region. Ben loves Colombia so much that he became a Colombian citizen when there was no need for it.

Colombia invariably betrays her lovers, and Ben has fallen victim to its political chaos, its institutional corruption, and its wondrously self-defeating perversity. Because of this he has lost his entire life's work, and has been reduced to living pennilessly on a beach far away from his farm and all the things that he struggled so heroically to create out of nothing.

To Ben I say thank you for lifting me out of England at exactly the right time in my life, and thereby changing the entire course of it. I suppose I might still have become a writer, but I would have been writing mediocre stuff about self-absorbed intellectuals having their dinner parties in North London. Thank you for saving me from that most terrible literary fate.

Thank you also for the great entertainment that you have always provided, and the many years of unavoidably intermittent friendship. Thank you too for this book which is a damn good read, and for giving me the honour of writing its foreword. I enjoyed every word of it, and only wish that it was longer. May it bring you much satisfaction, much well-deserved acclaim, and (as you might put it) may it get you off the bones of your ass.

—*Louis de Bernières*

Louis de Bernières is the award-winning author of several books including *Captain Corelli's Mandolin* (1994), *Birds Without Wings* (2004), *A Partisan's Daughter* (2008) and *Notwithstanding: English Village Stories* (2009). He dedicated his first book, *The War of Don Emanuel's Nether Parts,* to "The incorrigible Don Benjamin," who here gives his account of his adventures as the author of *Curucucú.*

ONE

A Chance Anecdote

I am a part of all that I have met
yet all experience is an arch
wherethro' gleams that untravell'd world
whose margins fade for ever and for ever when I move

— Alfred Lord Tennyson

Howler monkeys perched in a wild fig tree glared at our approaching jeep and roared in disapproval as it clattered over a protruding root growing across the forest roadway. A flock of macaws screeched indignantly and took to flight. Only a pair of blue morpho butterflies wafting peacefully through the shaded undergrowth seemed unperturbed by our intrusion. Ranch work had kept us occupied longer than we'd expected that afternoon in November 1957 and my host, Roland, was hurrying to show me a five hundred acre homestead before the sun set.

"The boundary starts just over there," he shouted above the din. It's a bargain. The owner's only asking the equivalent of five hundred pounds.

We passed under a feathery leafed archway of branches sprouted from rooted fence posts* lining both sides of the entrance track and came to a clearing where two wattle-walled, palm-thatched cottages stood amongst scattered fruit trees and clumps of wild flowers.

Roland's "Halloo" was met with silence.

"Looks like no one's here," he said, "but I'm sure it's O.K. with the owner for you to look around."

Gliricidia sepum, a copiously forked tree of the Leguminosea found throughout the tropics. Branches cut for posts take root and form a living fence.

Noticing that the plank door of the nearest cottage was held shut by a piece of string looped over a bent nail, I took Roland at his word. The door swung backwards and I looked into an empty room where evening sunlight stretched my shadow across the smooth earth floor to a whitewashed wall.

An open sided kitchen occupied one end of the second cottage. Balanced on three stones placed on top of a waist-high hearth, an aluminum cooking pot held a broken machete blade and spoons carved from the rind of a gourd. Four chairs, ingeniously constructed from twisted tree branches, encircled a roughly hewn table, and tucked between overlapping palm fronds in the roof I noticed an assortment of tin soup bowls and plates. The rest of the building was a communal bedroom. Ropes for securing hammocks dangled from the roof's crossbeams and pegs for hanging clothes protruded from the walls. From a rafter a resident gecko gazed at me inquisitively and swished its tail.

Outside, near toucans guzzling fallen ripe guavas, was a well trodden path which I followed to a stream cascading into pool. Kneeling, I tasted a handful of water and smiled in appreciation. Small fish darted around the drops as they fell from my beard; a basilisk lizard, defying gravity, scuttled over the water to the opposite side and two mottled butterflies flew to the trunk of a grey-barked tree, crackled their wings head downwards and disappeared in the protective coloration of the background. Everything I'd seen in the homestead seemed to co-exist in harmony and I was entranced.

"What do you think of the place?" shouted Roland. "Tomorrow, if you like, I'll take you to the river on the far boundary. It's too late to see it properly now."

As I came into view he started to reverse the jeep.

"Careful! There's a clump of flowers behind you."

"Something special about them?" he asked in surprise.

"I'm not sure but they're a part of something that is special about this homestead. What are they called?"

"Those? The natives call them *Caracucho*."

An owl-like bird alighted on a post.

"And that bird?" I asked.

"*Curucucú.*"

Pleased by the cadence of those unusual names, I clambered into my seat and, in the rapidly descending dusk, we started back to Roland's ranch.

"Don't have to look more than once at the lush vegetation to know the homestead's got good soil," he said. "The owner says it's over a metre deep. As soon as the railroad line from the interior to the Caribbean is completed, land hereabouts is going to shoot up in value. There's plenty of labour in the village, the farm has good timber and that stream is pure spring water safe to drink." Roland turned and gave me an encouraging grin." Buy the place. I'd sure like to have you as a neighbour."

"Hold on a minute! I'd thought of crewing on a yacht crossing the Pacific. There are dozens of islands I've always longed to see, and there's an uncle in Africa to visit before settling down."

"Settling down to what?"

"I haven't decided yet but I doubt if it'll be nine-to-five office work. I don't like city life and I'm not really an academic. My life seems to be guided by chance encounters." I paused and added confidently, "Something'll turn up."

"Look, pal, you don't often find good quality land like this at a pound per acre. It's a real bargain. Give it a try. If after a year it doesn't work out, you can sell it and go on to those islands in the Pacific. They're not going anywhere."

"But I don't know anything about tropical farming."

"In this climate you don't need to. Just follow nature. This is virgin soil free of diseases. Common sense tells you when things need a helping hand but most everything here thrives by itself. Look at the natives! If they can make a living, you should do brilliantly. I've been watching you for a month and there's not a job that seems to be beyond you or one you're unwilling to try. We get on. People like you. Not many people get the opportunity to start off in life as their own boss."

In England I'd given up any idea of farming or raising cattle. None of my relations were going to leave me several hundred acres and starting an agricultural venture with a mortgage was risking a life of penury. A couple of bad seasons or an outbreak of foot and mouth would mean either a foreclosure or spending the rest of my life working as an unremunerated bank asset.

Five hundred acres of fertile land, a pure water stream and a boundary river for five hundred pounds! It was certainly worth some serious thought. My capital wouldn't cover the costs of preparing and planting land with machinery. I'd have to clear the land with a machete, burn the vegetation when it was dry and, to keep myself solvent, plant a cash crop of maize. The first year or so would certainly be more slog than fun but, if I scattered enough grass seed, once the local ranchers had accepted me and seen my pasture, surely one of them would give me cattle in partnership.

If I bought the homestead a lot of people would say I wasn't making use of my Cambridge University degree, that I was turning my back on the culture that had made me what I was, and that embarking on a farming enterprise in a third world country without a tractor, implements or livestock was tantamount to lunacy. I'd have to produce some pretty impressive long term results if I were to show that my life hadn't been wasted, but dreams would never become reality if every effort to achieve them had to previously pass the censure of uninvited critics. Sod them! Sooner or later the decision of how I spent my life had to be mine. Working for a couple of years in the back woods of Colombia wouldn't necessarily be an unprofitable experience. Even if at the end it came to nothing financially, I would know myself a great deal better. Learning to recognize what values were real and which illusionary would be more than many people achieve in a life time. Moreover, it might be fun. What a lark it would be to construct a dam across the stream and divert an elevated leat to a water turbine for generating electricity! I was at an age when I disregarded conventional inhibitions with the ebullience of youth. If I could take what was unpalatable without resentment, and either accept or overcome difficulties as trials in the art of living, I was confident that I would find more to smile over than to make me weep.

It's curious how a chance anecdote can embark one on a series of unforeseen events. I would never have reached Colombia let alone Roland's ranch and the homestead if I had missed John Corner's University lecture on "The Explosive Spore Dispersal Mechanisms of Fungi."

Corner looked up from his lectern, gave us one of his engaging smiles and remarked, "I don't suppose any of you have ever had the opportunity of firing old forty-pound cannons?"

Aware that he was about to share one of the memories from his remarkable life that made his lectures unique, we had settled ourselves more comfortably and given him our rapt attention. Removing his spectacles and beginning to polish them, he described being sent to a Caribbean island by boat on one of the botanical missions of his youth and noticing, as he entered the harbor, old cannons sticking out from gun emplacements lining the parapet of the ancient fort guarding the town.

"Everything was mellowed under the tropical sun and the tempo of life seemed idyllically free from stress. Boys scampered up coconut palms to fell green nuts for their milk; women cooked breadfruit; men fished from hand-hewn canoes. Girls, balancing bunches of bananas on their heads, sauntered with sensual grace along the paths leaving their family small-holdings to the village. It was a friendly community whose unhurried way of life gave people time to smile benevolently at groups of carefree children playing in the street.

"The District Officer had few visitors, and when we had finished our official business he pressed me to spend the night at the Residence. After dinner he challenged me to a game of chess which I won. Magnanimously, possibly rashly, he asked me what I would like as a reward. Suddenly I had this marvelous idea. Shall I tell you what it was?"

Encouraged by our murmured assent, Corner continued.

"I reminded him that the next day was the King's official birthday and to fire the old cannons in the fort would be an appropriate recognition of the event. My host laughed delightedly at the suggestion and ordered his steward to bring another bottle of Scotch. The islanders possess an amazing bush telegraph service and by the following morning not only did everyone know of our plan but with unanimous accord had decided to take a day off. Homes were abandoned, the bank, the school and offices were shut and, in a festive mood, old and young gathered at the fort where a few enterprising families set up stalls selling home brewed alcoholic beverage by the calabash. To give the occasion respectability, pensioned army officers wore their medals, primed the cannons and prepared the touch holes. The District Officer, astride a parapet, delivered a brief but dignified speech. At his signal everybody shouted 'God save the King' and I, with other local dignitaries, was handed a lighted taper to ignite our appointed fuses. I can still visualize the scene. As a series of mighty BOOMS sent compressed rat's nests and flakes of rust shooting across the bay, startled bats emerged from nooks and crannies in the masonry and, in an impromptu flyover, swooped and darted around our heads."

Wrinkles of pleasure from the memory creased Corner's face and then, almost as an afterthought, he added, "Opportunities happen when they will. You can't force their pace or foresee the outcome but when they arrive be receptive. Some may change your life."

I had been left in a daydream wandering barefoot along a coral sand beach. Sparkling turquoise water lapped at my feet, a parrot screeched "pieces of eight," maidens offered me tropical fruits and the pressures of competitive academia faded into insignificance. A field botanist had moments of carefree enjoyment denied their more professionally ambitious colleagues who, behind laboratory walls, competed for academic advancement by publishing erudite monographs. What marvellous fun it would be to join a University expedition to some off-beat region of the globe!

Fortuitously in my second year I was introduced to Roger, a brilliant, debonair Edwardian. Even though he always wore a cravat or tie and I open necked shirts, we became great friends. I sometimes wondered if his determination to persevere unswervingly what he believed to be correct was influenced by his landlady, the widow of an Antarctic explorer whose equipment had been returned after what Roger referred to as "his unfortunate trip." Every morning she breakfasted at a table on her open air terrace paying tribute to the fortitude of her late husband by munching his favourite expedition food of raw porridge oats. No sub-zero gale sweeping across the fens could deter her. On such occasions, by encasing her head in his balaclava and fleetingly lifting its hem, she contrived to spoon the few oats that hadn't been blown away by the wind into her mouth.

Roger's parents were distinguished horticulturists and I was not surprised to learn that he and four other knowledgeable botanists were planning a long vacation expedition to collect bryophytes in Yugoslavia. For reasons which still elude me, as I could scarcely distinguish a moss from a leafy liverwort, he invited me to join them. It is not easy to find unrecorded plants in Europe. For centuries avid botanists have scoured the continent for additions to herbaria. Thus, it was greatly to the credit of the expedition's meticulous work that the collection was found to contain two previously unrecorded species for the Balkans. Using this kudos to full advantage, we agreed to plan another expedition after our graduation and explore a more distant part of the world.

That was the decade when Colonel Hunt's expedition to the Himalayas gave Hillary and Tensing the opportunity to make the first ascent of Mount Everest. The film recording their saga had world-wide success and produced an unexpected cash surplus which had to be spent in order to wind up the expedition's accounts with a zero balance. To achieve that end, grants were made available to finance approved scientific expeditions to mountainous areas. Shedding one of our group and replacing him with a cinematographer, we scrutinized maps for accessible but, to the world in general, unknown mountain ranges. We chose the Sierra Nevada del Cocuy in Boyacá, Colombia. The flora was uncharted, there were no recorded ascents for some of the peaks, and it would be interesting to compare England with a South American third world country where none of us had ever been. Rather grandly we called ourselves "The Cambridge Expedition to the Colombian Cordillera Oriental 1957."

According to our capabilities—and limitations—the expedition leader,

Peter Grubb, assigned us tasks. Roger and I were put in charge of soliciting grants from Trusts and Foundations, and food and equipment from firms known to be sympathetic to Oxbridge requests. "When in doubt, press on regardless," was Roger's motto and it always seemed to get results (although later, in a moment of confidence, he admitted that applying it to his final examinations had probably been detrimental to his being awarded a first class degree).

In addition to the Mount Everest Foundation, we received help from the Shell Oil Company. Possibly it was hoped that some of us would join their Colombian team analyzing core samples for spores indicating oil rich strata. Perhaps their Oxbridge employees felt a surge of nostalgia for their Alma Maters and wished to be associated once again in University projects. In either case, Shell Oil (Colombia) offered us transport from Bogotá to the Sierra Nevada del Cocuy and, once there, the use of ten mules. To celebrate all these developments and meet some of our sponsors, the expedition members were invited to a cocktail party in Shell Mex House, London.

Access to a well-stocked bar and the continuous circulation of waiters carrying trays laden with drinks and snacks put us at our ease and in less than half an hour we were convinced that Shell Oil was a jolly decent company. At that point, a serenely mellowed Roger found himself questioned by a distinguished looking gentleman concerning the purpose of our previous expedition. Pursing his lips, Roger pontificated, "You are no doubt aware of those funny little mossy plants that one usually treads on but never really notices. Well, in scientific nomenclature they're known as bryophytes." Beckoning the gentleman to come closer, Roger leaned forward and, as though imparting a piece of classified information, confided, "We collected 'em."

Before Roger had a chance to elucidate on other more meaningful accomplishments, a waiter excused himself for interrupting and announced, "Professor, there's an urgent telephone call for you in the main lobby."

Somewhat put out by the professor's abrupt departure, but true to his motto, Roger queried, "Waiter, who was that worthy gentleman?"

"Professor Adams, sir, is the President of the Royal Society."

"Ah yes. I remember the name. Perhaps we'll be able to continue our little chat on another occasion."

I don't believe any of us were ever purposely disrespectful where manners or courtesy were due. Definitely not Roger. But underlying Cold War tensions were shaking the foundations of blind subservience to tradition. We were the first generation to live under the threat of an atomic holocaust and I, certainly, was repulsed by a strategy for world peace based on stockpiling weapons of mass destruction. If ever used, the least harmful scenario would be indiscriminate, international homicide, the worst, the annihilation of life on earth. Quite apart from moral considerations, I was not content to be a dutiful but expedient puppet pending a sacrificial order from the Old Men in Whitehall whose wisdom had so often been conspicuously absent.

If my views were unconventional, they were the outcome of an unusual background. My father, W. B. Curry, was the founding headmaster of Dartington Hall School in Devon. Allowed by the trustees, Dorothy and Leonard Elmhirst, to practice what he preached—and greatly influenced by the ideals of Bertrand Russell—he, my mother Ena Isherwood and her sister Margaret, pioneered progressive education in England. Although my parents divorced, my memories are of a happy childhood. My aunts and uncles took a kindly interest in my upbringing but what impressed me the most was the sheer goodness of my maternal grandfather, A.A. Isherwood, the vicar of a small village in Wiltshire. Before members of his family were allowed to sit down to their Christmas dinner, each had taken a plate of food, suspended in a starched linen napkin, to a destitute parishioner.

At the outbreak of the Second World War I was evacuated with my mother and elder sister to the United States of America. Funds taken out of England at that time were strictly controlled. For the first few months my sister and I boarded with friends in Cambridge, Massachusetts, where we attended the Shady Hill school. This freed our mother to work for the "Save the Children Organization" and find foster parents for other evacuee children. At the end of our first year in the States she was offered a teaching post in Colorado and we moved west. One of my aunts, Helen Isherwood, who had been working in America for several years, offered to pool her resources with any money that my mother had been able to save from her salary and buy a home for us all in the equitable climate of Southern California. There was just enough to purchase a simple wooden-frame house with a garden shed in Laguna Beach. The seller, in sympathy with our impecunious state, kindly left us four beds, a refrigerator and a stove. At the foot of my cot in the shed was a workbench that looked as though it had been put together from pieces of drift-wood. I walked along the beach looking for what else had been washed up by the sea that could be nailed together and furnished our dining room with a much needed table. In the pioneer climate of California it was accepted that youngsters be useful. During weekends, and school holidays, my sister worked as a waitress or babysitter and I apprenticed myself to a neighbor who spent Saturdays and Sundays building an extension to his house. Barefoot and clad in shorts, I also cut lawns, washed cars and at the end of the day collected soft drink bottles—discarded along the shoreline by picnickers—which I returned to a supermarket for their refundable value. My sister and I never thought it a hardship to contribute to improving the standard of living in our home. We were both proud and happy to be able to do so.

In 1944 I was awarded a scholarship to Fountain Valley, a select boarding school for sons of the wealthy, at the foot of the Rocky Mountains on the plains near Colorado Springs. It exposed me to a different world. Boys boasted about the price of their parents' new cars, I won an arts award for an inlaid chess board that I made in the carpentry class and another pupil introduced me to what was commonly done on the night before the weekly change of sheets. Unluckily in my first year I was hospitalized with bulbar infantile paralysis. It is probable that I would not have recovered had it not been for Ishbel Campbell, the English master's wife, who handed her signed chequebook to my mother to pay for the expenses of my recuperation. That unforgettable gesture of generosity and trust changed my perception of friendship.

Six years later when I had regained my health and graduated from Fountain Valley, I returned to Dartington to attend my father's co-educational school. There, children had always been allowed to develop non academic skills but in the austere post-war conditions of England when costs were rising but the school's income remained fixed, student help in maintenance became an economic necessity. For the first hour of each school day every pupil in the senior school participated in some aspect of the work associated with keeping the buildings and their contents in good working order. This "useful work," as it was called, altered the students' attitude toward responsibility. Previously it had been assumed that "someone else" would do the manual work and that furnishings and equipment were there to be used or abused. Finding the faults of, and fixing, worn out electrical machinery, mending broken furniture, glazing windows, cleaning rooms and helping in the kitchen developed not only unsuspected skills but a proprietary feeling about the school where everyone's effort was appreciated.

When in 1925 Dorothy and Leonard Elmhirst purchased the manor house and estate known as Dartington Hall near Totnes, Devon—once owned by John Holland, the half-brother of King Richard II—their vision was to revi-

Oxen pulling a primitive plough.

talize the lives of the residents in the economically depressed area. They began by financing a wide range of rural industries, a progressive school and creating a community where every aspect of the arts could co-exist and flourish. I spent two exciting years there gaining an appreciation of the community that develops when dedicated professionals—many of whom were permanent residents—are encouraged to add their expertise and ideas to enriching society. Then, in 1953 I was accepted by Sidney Sussex College, Cambridge, to study for a degree in Natural Science.

On the day I received my degree, I was free to do whatever I chose. I had no dependants, a few savings and an ambition to see the world. The expedition to Colombia would be a stepping stone to unimagined adventures.

✄ ✄ ✄ ✄

With funds and equipment collected, the expedition sailed in July 1957 on *La Reina del Mar*, one of the last passenger liners to make regular runs from Liverpool to South America. Cartagena, the fortified treasure city

Close-up of a primitive wooden plough being used.

where the *conquistadores* stored New World gold before shipping it to Spain, welcomed us to Colombia. Had the British Consul not previously arranged for our expedition gear to by-pass the usual venal import procedure, our belongings would have been pillaged by customs officials. Denied any baksheesh from us, they compensated by tearing furiously into the baggage of returning citizens. It was our first lesson in survival techniques necessary to prosper in Colombia.

Members of the British community greeted us at Bogotá airport and, hospitably dividing us among their homes, generously wined and dined us for a week. Then we climbed into two Shell Oil trucks and were off to Guicán, the highest village in the Sierra Nevada del Cocuy. The Andean scenery was superb, the air crisp and clean. *Campesinos** with black homburgs firmly pulled down to their ears and *ruanas** flung back over their shoulders, hoed

---

*Country folk, farmers and others whose livelihood depends on rural occupations. Synonymous with the term "peasant" but without derogatory overtones.

strips of potatoes. Similarly dressed small children with ruddy cheeks and shy smiles tended tethered cattle foraging between fences and the roadway. Occasionally we passed fields being tilled by yoked oxen pulling a simple wooden plough. It was all very new to us and we frequently asked the drivers to stop so that we could take photographs or collect specimens of spectacular flowering plants. White, yellow and scarlet daturas—some reputedly emitting narcotic odors at night—adorned peasant doorways and at the side of the road grew unfamiliar shrubs with brilliant pink and purple flowers that even Peter Grubb could only identify as belonging to the family *Melastomataceae*.

The first evening we reached Capitanejo, a small township situated in a valley at the base of the Sierra Nevada del Cocuy. Snow-capped peaks, glistening among wisps of cloud, looked cold, challenging and enticing. Perched on the roof of the only hostel, a row of scrawny vultures stretched their necks and glowered at us hungrily. We'd been regaled, before leaving Bogotá, with macabre accounts of pieces of missing persons appearing in the kitchen stews of such places. Without a single dissent, we declined the owner's offer of accommodation and, pitching our tents between the trucks, slept at the side of the road.

We received a more gracious reception in Guicán. Upon reading the letters of introduction supplied to us in Bogotá, the town's courtly patriarch, Dr. Nepomuceno Arango, respected political scientist, lawyer and scion of colonial estates, ushered us into a drawing room furnished with ornately brocaded chairs. He and Roger immediately recognized in each other their mutual gentility and for the remainder of our stay we were received in Guicán as personages of note. Roger's charm combined with the academic brilliance of our leader, Peter Grubb, persuaded Dr. Arango that we were worthy of his patronage and to our joy he sent a message to Don Juan de la Hoz, the administrator of his high cordillera estate, Hacienda Ritacuba, stating that a paddock was to be reserved for our mules and the barn made available for our use. It became more than a base camp where we slept and stored gear while foraging into the surrounding mountains, it became a home where Don Juan's family always made us feel welcome.

"As you will be working in the countryside for the next two months," our patron cautioned, "you may come across Marxist agents inciting peasants to overthrow the government. I must warn you that you will loose your welcome

---

*Native woven blankets squares worn as a cape with a slit in the middle for the head.

if you have anything to do with them."

"Are they a threat to Colombia's stability?" I asked.

"Since Simon Bolivar's battles with Spain, that led to our becoming a sovereign republic in 1830, two political parties, the Liberals and Conservatives, have controlled Colombia. As you may know, during the last hundred and twenty-seven years they've jockeyed for power by engaging in nine brutal civil wars and dozens of minor skirmishes. Despite political fanatics slaughtering each other by barbaric methods such as that of a thousand cuts, the redeeming feature—if one can call it that—is that every confrontation was an internal dispute between citizens who cared about the good of their section of Colombia. Marxism is an alien menace led by agitators financed, controlled and brainwashed by Russia whose object is disrupting and causing chaos to the social stability of our country. Clearly, they have to be dealt with."

"Brutality is a global phenomena," I said. "In England, a few centuries ago, opponents of the crown, proven guilty of treason or not, could be publicly hung, drawn, and quartered and have their heads skewered on a spike on London Bridge. Please rest assured, Doctor Arango, that none of us have the slightest intention of encouraging Marxist agitators here or anywhere else. The possibility of meeting them, though, is disturbing. May I respectfully ask you a question concerning the reason for their presence?"

"Please do."

"Does the Marxist propaganda, as I understand it, that the poor are getting poorer and the rich richer correspond to the reality of most present-day Colombians?"

"Answering for the vast majority of modern Colombians, the reply is a categorical no. The new generation is on the threshold of a brighter future than their parents ever thought possible. I'm assured that in less than twelve months the Liberal and Conservative politicians will have adopted a system of peacefully alternating governments every four years with an agreement called *El Frente Nacional*. Education, communication technology and mass produced luxury goods are providing the conditions where nobody will be excluded from a middle class standard of living. Peasant society as you see it today will have largely disappeared by the end of this century. If you have criticisms about present conditions in Colombia, reflect for a minute on the thought that our respective countries belong to different centuries and Democracy evolves slowly."

"Yes," I replied, "that's certainly so. My mother was a suffragette. She often reminded me that while the Magna Charter was signed centuries ago, women in England only gained the vote in 1917."

Dr. Arango smiled appreciatively. "Thank you for mentioning that," he said. "In certain aspects Colombia is still feudal. Citizens have the right to vote and own their homes and businesses but ultimate power is still held by the large land owners who expect allegiance in return for protection and favors. Every village has a Catholic church and, as was recently common in Europe, the priest levies an ecclesiastical tax of ten percent on all agricultural produce. But traditions are crumbling. Modern Colombians, whether Liberal or Conservative, Catholic or Evangelical, neither accept nor believe that their future be limited by their parent's position in society. I promise you one thing, however, while you're under my patronage nobody in Guicán will dare bother you."

We each thanked Doctor Arango for his kind welcome and promised to be worthy of his trust

Situated at an altitude of about twelve thousand feet, Hacienda Ritacuba's buildings, adobe walled and roofed with Spanish tiles, stood around three sides of a cobbled courtyard. At dusk a palpable coldness descended from the permanent snow on the adjacent peaks. In one wing Don Juan de la Hoz lived with his wife and herd of children. In the other were the rooms reserved for Doctor Arango. In the middle section was the barn allotted for our use and the kitchen—the only room with any warmth and the communal meeting place even though every permanent fixture in it was blackened with soot. From the one and only chair, Don Juan's wife, attired in sensible black shoes, long black dress, black *ruana* and a black homburg hat perched above a luxuriant black plait, supervised the activities of her household. Everyone else sat on logs arranged in a circle around the open fire which was never allowed to go out. From a trestle, hung a black iron cauldron containing the day's stew. It bubbled constantly and, when the level dropped, was replenished with whatever was at hand and thought edible. In the weeks we were there we never saw the pot either emptied or washed. The kitchen lacked windows and the only rays of light to penetrate the gloom came through chinks in the walls, as the doorway was usually shut to keep out icy draughts. Smoke filled the kitchen before escaping through a specially designed hole in the roof. From opaque depths emerged and disappeared poor relations, the family idiot* and various dogs. Sometimes we were invited for a meal. Choosing a place on the commu-

---

*Discretely displayed by many families as proof of the purity of their Spanish lineage.

nal log, we balanced bowls of stew thick with potatoes, broad beans and onions. What couldn't be managed with the wooden spoon provided was picked up with our fingers. At times the stew contained curious cross sections of meat which, when we felt observed, we politely chewed and swallowed. But, when nobody was looking, surreptitiously passed to the ever-hungry dogs behind us. After the meal we went outside and rinsed our hands and mouths in a glacier fed stream which provided water for the kitchen.

Don Juan's eldest daughter, whom we nicknamed "Snowflake," was a cheerful, simple soul, somewhat plainer than pretty and of the ample proportions popular in proletarian statuary. Although thirty years old she had remained unmarried, a state attributed to her penchant for embracing any dancing partner in a manner that left his feet dangling in the air as she twirled him around. Not only had she inherited her father's booming voice by which, we were told, she had once stood at the top of a ridge beside their house and ordered provisions from the shops in Guicán a thousand feet below, but had developed formidable pectoral muscles by lifting two hundred pound sacks of potatoes on to the backs of mules.

Once a week at the crack of dawn she would appear in the doorway to the barn where we would be lying warmly in our sleeping bags and ask for volunteers. She was clearly smitten by Roger's impeccable manners and winked at him invitingly, although for the help she needed she might as well have winked at any of us for we were equally incompetent. Taking turns, two of us would put on our anoraks and go out into the freezing mist of the courtyard. Her brothers were never there. Having caught ten mules and tied them to posts in the courtyard with their cargo saddles securely cinched, they had left Snowflake to her own devices and gone off to the fields to dig more potatoes. To avoid being kicked, Snowflake would take off her *ruana* and drape it over the head of the mule to be loaded so that it couldn't see what was happening. Then, casually picking up a sack of potatoes, she would place it against one side of the cargo saddle in the hope that we were doing the same on the other side. It may have been the lack of breakfast or that lifting two-hundred-pound sacks of potatoes shoulder high was a knack that Cambridge had failed to teach, but in either case we could seldom raise our sack more than a couple of feet off the ground. With the indulgent smile of a fond mother wishing to spare her retarded children humiliation, Snowflake would tell us to keep the one she had just lifted where it was, move around the mule and toss the second sack into a position where it balanced the one we were holding. Supporting its bulk on a raised knee she would tie the tops of the two sacks together and with a few more twists and turns of rope secure the first mule load.

Learning skills in the art of primitive living by members of Don Juan's family was a salutary experience.

✦ ✦ ✦ ✦

Ricker Laboratories had commissioned us to collect a hundred pounds of the sessile alpine plant, *Draba litamo*, reputed to contain medicinal properties. On the day we climbed to its habitat along the snow line, Roger felt ill. We left him in Dr Arango's guest bedroom, where Snowflake assured us she would happily provide his meals. Don Juan's eldest son, Pedro, lent me his horse and as soon as Fermin, his brother, had secured our equipment to the mule saddles we set off for the three-day trip necessary to gather and sun dry the requested plants which grew above a glacial lake at about fourteen thousand feet. On arrival we pitched our tents and spread a ground sheet over a sun-warmed slab of rock where Pedro could turn the gathered material. The morning's moderate wind and open sky made perfect conditions for drying but, as the afternoon advanced, clouds threatening rain compelled a halt to the day's work. Pedro mentioned that the glacial lake had been stocked with trout and that he'd brought a fish hook. The chance to change our diet overcame angler etiquette. We baited his hook with a lump of mutton fat, tied it with a boot lace to a tent pole and told him to try his luck. A hungry trout snapped at the unexpected treat, leapt into the air and crashed back fighting. Pedro whooped in excitement and we all rushed down to help. Fermin with another tent pole, I with a .22 rifle.

"Don't let it go, Pedro," I shouted. "We're on our way!"

Fermin waited for the trout to swerve near the bank. Intending to kill the approaching fish with a wallop on the head he leaned forward to strike but slipped. The spike at the tip of the descending tent pole severed the boot lace and the stupefied fish reeled away out of reach. I took aim and fired. My shot stopped the trout but brought it no nearer. Thinking the lake could not be much colder than the English Channel, I stripped, swam out and brought back our supper.

My blue goose flesh discouraged any further attempt at fishing so we climbed back to where we'd left our gear and I lit our primus stove. Fermin said he knew a recipe for cooking trout and we left him to prepare the evening meal. As we were all hungry, the mashed trout and potatoes fried in mutton fat and topped with sliced spring onions seemed delicious.

If we wondered how Roger was faring, little did we imagine that he was being offered one of Snowflake's culinary specialties.

"She appeared in the doorway," he told us on our return, "and asked if I was hungry. I'd eaten virtually nothing for two days and was famished. Images of my mother's Sunday lunches flitted through my mind: a haunch of beef, golden Yorkshire puddings, roast potatoes with gravy, Brussels sprouts, gleaming tableware and a carefully selected claret waiting to be poured from a cut glass decanter. Snowflake, glowing like an animal on heat, reappeared carrying my supper on an oval plate. I struggled eagerly into a sitting position to see what she had brought. Stretched between two potatoes at the far end of the platter lay the full length of something which must have belonged to a bull." Roger winced at the memory. Since Snowflake's offering he had tightly shut his eyes and remained in a prostrate position waiting for our return.

"Well? Go on. Tell us. What was it?" we naively queried.

"Peering at me over the edge of the platter was the knob of a boiled penis."

Roger waited until we had wiped the tears of laughter from our eyes and then suggested that if what he'd seen were cut into short lengths they would be indistinguishable from the cross sections in the kitchen stews that we had so often felt obliged to swallow.

The Cocuy Massif extends on a north-south axis. At the end of the first month, having completed a representative collection from the western vegetative zones, we loaded our equipment on to the mules and set off to a cabin at Cobagón on the eastern flank. Our path zigzagged upwards to the *páramos* where a stiff wind sent clouds leap-frogging exuberantly over the summit ridge. Even the mules felt the exhilaration in the air. Kicking up their heels, they scampered into a pasture scattering a flock of sheep up a hillside. It took the combined effort of ourselves and two small shepherd boys to coax our recalcitrant pack animals back to the trail.

Giant *espeletias** brooded on the high moorland *páramo* like a massed array of hooded friars. Many a traveller caught in a mountain blizzard has saved himself from hypothermia by putting together a crude "log type" cabin

---

*A plant of the *Compositae* unique to the northern Andes, growing to three metres in height and locally known as *frailejones*.

The author on Pedro's borrowed horse crossing the páramo.

shelter from fallen stems and warming himself by a fire made by igniting the resinous leaves.

Skirting around the base of the snow line, we crossed the divide and descended into a belt of cloud forest. Along mist dampened branches bromeliads of the genus *Tillandsia*, mosses, the ubiquitous lichen *Usnea* and spectacular orchids vied for space. Collecting specimens meant a hazardous clamber through trellises of slimy aerial roots beneath which weird fibrous growths, resembling tentacles of some giant octopus, entangled those who fell.

Rumbling cumulus clouds streaked with flashes of lightning persuaded us to seek accommodation for the night in a mountain hostel. There were two bedrooms, one for women and the other for men. In each a wide communal bed, constructed of split saplings laid at right angles over two horizontal logs, was wedged between opposing walls five feet six inches apart. Three uncured sheepskins sewn side by side with the wool facing up served as a mattress. The coverlet consisted of three more skins sewn side by side with the wool

Mules laden with the expedition's equipment crossing the páramo between Guicán and Cobagón.

facing down. An impediment to a good night's rest was the differing lengths of bodies lying next to each other and the consequent unsolicited and occasionally intimate proximity of another's knee. Moreover, a tug of war using the top sheepskin inevitably took place between those lying at the edges of the bed. When the person on one side rolled over and faced outwards he was obliged to pull the sheepskins over his knees to keep them warm. That action uncovered the person on the other side, who yanked the coverlet back again. The caress of unwashed sheepskin pulled back and forth over the faces of our group in the middle snapped the willingness some had expressed to expose themselves to a genuine ethnic experience. Crawling over cursing bodies they disappeared into a cold mountain rain to pitch tents on uneven stony ground.

In the morning it was difficult to decide who had fared the worst, those on the split saplings or those on the stones. We all looked dishevelled. All of us, that is, except Roger. Never for one moment had he entertained the notion of sharing a communal bed. He had pitched his tent on the only level and smooth spot available and, upon retiring, had neatly stretched his trousers beneath his inflated air-bed. As usual, he emerged dry shaved, a crease in his trouser leg, boots gleaming, and wearing a clean cravat. From under the rim of the deer stalker hat set jauntily on his head he initially regarded us as an unfamiliar species. Then, courteously enquiring whether we had slept well, he savoured an early morning cup of coffee sent especially to him from the hostel kitchen by the owner's wife. She could tell who was important. Several hours of being outside in the pure mountain air were necessary for the rest of us to clear from our nostrils the pungent odours of rancid sheep's wool and muleteer's sweat.

The cabin at Cobagón stood in the middle of a forest clearing. It belonged to Don Juan. No one lived there permanently but the door was left unlocked so that weary travellers could take advantage of its shelter. It suited our purposes admirably. There were two rooms. The first, a rudimentary kitchen with a raised hearth and trestle table. The second, a bed room large enough for us to spread our sleeping bags and equipment. Wild turkeys provided us with meat and close by ran a stream with water a few degrees above freezing in which it was bearable to wash. We established a harmonious work routine. Every morning the mules not needed for an excursion were hobbled and allowed to forage in an unfenced paddock. The muleteers then swept the ground around the cabin, collected firewood, put new palm leaves in the roof where old ones had rotted, hunted for game, and generally helped us in any way they could. We went in pairs to collect plants and usually found enough new material to keep us constantly occupied sorting and labelling material before carefully arranging it in our portable plant presses.

Occasionally passers-by would break their journey and run their eyes appraisingly over our equipment. Why were a group of foreigners collecting and drying local plants which were neither good to eat, smell, smoke or sell? Had we discovered something of value? Cobagón was far from any authority and we were very much aware of our vulnerability should anyone wish to pillage our belongings. As none of us were sufficiently fluent in Spanish to convincingly explain what we were doing, we crossed the linguistic barrier by adopting one of Colombia's cultural successes. A pot of coffee was always kept at the back of the fire pit ready to offer anyone a *tinto*. The results of that simple gesture were magical. Looks of distrust were replaced by friendly smiles and, even if what we were doing remained incomprehensible, a communion had been established that sent visitors peacefully on their way.

We completed our collection of plants in the environs of Cobagón just as changes in the weather foretold the imminent arrival of the rainy season. Sunny days gave way to drizzle and we knew that to ensure the professional preservation of the accumulated specimens we would have to return to Bogotá without delay and place them in the special drying ovens available in the National University. We had amassed some four thousand herbarium specimens comprising over one thousand four hundred "numbers" which contained about one thousand two hundred species. The collection was divided equally into three parts. One was sent to the Smithsonian Museum of Natural History in Washington DC, the second was donated to the National University in Bogotá and the third went to Cambridge with the other expedition members.

For them, their time in Colombia had been an enjoyable and interesting hiatus between graduation and a career. With guaranteed employment waiting in England they were happy to return to familiar surroundings and establish their niches in the security of a society they understood.

I was still undecided about my future but I knew that whatever I chose would have to have freedom, beauty, and a sense of adventure. Colombia's diversity offered the opportunities of an "un-travelled world." Endowed with one thousand six hundred species of birds, two thousand species of orchids, an abundance of mineral wealth, three mountain ranges rising above both Caribbean and Pacific coast lines, climatic zones and vegetation varying from the alpine to the tropical and an uncongested heterogeneous population virtually devoid of ethnic discrimination, the country might be a good place to settle. I could afford to look around for a few months and if I found nothing of interest in which to immerse myself I would move on. John Corner's smile and advice about opportunities were still fresh in my mind.

TWO

Let's Go For It!

When I was young, every day was the beginning of some new thing,
and every evening ended with the glow of the following morning.

—Inuit verse

Rose K. Gaul's boarding house for gentlemen became my temporary home. In the early nineteen hundreds it had been the only hostel in Bogotá recommended by the *South American Handbook*. Rose, affectionately known as "Mother Gaul" by her permanent residents, had left England by herself at the turn of the century to marry her youthful sweetheart employed by the Erricson Company in Bogotá. Shortly after her arrival in Colombia he died of yellow fever. Finding herself destitute she opened a hostel and, using a treasured family recipe, made English breakfast sausages. Every Thursday the British community loyally telephoned their orders and every Friday a dilapidated taxi, driven by a grateful pensioner wearing a dark suit shiny with age, delivered them.

Mother Gaul never quite fathomed why Colombians obtusely conversed in Spanish and her attempts to speak in that language were usually only understood by her faithful maid, Graciela. To the world at large she communicated in graceful, old fashioned English. It was rumored that she was the only non-Colombian living in Bogotá without a resident permit. On being questioned about her status by a bilingual immigration inspector her reply, "I couldn't possibly be a foreigner because, don't you see, I'm British," had been delivered with such sublime assurance that she not only received an apology but had her name removed from the list of aliens.

A nucleus of long term lodgers protected Mother Gaul from accepting any newcomer for more than a few nights if they found his manners and conversation sub standard. The rooms were economically priced, the bathroom fittings period pieces and the meals enlivened by a parrot. This parrot, as old and wrinkled as Rose Gaul herself, was sacrosanct. It lived in the dining room and at mealtimes found amusement—if it saw an unfamiliar face—in leaving its perch and waddling along the communal table to the newcomer and squawking, *Quiere cacao?*" (Want some chocolate?) It upset condiment jars and might even leave droppings as it exerted itself to climb over some particularly difficult obstacle. There was a tacit understanding that it would be bad form to suffer from psittacosis* and, miraculously, nobody staying there ever did.

I managed to cover my expenses by giving private English lessons. Their infrequency provided me with ample time to explore areas of Bogotá seldom visited by affluent tourists and there, in sidewalk bistros, university students introduced me to some disturbing facts. Colombia was emerging from ten years of politically incited mayhem, known as "*la violencia*," following the 1947 assassination of Elieser Gaitan, a popular left wing aspirant to the presidency. The internecine abuses of that time between the Liberal and Conservative parties had so discredited the country's political leaders that in despair many students had joined Marxist cells. A student who came from Barichara in the Department of Norte de Santander told me that in that area during the "*la violencia*" not only had the Conservative majority forced Liberal farmers to flee for their lives but, having taken over the abandoned properties, arranged a fire in the municipal registry office which conveniently incinerated all the Liberal's title deeds. Authenticated reports of inciting violence mentioned pronouncements of Catholic priests from their pulpits—in both Conservative and Liberal village churches—that it was not a mortal sin to kill someone of the opposing political party.

I felt that some of the more rabid students were trying to arouse my indignation in the hope that I, as a representative of British youth, might join them in some revolutionary demonstration. I remembered Dr. Nepumuceno Arangos's positive predictions for a stabilized society and preferred not to get involved. No country welcomes foreigners who participate in protest movements.

---

*A parasitic disease of parrots transmissible to man.

An invitation from the wealthy patriarch of an expatriate Welsh family, Don Hywell Hughes, offered a very welcoming change of scene. Would I like to spend two months as a working guest on the tropical ranch he had recently purchased? He had installed his youngest son, Roland, as manager and the four-seater family plane which was making a trip there in a few days time could take me. Roland I was assured would welcome my companionship. It sounded delightfully free of intrigue and a perfect opportunity to see another aspect of Colombia.

The ranch purchased by Don Hywell had been founded by three quixotic Spaniards with visions of the fortunes to be gleaned from growing rice on the fertile plains around a growing settlement located in the foothills of the Perija Mountains on the north-eastern Colombian-Venezuelan border. Cartographers failed to recognize the village, but to the people living there it was known as Poponte.

From Barranquilla, the Spaniards transported by barge three tractors fitted with solid iron rear wheels, three trailers loaded with ploughs, harrows, rice seed and fifty-five-gallon drums of diesel fuel approximately one hundred and fifty miles up the Magdalena river to a landing forty miles distant from Poponte. Forging a cross-country track to their destination took six days. Within a year one Spaniard had been killed when a tractor rolled over on top of him, the second went bankrupt and the third, declaring that he would rather be in Hell than continue, sold what was left of the enterprise to Don Hywell. Recognizing the impracticality of administrating the ranch as it was from Bogotá, he ordered that two fields be joined to make an airstrip.

Before that modernization, at least for most travelers, a horse, a four-wheel-drive vehicle carrying a canoe, or a pair of sturdy legs and the ability to swim, was needed to reach Poponte. One unpaved, rutted road—with occasional side tracks—straggled on a south-to-north axis between Colombia's Cordillera Oriental and the Magdalena River in an attempt to connect the region's settlements and townships. As bridges for the many rivers that traversed the road from east to west were still in the planning stage, after heavy rain falls in the cordillera, flood plains several meters deep in water discouraged all but the most intrepid.

The pilot nudged me in the ribs and pointed downwards. Beneath us cowboys were chasing cattle off the runway. "Can't land till they get those animals out of the way," he said. "Lets buzz the ranch house." He banked the Cessna into a tight turn and we flew over what looked to me like a Wild-West movie set. A picket fence enclosed a long, whitewashed, single-story, clapboard building. Pigs cooled themselves in a mud bath beneath an elevated water tank and, tethered in the shade of a tree, two sweat-streaked horses flicked their tails in attempts to dislodge blood-sucking flies.

Squawking chickens scattered to either side of the plane as it taxied up to the garden gate. Ranch hands unloaded boxes of provisions and replaced them with ice chests packed with meat and cheese to be taken back to Bogotá. Roland shook my hand warmly and leading the way into the house, showed me where I was to sleep. The cook prepared tea. Someone started a diesel motor and the fan in the ceiling sprang into life. A horse galloped up to the door and Roland's foreman, Don Vito, dismounted. He went into a huddle with Roland and started to talk. On the journey the pilot had mentioned several interesting things about Don Vito. That he had sired forty children, had worked loyally for Don Hywell for thirty years and having earned the respected prefix "Don" by his ability to get things done, had been sent to help Roland sort out any problems the ranch.

It appeared that another three cows were missing and Roland was being asked what to do with the body of the thief if he was caught? I had been warned in Bogotá that Don Vito was rough-cut and, overhearing his comments, I had the distinct impression that I would find my visit to the ranch much more agreeable if he decided he liked me.

I found the ethos of the community extraordinary. Were there no law enforcement officers to capture cattle thieves and, with due process, put them on trial? How did Don Vito justify forty offspring? Most civilized societies would have attached a stigma to a man who sired an excessive number of children with a series of casual partners. In Poponte, could one go through life unhindered by conventional concepts of social obligation? I looked at him curiously. With his small porcine eyes set in a heavily fleshed face, it was easy to imagine him dispatching someone whom he considered a nuisance with the indifference of butcher slaughtering a goat.

Roland was called outside by the pilot, and I was left alone to make conversation with Don Vito. The only words I had received from him up to that moment had been his rather brusque "*mucho gusto*" (pleased to meet you)— and now it was being followed with a bleak stare. Clearly it was up to me to think of a topic that we might have in common to chat about but nothing came to mind. In desperation I asked what he did with all his progeny.

"Left the first ten with their mother."

"She didn't mind?"

"She had a good business. Why should she?"

"Really? What did she do? What was it?"

"She was the madam of a whorehouse."

I wasn't sure if I should commiserate, be shocked or proffer my congratulations. I chose the latter option and Don Vito, relieved that I was not a narrow-minded, censorious bore, smiled. By the time Roland returned he had even offered to take me on a tour of "the sites."

Riding with the cowboys, sorting, branding and vaccinating, days passed very agreeably and I came to appreciate the long-eared Cebú cattle. They were hardy animals reared for beef. Only a few cows were worth milking so the majority of calves ran freely with their mothers suckling at will for the first seven months of their lives. In that climate they out-pastured all year round so the toil, stress and expense of making hay or silage was both unknown and unnecessary.

When there was no cattle work, I helped the carpenter construct a garage and workshop for Roland's tractors and implements. As the only standard building supplies for sale in Poponte were nails and cement brought from Barranquilla at enormous cost, initiative and ingenuity were needed to find local material for archways and columns which would be immune to the ravages of termites. Pieces of iron salvaged from the Spaniard's cemetery of discarded machinery were welded together to make skeletons for vertical concrete pillars but hard-wood tree trunks were the preferred material for overhead beams. Every day offered something of interest and I found living in an environment where necessity honed improvisation enormously satisfying.

One afternoon I decided it was time to go and see what Poponte had to offer. As no bearded foreigner had ever ridden into the village before, the inhabitants were, at first, uncertain how to regard me. Some mothers decided to tell their children that if they were not "good" the bearded bogy man would eat them. It was the beginning of a game that soon made me a popular figure. On subsequent visits I got off my horse, hunched my shoulders and, with open fingers waving in front of me as if to grab a wayward child, walked down the one and only street like a bandy legged, drunken King Kong. Mothers welcomed me with genuine shrieks of laughter, children with uncertain squeals of fear.

Wandering through the nearby forest at dawn made an uplifting contrast. Early morning rays of light illuminated tree trunks soaring like cathedral columns into a branched tracery and emphasized the reds of bromeliads and yellow tints of turning leaves. Sounds seemed sharper in the coolness of early morning and one was aware that there were many more varieties of bird song than could ever be heard in England. In overhead canopies monkeys rubbed their eyes and at the edges of streams delicate footprints showed where dwarf deer had stopped to drink. A disturbed tapir might crash through the underbrush and once I caught sight of an ocelot. After rain storms butterflies, gathered around patches of glistening mud at the edge of hollows, would rise and dance around my head. Amidst all this splendor I sometimes forgot to scan the ground for snakes. In a wooded declivity between two mountain bluffs Motilone Indians had left crossed arrows to mark the entrance to their territory and one morning I saw an Indian fishing in the river there with bow and arrow. He must have sensed he was observed for like a wild deer he silently disappeared into the underbrush.

Life was delightfully free from conventional inhibitions and restrictions. For most people business transactions were concluded with a shake of the hand and an exchange of cash. Cheques were rarely received as so many had bounced on presentation in the nearest bank some fifteen miles away. Account books, for those who needed them, were a way of presenting facts for whatever it was that needed to be proved. One set of books might show a profit to obtain a bank loan; a second could show a loss to include with income tax forms and the third, fictitious births and deaths of livestock to show an associate. Impecunious accountants could always be relied upon either to produce, or fabricate, invoices and receipts to give credibility. Reliable financial details were kept safely in the interested party's head.

Halfway through my stay Roland took me to see the homestead that he suggested I buy. He'd found managing his father's ranch socially restricting and welcomed the thought of a neighbor with a European background. Clearly he had far more resources at his disposal than I but we were both young and keen to make something of our lives. Moreover he volunteered his support and the benefit of his experience . This was an offer not to abuse but certainly one not to dismiss. Something inside me responded favorably. Rather than being constrained by the parameters of conventional employment, homesteading offered me the rare opportunity to mould an environment to my liking.

---

*A parasitic disease of parrots transmissible to man.

As we drove back to Roland's ranch it struck me that all my life I'd received the benefits of other people's efforts without contributing much in return. Perhaps it was time to add my worth to what Siegfried Sassoon termed, "The old proud pageant of man."

Hours ticked by, sleep evaded me and doubts wracked my mind. "What the bloody hell am I thinking?" I muttered as I pulled the sheet over my head to shut out the noise of a whining mosquito. I must be half witted! Nobody in their right mind enters into the life of an alien community and embarks by themselves on a project they know nothing about. I tossed and turned. I saw myself as prosperous, as a pauper, as a respected member of the community and shunned as a pariah. It was not until daybreak that I slept. During the next few days I walked over every square meter of the homestead, met my prospective neighbors and enquired about local services. There weren't many. Roland took me to market towns and introduced me to shopkeepers. Finally, I went into the village, not as a bogy man, but to appraise the advantages, drawbacks and characteristics of the community.

The cluster of basic dwellings known as Poponte, situated a mile from a river called La Mula, had been founded in the early 1900s by adventurers settling on traditional Motilone Indian hunting ground. Land was free for the taking and newcomers not only built homes for themselves next to the last house in the single street but staked out farms for themselves in the wooded foothills. Homes were simple dwellings with palm leaf roofs, walls of bamboo or mud and wattle and a rudimentary palisade door. In the fertile soil cacao (the tree from whose pods the chocolate bean is harvested), yucca (the plant whose tuber supplies the staple carbohydrate of the tropics), maize, breadfruit and bananas flourished. Although much woodland was felled, countless acres were left in a virgin state to serve as a living warehouse. Despite the influx of new settlers, Poponte had neither a church, bank, post office or hotel. In 1957 the only buildings serving the public were a general store and a saloon with a diesel-powered light plant.

The latter business was owned and managed by a cadaverous miscreant named José Chiquito who found weird amusement in embarrassing newcomers by hunching his back and groping obscenely in his ill-fitting trousers to adjust a ruptured testicle. He supplied cold beer, a pool table fitted with a stained and cigarette-burnt felt and, in a row of cubicles at the rear, whores who had dissipated the best years of their working life elsewhere. His sales pitch as he proffered their services was "Catchee money nice price." For many hard-working *campesinos*, living basic lives on isolated farms during the week and trekking on Saturday afternoons into Poponte to buy provisions, a night cavorting in José Chiquito's saloon with its bright lights, cold drinks and cheap women seemed like a preview of Paradise.

There was no other electricity in the village. No water mains, drains, police station, telecommunication center or launderette. When an early morning sky indicated a sunny day groups of women balanced bundles of dirty clothes on their heads and sauntered with sensuously twitching buttocks to the river's edge where astride flat stones they pounded the garments to be washed with stout wooden clubs. When clothes were considered clean they were laid over warm stones to dry. The gossip exchanged as they worked made the day more of a social outing than a chore. Should a man's contraceptive float out of a pocket there was always raucous laughter followed by ribald speculation as on whom it had been used. To dull pangs of hunger the washer women smoked short lengths of locally rolled cigar. The butts were never thrown away. With a clever flick of their tongues the burning ends and the soggy stumps were reversed. Saliva reduced the stumps to a mush that when slowly chewed released flakes of tobacco which were savored at leisure.

The village, shut off from the rest of the world without even a television transmitting station covering the area, was an anachronism in the twentieth century. The one celebration that united the community occurred at the stroke of midnight on New Years Eve. Old and young gathered in the main street to embrace each other and fire their home-made pistols and iron-pipe shotguns into the air.

The palm fronds used to roof homes grew locally and provided a cool shade from the midday heat. Their drawback—before tons of DDT were shipped for widespread spraying in rural Colombia after that chemical had been banned in the United States as a health hazard—was that they provided a labyrinth where cockroaches bred in hundreds of thousands. The only practical way of controlling these pests was to allow chickens to roam freely inside the house. While cockroaches falling to the floor were recycled into tasty eggs, poultry droppings on the floor were messy underfoot and attracted flies.

I supposed that the economical construction of homes was due to the owner's desire to put his resources into something that provided an income. In the equitable tropical climate villagers tended to socialize more under the shade of a tree at the side of the street than in their homes. A home was a place to keep one's clothes—usually in a cardboard box—and where one went to sleep at night. Typically it had a door back and front, two bedrooms with a small window in each and a kitchen shed in the garden. The bedroom furnished with a wooden planked bed and a chamber pot was reserved for the owner, the spouse of the moment and any new born babies. Everyone else in the family slept in the other. Anyone lucky enough to own a hammock slung it at nightfall from the rafters while those less fortunate lay on rush mats spread over the earthen floor. During the day hammocks and sleeping mats were rolled up in a corner or put outside in the sunshine to air. In a corner would be an axe, a machete and probably a tool for loosening soil around yucca plants. But not everything was utilitarian. Pasted to the walls were colorful, full-page advertisements from glossy magazines salvaged from Roland's rubbish heap. The kitchen sheds were of rudimentary design being open to the elements on three sides but with a wall on the fourth to shelter the waist-high hearth from horizontally blown rain common during tropical storms. Attached to the wall, smoke blackened shelves held assorted foods wrapped in banana leaves. Fire wood was stacked under the hearth, pots and pans above it and the grill was made from broken automobile leaf-springs collected when overloaded communal taxis crashed into potholes dotting the unpaved road between Poponte and the Municipal centre of Chiriguana. When members of the household chose the kitchen table as a place to play an evening game of dominos, geckoes took advantage of the swarm of insects attracted by the kerosene burning lanterns to gorge themselves.

Affluent homeowners washed themselves in patio cubicles—discretely screened from the view of passers-by with plastic sheeting—using dippers to scoop water from an open fifty-five-gallon fuel drum filled either during rain storms or from the wells that supplied the village with potable water; impecunious villagers went to the river. Pigs rooted happily at the bottom of gardens or in the many copses at the edge of the village where people went to defecate and I finally understood why in many countries, though curiously not in Colombia, pork is considered unclean food.

Most women knew that their liaisons would soon end if they made wearisome complaints about childbearing. Pregnancy—the accepted fulfilment of the female role—was proudly displayed, but when age put an end to that possibility, sex still flourished. Don Vito assured me that after years of assiduously practising the art of inducing memorable climaxes, certain women had acquired the skill of transcending the ordinary gonadotrophic spasms of their partners into the bliss of a total body orgasm. Thus there were unions where a strong matriarchal figure dominated the home. The husband might be allowed moments of infidelity—for these proved his virility in the eyes of the village—but such affairs could be expensive should the wife discover that another woman had been taken to the matrimonial bed. When that happened, the wife was more than likely to burn both bed and bedding and refrain from any marital sex until her penitent spouse had shown his adoration by the purchase of new bedroom furniture. Such reconciliations enhanced the public image of each partner.

The penchant for promiscuity resulted in a bewildering array of progeny of uncertain paternity but I saw no dysfunctional children. The custom of breast feeding babies for their first year bonded mother and child and the experience gave each successive sibling both a sense of security and, in the knowledge of being lovable, a confidence in themselves. Such attributes helped to sustain them when exploring their surroundings, making tentative contacts with others of their own age or playing quietly by themselves. When torrential rain fell, as it often did in the afternoons, children unabashedly stripped and showered with bars of blue laundry soap under water cascading from their roofs. In their imaginations old tin cans pulled by lengths of vines became toy cars. Banana leaves, sprays of exotic flowers and sun bleached bones provided material for ingenious games. Scraps of coloured paper and striped plastic bags strung across the street at Christmas time gave the village a festive air. Pleasure was its own reward when something they created was successful, and if what was attempted proved disappointing they tried something else. The simplicity of children's surroundings encouraged the development of self-reliance and competence. Smiles were not put on to please adults, they emerged as joyful expressions of being in harmony with their environment.

Had the youth of Poponte been permanently isolated from the outside world, their seemingly idyllic formative years—as I initially thought them— might have been ample preparation for adult life. But children growing up in economically deprived homes where communal ownership of possessions is as natural as breathing seldom understand conventions regarding private property. How could a child learn the consequences of pilfering something of value when there was nothing of value to pilfer?

Emel, as a lad from a poor home in Poponte, had often been sent into the street without breakfast and told to fend for himself. Sometimes he went to the river with hook and line intending to fish but if that proved unsuccessful and he returned mid-day with a bunch of cooking bananas and a wandering chicken to put in the stew pot he was neither reprimanded nor his booty questioned. Relations who might have done so were not invited to share the free meal. He reached manhood untroubled by qualms of conscience concerning occasional acts of petty thievery and proceeded to the lucrative practice of stealing calves from the herds of cattle pasturing on the unfenced savannas near Chiriguana. When apprehended and sentenced to a short term in jail, his reaction was that of being unlucky, not of having done something wrong. Next time he would have to be more careful. The ease of stealing calves was too attractive. Although capital punishment is proscribed in Colombian law, after Emel's fourth conviction special police drove him to a deserted savanna where his body was later found by a cowboy investigating a flock of squabbling vultures. The community gave him a decent burial in the cemetery but agreed that the means of his passing was a fitting retribution on a member of society who had made a habit of by-passing the accepted norms of working for his daily bread.

In other respects the people showed a mature tolerance to eccentric behavior. One elderly peasant set off to work every morning conventionally dressed. Out of sight around a bend in the track that led to his smallholding he took off all his clothes and put them, carefully folded, into a sack which he carried over his shoulder. Unworn clothes, he reasoned, stay new; torn clothes have to be mended or replaced but scratched skin heals itself. He continued on the path wearing only his straw hat which, if he met anybody, he doffed politely and then held in front of his private parts as greetings were exchanged. While working in his clearing he wore a tattered singlet and a red cotton loincloth to protect himself from the sun's rays. The waterfall under which he bathed at the end of the day pummeled away his sweat and massaged the aching muscles of his back. Like many others, he found there was a sensuous pleasure in scrubbing himself with handfuls of sand till a cleanliness tingled the length of his body. Having washed himself, he rinsed his singlet and rectangle of red cotton and hung them under a palm leaf shelter to dry overnight. Nearing Poponte he untied his sack and returned to the village a model of propriety. Blessedly, commercial television programs aimed at making non-conformity a cause for neurotic anxieties—and non essential luxuries, necessities—had not yet been transmitted to the area. Villagers went through their lives happily unaware that they should regard themselves as inferior because they failed to conform to the images of sanitized people depicted on commercials.

Lacking the sophistication to indulge in theoretical concepts of male and female roles in society, fathers and mothers in Poponte provided a prototype of masculinity and femininity for children to copy. Men provided what was necessary for the women to keep the home, bear and cherish their children and produce meals. While there were no obvious signs of competition between these roles, as the work of each was necessary to ensure the stability of village life, primitive instincts of masculine sexuality in pursuit, penetration and pride in the number of progeny made Poponte a macho dominated society. Pent up frustrations, while occasionally liberated in bouts of drinking, customarily found an outlet in the rugged physical exertion of wielding an axe or machete while clearing land.

The police and municipal employees of Chiriguana no longer had recourse to such outlets and social invitations were likely to end in scenes of carousal. I heard that late one evening Chiriguana had resounded with the sounds of a celebration coming from the Mayor's residence. In small towns the participation of functionaries in communal amusements assume a camaraderie seldom witnessed in cities. Shortly after midnight the Mayor, followed by his political cronies, the police and most of the town's adult population all in the nude except for chicken feathers stuffed between their buttocks, had lead a conga line down the main street in the popular "Dance of the Plumes."

The schoolmaster was a disappointment. One day I noticed children playing in the street, the school house closed and the schoolmaster, too drunk to stand, seated in the shade of a tree. He was the centre of a roistering crowd of well-wishers singing bawdy songs and guffawing over each other's wit. Clearly he has received good news I thought as I was called over to join them. Without the slightest embarrassment he boasted, "I've got two more sons! Come, a celebratory drink to their health. Last night both my mistress and my wife gave birth!"

Rather worryingly, academic accomplishment appeared to be limited to a competence in the three "R's," the knack of writing on a typewriter with two fingers rather than one and the ability to recite religious tracts from memory. Young people aspiring to a position in a government related office needed a relation who could offer a politician a block of family votes in exchange for the appointment. Even with a patron, tenure was hazardous. With each change of government non-essential personnel were replaced by supporters of the new regime. Keeping oneself on the payroll in an office largely staffed by incompetent party stalwarts required a willingness to "satisfy" the patron in any and every way.

Occasionally an itinerant dentist visited Poponte. The only cure for all dental problems was the pair of pliers carried in his trouser pocket. The patient kneeled open mouthed, the dentist put his knee against the sufferer's chest and even if the pliers slipped on the first tug the second usually removed the offending tooth. Should, in the dentist's absence, an extraction be required, the sufferer tied one end of a piece of string around the tooth causing pain and the other end to the latch of an open door. Then he braced himself in a chair and a friend dislodged the tooth by slamming the door shut. Quite understandably there was much excited commotion when a machine for "fixing" teeth rather than pulling them arrived in the village. The drill, driven by a foot treadle from an old sewing machine, was worn and probably months had passed since it had been properly sterilized, but the apparatus filled the villagers with admiration. Only the chair caused concern. The dentist had attached arm straps to it after a patient had punched him on the nose.

The nearest medical doctor, a virile, jovial man, lived in the neighboring village. He practiced both general medicine and gynaecology but was better known for the latter. Women flocked to his surgery and it was accepted knowledge that over the years he had sired twenty-two children in his consulting room. Prominently displayed on the wall of his office hung a gilt-framed and glazed diploma from an American correspondence college written in English. It gave him great prestige, as none of his patients could translate "Certificate of Proficiency in First Aid Awarded to...." Along the shelves were an array of technical pamphlets sent by pharmaceutical companies to advertise new products. These he pursued when he thought a patient's complaint interesting, or when somebody went to see him after other doctors had failed to find a cure. He often invited me to his house to drink beer as it gave him an opportunity to practice his English. Having worked in Bristol as a hospital orderly during the travels of his youth he enjoyed reminiscing about his night time escapades in the nurse's dormitory. One evening he confided, "I've had a happy life, and I'll tell you why. I discovered the secret about doctoring. Seventy per cent of patients recover from their illnesses due to natural powers of recuperation, fifteen percent can be cured with antibiotics, but no matter what's prescribed, the rest will die. What other profession gives an eighty-five per cent success rate and provides the opportunity for so much pleasure?"

I enjoyed his beer and the prestige of his friendship but kept our relationship on a non-professional level.

Poponte's nurse was both illiterate and opinionated. She insisted that the one and only syringe and needle in the village could be adequately sterilized by being rinsed in soapy water and then dipped in a bottle of alcohol. Remedies, whether for humans or livestock, cluttered a shelf in her kitchen. By the shape of a bottle or the color of its label she chose which medicine to use. She met her nemesis after injecting a man with what she thought was penicillin with a purge for expelling afterbirth from cows. The unfortunate fellow reached the street writhing in agony. There he pulled down his trousers and became the object of animated conjecture to passers by as, with the exception of his ears, spectacular emissions spewed from every orifice of his body. The nurse was dismissed but her replacement, enjoying the company of men and exhibiting a predilection for drinking alcohol with them, failed to endear herself to the women of the village. One night she passed out while trying to finish a bottle of *aguardiente*—a distilled drink which translates as "fire water"—which her drinking companions had wagered she couldn't do. Her insensate body was carried to the room used as an emergency health centre and left on a cot. The news spread quickly and by dawn nearly every able-bodied man in the village had taken advantage of her. Women were neither unduly surprised nor upset that their husbands or partners had been momentarily unfaithful. After all, that was how most of their own liaisons had begun. A few mothers were even pleased that their young sons had progressed along the sexual route to orthodox fatherhood with a woman instead of satisfying their youthful lust with a donkey—commonly, I was told, the first heterosexual partner of pubescent boys. Be that as it may, the village agreed that it needed the services of a competent nurse who commanded respect and would be available as a midwife at any hour. Using their momentary solidarity to effect, the women commandeered an ancient truck that carried passengers between Poponte and Chiriguana and descended on the Mayor like a swarm of angry hornets. To my amazement, a first-class nurse was found and appointed. She later attended the birth of my own children.

There was a hospital building in Chiriguana. Those who couldn't afford to go anywhere else, or needed emergency treatment, were taken there for surgery. A coffin maker—there were no undertakers as relations buried their own dead—worked at the front entrance and was constantly busy. When one of Roland's workmen, José, developed a ruptured hernia, I volunteered to drive him there in the ranch jeep. It was a vivid experience. Lying on the floor inside the operating room was a mutilated human finger. Without any preliminary tests, José was ordered to strip. Then, strapped to the table, he was swabbed with alcohol and injected with a local anesthetic. When the doctor cut an exploratory incision, José screamed, "Ow, I can feel that!"

"Steady, José, steady," growled the doctor. "Some of these anesthetics need time to take effect." Turning to the nurse, he added, "Give him another fifteen cc's."

I remembered seeing a painting of a surgery by Hogarth where the anesthetic is a bottle of rum and dashed out to buy one. The doctor was pleased to have it as, when I returned, José was unconscious.

The community was not attuned to equal job opportunities for the sexes and when a woman was appointed as Inspector of Police for Poponte her tenure was memorable for its brevity. The unfortunate lady arrived to take possession of her office only to discover a liberal layer of human excrement embalming the padlock securing a hasp to the door. She couldn't insert the key without sacrificing her dignity. Hearing peals of raucous laughter from a group of nearby men, doubtless anticipating further hilarious anecdotes at her expense, and not relishing the prospect of becoming the object of a merry morning ritual, she immediately resigned.

Nowhere in the municipality of Chiriguana were there regulations concerning the sale of alcoholic drinks. Over weekends bars remained open twenty-four hours a day. Early morning disagreements between inebriated campesinos often led to machete fights and even loss of life. The Inspector of Police, usually a local civilian with no greater authority than the force of his own personality, wasn't paid to leave his bed during the night to intervene in drunken brawls and had he done so his presence would not have been appreciated. In any case it wasn't needed. Over the years the community of Poponte had evolved its own way of coping with altercations that led to the death of the loser. The survivor was given several hours to collect his possessions, saddle his horse and head for the hills. The lacerated limbs of those who had attempted to intervene were treated by the resident nurse who applied iodine before stitching up the cuts.

Apart from a ritual outpouring of grief at a burial, sentimentality about birth and death was rare. When you were ready to be born, you were. When it was time to die, little was done to postpone the inevitable. Decisions regarding life or death depended more on gut reactions than sentimental morality. A woodcutter called Trino displayed the former when his mother took to her bed. He left an open coffin for her to contemplate while he went to work. When he came back, she was ready to be placed inside it.

As public participation in regular church services was minimal, to ensure that the procession down the single street to intercede with the Almighty for rain when thunderclouds were rumbling after a prolonged drought would be impressive, the priest from Chiriguana brought with him a cadre of devout women to chant the responses and incantations. The priest's visits were seldom acts of Christian love. Transport, a chicken lunch and a generous contribution to the Church were the demanded prerequisites.

I first met the priest one Sunday afternoon at Roland's ranch. He'd arrived with two women in a jeep and after being invited into the house for a lemonade had asked permission to pass to a swimming place in the river. On going outside to see them off, Roland noticed that there were neither towels nor swimsuits. Would they like to borrow some towels? The offer was refused. There was no pretence, no apology, nor any sense of the need for one. A priest of the people occasionally indulged in worldly pleasures. Surely confession restored grace after a sinful lapse?

The Pentecostal faithful offered another religious option. Daily meetings resounded with "the words of the Lord" and revivalist songs. During the latter everybody swayed happily and either raised their arms to Heaven or clapped in unison. New members were attracted by the demonstrative joy of gatherings at the river's edge where converts were baptized by total immersion but the congregation never increased significantly. Inflexible adherence to the demanded code of sexual behavior was irksome, incompatible with natural urges, and the cause of frequent defections.

If I decided to buy the homestead, these people were representative of the population that would be my daily contact with the human race. It was a sobering prospect. Whereas in England the countryside is liberally sprinkled with professionals, academics and eccentrics all actively interested in their vocations, intellectual interchange in the municipality of Chiriguana appeared to be non-existent. There was no public reference library, and the dilatory postal service ensured that if one wrote away for technical information the reply would arrive long after the need for it had passed. I could forget about Social Services. If I became ill and died, I would be buried within twenty four hours—a necessary hygiene in the heat of the tropics—and be forgotten. Luckily, material comforts had never been of great importance to me. I enjoyed them when they were there, but having lived in both basic and affluent surroundings I realized that they were merely worldly adjuncts to a sense of well-being, not essential components of happiness.

✐ ✐ ✐ ✐

Roland was called for dental treatment in Bogotá and I was left with Don Vito—a man who didn't tolerate ditherers. Each morning a placard on the dining-room wall with the inscription "Guests and fish smell after three days" reminded me that welcomes were limited. However graciously the Hughes family had treated me in Bogotá, I couldn't help but feel that I was being urged to determine whether to start farming or not, and soon.

In the hope that if I spent a night in the homestead I'd become aware of a signal to decide me, I borrowed a hammock, rolled some rice, yucca and boiled meat in a banana leaf and walked back along the jungle track to the howler monkey tree. A breeze waved branches along the avenue of sprouted fence posts and Caracucho flowers in friendly welcomes; fallen coconuts waited to be collected; lemons and grapefruit were ready to be picked and from a rafter in the kitchen the Curucucú nodded his head sagely as if to say, "I knew it." I felt accepted and didn't feel any need for human company.

I slung my hammock between two coconut palms with trunks leaning away from each other and took my supper to the stream. The water was as translucent as I remembered and the surroundings to the pool as magical. As darkness descended the tuneless rasping of cicadas faded into silence. Stars appeared through the overhead canopy of branches and peace permeated my soul. I stripped by the light of an emerging moon and, entering the pool, floated on my back admiring the firmament.

You're not going to find any signals gazing at stars, Curry. Get out of your bath and think why you're here.

Chagrined, I put on my clothes and returned to the hammock. Random thoughts swirled in my head as I swung to and fro but the only thing that came clearly to mind was the tale of a cadet at a famous military academy in his final examination. The question presented was, "What procedures would you adopt to put up a nine-meter-long tubular flagpole of half-inch galvanised iron with an external diameter of eight and a half inches, on an island of coral rock subjected to force six gales blowing from the north to north-east quarter for three months of the year? You have two hours in which to write your answer." The brightest cadets got out their slide rules and started to work out the stresses and strains of wind-warped tube as related to metal fatigue, the necessary tensile strengths of retaining cables and—if such a thing exists—the compactability quotient of coral rock. The least bright cadet, Willie, scratched his head and scribbling a sentence on his answer form handed it in and went out into the sunshine. The other cadets smiled smugly, shook their heads and while continuing their calculations thought, "It's a pity about poor old Willie." His answer, however, was the only correct one: "Sergeant, take a detail and erect a flagpole."

My reverie was broken by a falling coconut missing the hammock by inches and thudding into the ground and I became aware of scurrying nocturnal creatures underneath me getting on with their lives. Suddenly the sequence of Willie's answer, the falling coconut and the busy animals seemed to have significance. Were they the signals?

You mustn't expect signals to be answers, Curry. They're only omens to be guided by.

Obediently I went over them one at a time.

Willie: When confronted by imponderables choose a pragmatic solution.

The falling coconut: Dangers abound but if sensible precautions are taken things that can harm have their use.

The scurrying animals: Animals getting on with their lives don't wait for the sun to shine.

I looked over the edge of my hammock to consult my moonlit shadow which was patiently waiting for me to make a move. "What do you think, partner. Shall we buy the place?" As I gave a questioning bob of my head my shadow simultaneously responded with a nod. "O.K. It's settled. Let's go for it!"

THREE

Hacienda Curucucú

That which I have not conceived lures me constantly,
and where I have never been receives me always.
Into the inexplicable I was born and that I learned was home.
Others went astray and wandered helpless among the known, while I
guided by the Hidden-Real, straightway find forever the impossible.

—Harper Brown

The belaboured sighs of a slowly rotating ceiling fan in the Notary's office merged with the undulating drone of the Clerk's voice as he read me the contract transferring ownership of the homestead, and I found the legal jargon difficult to follow. I was on the point of giving up when I caught the words "the property La Pretención."

"Stop!" I cried.

The notary glanced irritably in my direction. "There is a problem?"

"It's that awful name, La Pretención. I insist it be changed."

"You have an alternative?"

I hadn't, but suddenly I remembered the owl. "Of course," I replied, "Curucucú."

The clerk raised his eyebrows in disbelief. Give a farm the name of a bird? Ridiculous.

What did I care? I'd given the homestead a name and it was mine!

Later that afternoon it occurred to me that I was decidedly odd in my feeling of elation. I'd severed myself from the accustomed luxuries associated with electric power, piped water and modern household equipment and ought to feel despondent. But I didn't. I felt confident in my ability to tackle all the improvements waiting to be made, but I must confess, in the course of that first week my spirits oscillated. The purchase of a sturdy second-hand, four wheel drive Willy's pickup truck which a friend of Roland was selling allowed me to become independent of Hacienda Poponte and with it I was able to bring building materials to improve the comforts of my new home. An uncomfortable night in a narrow hammock prompted me to buy some carpentry tools and some rough-hewn planks to make a work bench and a bed. The results pleased me and were followed by a rustic chair, a table, and a dresser with two cupboards. An attack of diarrhea slowed my work and convinced me to buy— apart from a cotton mattress—my only luxury, a second-hand refrigerator cooled by burning a kerosene-soaked wick. It seemed contrary to reason that such an apparatus would make ice, but make ice it did and by keeping food from spoiling helped to keep me healthy. Once a week a lorry from villages over a hundred miles away in the Department of Santander entered Poponte selling cool climate vegetables. Undoubtedly a cookbook would have provided some welcome recipes to make dishes of boiled cabbage, carrot, potato and onion more interesting, but even if I had possessed such a book, two saucepans on a wood burning hearth precluded most culinary experiments. Mixing whatever the lorry brought with the meat, fish or eggs on sale in the village I invented healthy meals which were easy and quick to prepare.

For the majority of the local populace I was an enigma. They couldn't understand how a person who knew how to do so many things could be so ignorant about the basic aspects of the environment known by every young child. A book on tropical husbandry had informed me that tubers of the yucca plant, *Manihot esculenta*, contain prussic acid and were fatal if eaten raw. If yucca plants had developed such an effective protection against the ravages of rooting foragers how, I wondered, could peasants safely feed raw chopped tubers to their pigs? A friendly neighbour patiently explained the conundrum. "That guy who wrote that book sure didn't travel much in the tropics. You see, there're two varieties of yucca, bitter and sweet, and only the bitter contains prussic acid. Indians in the jungle cultivate the bitter variety but neutralize the acid by cooking the tubers. Here *campesinos* cultivate the sweet variety. Simple huh?"

He later invited me to a lunch of stewed chicken. When he casually tossed a leg bone over his shoulder, I cried out in alarm. Any one of the circle of dogs around the table could have snatched it in mid air. I had been brought up to believe that crunched chicken bones could splinter into shards and perforate a gut. He treated my concern with derision. "Where the heck do you think you are? My dogs are hunters. All the animals they catch have bones and believe you me, after they've eaten all that's left are feathers or fur." To retrieve my host's respect and restore my self confidence I had to catch a gecko, which he believed to be poisonous, and hold it in my hand.

✐ ✐ ✐ ✐

Having attended to my basic creature comforts, my next priority was to plant a cash crop. If I put up the farm as surety for a bank loan to pay for clearing the land with a bulldozer and lose the crop due to my lack of experience or bad weather I would lose everything I was hoping to achieve. I resolved to prepare land peasant fashion with an axe and a machete. But before beginning I asked my neighbour to show me which trees could be felled and which, valuable for their wood, shade or beauty, should be left standing. With that done, I braced myself and went out under the blazing tropical sun and started to hack away at the undergrowth. After a few hours I could barely move my fingers for the blisters. While undoubtedly my predicament caused much good humoured laughter among my neighbours, all of whom had hands calloused by manual labour, my efforts were treated with respect. Two unemployed labourers glad to earn some money enlarged my feeble four square yards of severed scrub into an area of three acres and then persuaded me that setting fire had advantages over composting. Venomous snakes and insects, branches and twigs would be incinerated and ashes rich in minerals would immediately become available to nourish the seeds I planted.

After the first rainfall I tied a basket filled with maize kernels to my belt and clambered among the tangle of unburned residue from the fire with a pointed stick. With it, using my left hand, I jabbed holes in the soil at metre intervals into which, using my right hand, I dropped four or five kernels of maize. To protect them from mice, I had to give them a foot scuffed covering of soil.

Within a week maize was shooting up but so were tropical weeds which I had either to pull up by the roots or sever with a machete at ground level. Sometimes as I paused to straighten my back and flex my shoulders I wondered what my Cambridge colleagues would think could they see me: It's a

A neighbor demonstrating the art of planting maize.

pity about poor old Curry? Our paths had certainly diverged. I had chosen the less travelled one, and they the other. Although my vision was momentarily blurred by the sweat of manual toil, when I envisaged the ranch I would make, in my heart I was happy at having taken the path of my choice.

While I exchanged friendly greetings with the men, women and children who passed through the homestead, some with donkeys to collect firewood others taking bundles of washing to the river or going there to fish, I seldom took time off to join them.

On rare occasions I went to Chiriguana in my pickup truck in search of what Freud termed "some indispensable palliative remedy to counter the pains and disappointments of life," but found that sex in the brothel there was more of a brief physical romp than an experience satisfying an emotional need. A row of beds, placed about one metre apart, were separated by curtains suspended from the ceiling by lengths of string. Sounds of shoes dropping on to the cement floor, squeaking wooden frames and the sighs and moans of the clients gave ardent intensity to the atmosphere. But when, as often happened, a voice cried out that his money had been stolen, pandemonium ensued. Curtains separating cubicles were brusquely ripped to one side by scantily clad jokesters demanding that the mating couples stand and submit to total body searches. It was always possible, the intruders maintained, that the money having been passed under the curtains was secreted in the cleft between the buttocks or under the armpits of an accomplice.

In spite of Don Vito's well meant introductions to some of his accomplished lady friends whose pulsating vaginas acted on an inserted penis like a milking machine on the teat of a cow, I always felt after such an event, no mat-

Using two stones, a neighbor's wife grinds maize into flour.

ter how momentarily exhilarating, that I was no more than one of a line of faceless clients who, far from being conscious of some special shared affection, had paid to experience an impersonalised circus trick. If my aim was to real-ize a dream of making Curucucú a successful cattle ranch I couldn't get involved in some amorous entanglement in the village which would curtail my independence, dissipate my energies, deplete my resources and very likely end in commitments which I was not ready to make. Somerset Maugham's stories of isolated British planters in the Far East were warnings of the cultural incompatibilities which could so easily impair a long term relationships with a local girl. Still, like most people who live alone, I secretly yearned for a faith-ful companion with whom I could share feelings of love.

Heraclitis filled that void. He came from a litter of mongrel puppies and, although he had the freedom to run freely, he would return from a hunting foray with a leap as if to embrace me. If he didn't stink of decayed carcass I allowed him to lick my face and I, laughing at his exuberance, would give him a hug. In the evenings, with a lantern on the table and Heraclitis at my feet, I relaxed with a book or, if I had the energy, wrote in my diary. One entry, recorded in doggerel, parodies A.A. Milne's poem "The Old Sailor":

A horse and a cow I most certainly need
with well kept fences and grass for their feed;
but a post needs an axe and a hole needs a spade
barbed wire's so expensive I'm really afraid
that my funds'll run out at a lickety hop.
I must shelve all these plans and attend to my crop!

By the end of the second harvest and third burning, most of the felled tree trunks had been converted into ashes and only the stumps remained. Although I spent every spare moment cutting and chopping, by the end of the year there were less than seven acres cleared. I realised that I had underestimated my need for a tractor—without one I would remain at *campesino* level for a long, long time. With confidence in my new-found understanding of tropical agriculture and with encouragement from neighbouring farmers who promised me contract work, I decided to buy a Massey Ferguson. By selling the pick-up truck and borrowing money from my family, I covered the down payment and financed the remaining costs by signing promissory notes in a newly opened account in the Chiriguana bank. When the tractor finally arrived pulling weakened stumps and gathering them for burning became fun! As soon as the land was cleared, I borrowed a heavy disk harrow from Don Vito and planted sesame.

With abundant rain the crop grew well in the new soil. Some two months later I was happily singing while preparing my lunch when I chanced to look up. A lanky, grey-haired Negro, with a hammock slung around his neck, was approaching the kitchen. He wore his clothes with the insouciance of a scarecrow but, as he came closer, I was attracted by his honest weathered face. He had kindly crinkles in the corners of his eyes. I looked at his hands. They were gnarled in a manner only attainable after years of manual toil. He asked if I had anything for him to do. My stock answer to requests for work was that I didn't have the money to employ anybody, but that morning I was in a charitable mood.

"*Como se llama*? (What's your name?)," I asked.

"Crisanto Forbes Archibald, sir," he replied with a smile.

Well, I thought, that's a good old piratical surname. I wondered what his background was. Perhaps I could offer him work. I was soon going to need help harvesting the sesame.

"*Y de donde viene* ? (And where have you come from?)"

"I be born on San Andrés Island, sir," he answered in English.

"Good Lord! Where did you learn English? Isn't San Andrés Colombian?"

"British buccaneers live der long before de island become Colombian, sir. Many of us speak English."

It was refreshing to converse in my native tongue. There was possibly enough lunch for two and he looked as though he could do with a meal. "Have you eaten?"

"No, sir," he said. "What cooking in de pot smell mighty fine to me."

His vernacular amused me, but I had the uneasy feeling that his English was probably better than my Spanish. Locals had often replied, "Yes, sir," to me, and then asked a companion, "What did he want?" Chuckling to myself I said, "OK, I'll add more water to the stew and we'll divide it. Go and pick some lemons and we'll make a jug of lemonade."

As we ate, I discovered that while Cristano was willing to help in any job, on his island he had worked as a carpenter.

"I work at everything, but mostly I enjoy de work shaping tings from wood."

"You could make me a couple of rocking chairs?"

"I surely could."

"I might not be able to pay you regularly."

"Oh dat's just fine, sir. I've left my family so I don't needs money all de time."

"I can only offer you work till the sesame is harvested."

"I's glad to help you, sir."

When we'd finished eating he slung his hammock in the room next to the kitchen.

It was still too early to cut the sesame and while we waited for the pods to mature Crisanto went into the village to find lengths of native hardwood suitable for the rockers of the chairs he was making. Like many men who drifted into Poponte he harboured a defect and it didn't take long to discover what it was. He was incapable of resisting the lure of drink and when paid headed straight towards José Chiquito's bar. Soulfully serenading the dawn with songs he composed about being far away from home, he would return with an abashed grin and a piece of meat tied to his wrist by the butcher. "If I goes to my hammock for a little sleep till breakfast, I's mighty grateful if you save me a piece of dis." The meat he gave me wasn't a sign of remorse for his intemperance but a recognition that as I had shared my soup with him he would share what he had with me. Although I was tempted to throw him out on such occasions, reflecting that no one is perfect, I refrained from doing so. Drink comforted his disappointments and I could scarcely claim to be free of eccentricity. What was of more immediate importance was his philosophic acceptance of the loss of a day's wages and his companionable contribution to the larder.

One morning I was startled out of my sleep by a shriek of terror followed by muted gurgles of fear coming from Crisanto's room. If he was having an attack of delirium tremens I didn't know what to do but I felt I ought to go and see what was troubling him. A boa constrictor, bulging with something probably caught in the thatch, was dangling from a rafter and using Crisanto in his hammock as a ladder to reach the ground. It was quite likely that all the snake wanted was a drink of water. To Crisanto, however, awakening to the feel of sliding reptilian scales starting around his neck and continuing down to his midriff had been unsettling. I pushed the door wide open and stood to one side. The boa, as if offended by Crisanto's boorish manners, dropped indignantly to the floor and slithered past me towards the stream.

After that I kept back Crisanto's wages to prevent him missing a day by having a hangover. His help was vital to cut the sesame stalks and arrange them in stooks while the pods were still closed. After a week of dry weather the pods would open and the stooks would be ready to be threshed. Then the seed could be winnowed and bagged. Tractor payments were due and I desperately needed a good harvest.

I didn't get one. Rain fell every night for three weeks. The alternate drenching by night and steaming by day caused the sesame to mildew. The pods rotted and continued bad weather blighted my hopes. It was a disastrous season. *Campesinos* also had bad harvests and when they came to request tractor work on credit I had to turn them down. Nobody supplied me with diesel fuel on "pay later" terms. Luckily Crisanto's needs were simple. He was happy with a bottle of alcohol and a bar of laundry soap to wash himself, his clothes and his teeth.

The day came when I was literally without a peso. I'd often gone barefoot for pleasure, now it was a necessity. My last pair of shoes disintegrated and my only other foot-ware were sandals with canvass tops and truck tyre soles. There was nothing in the larder and we would have gone without breakfast had Crisanto not noticed a fallen coconut. As we sat down to share it I turned to him in desperation and appealed, "Is there nothing this farm could produce and sell?"

Crisanto raised the knife he had been using to prise coconut meat out of his piece of shell to pensively scratch his scalp. Finally he gave me an embarrassed grin and confessed, "I knows how to distil liquor, sir. You got two fifty-five-gallon fuel drums that'd do fine fo de still. If you gets some *panela** on credit, I knows where to get me some ferment."

"Come on, Crisanto. You know jolly well that backyard breweries are illegal. What if we were caught distilling? You might get away with it, you're Colombian; but if they found me, I'd be nailed."

"Oh, dey wouldn't do dat, sir. In Colombia brewing's not dat illegal. Big guys do it, little guys do it, and custom make it right. Most everybody enjoys a little drink now and den. I's of de opinion dat distilling's honest work. It makes us money so us can eat and don't have to steal or kill or do nuttin wrong." For him the logic was irrefutable.

For eighteen months I'd put everything I had into Curucucú and more than once teetered on the verge of bankruptcy. It would have been virtuous to have engaged Crisanto in some pedantic quibble in order to show him the errors of his reasoning, but it would be a hollow victory if I deprived myself of the income to keep going. I'd have to give up the farm and return to England a failure. Hunger, the determination to continue, and a perverse curiosity, forced my lips to utter, "OK. Let's try it. How do you make a still?"

"Well, sir, I cut de top off one fifty-five-gallon barrel and der's mi cauldron. I cut de top and bottom off de udder and der's mi chimney. All right?"

I nodded.

"So den I arrange three stones so mi cauldron balances on de top. I puts water in de cauldron and adds bananas, all chopped up fine, de *panela* and den de ferment. In about two days, sir, de mixture heaves and bubbles and I puts de chimney above de cauldron and on de top of dat a big aloominum bowl dats got a tit knocked in the bottom side." Crisanto opened his arms as if to embrace a large washing up bowl and then, in pantomime, caressed a teat beneath it with the fingers of his right hand. "Now I gets to be really busy, sir. When I lights a fire under de cauldron, I got to fill de aloominum bowl wid cool water dat's got to be changed all de time so de alcohol ferment dat's rising inside de chimney finds a place to condense. Mighty soon der's a trickle of pure alcohol running off de tit."

"But if the tit is inside the chimney, how do you collect the alcohol?"

Crisanto gave a blissful smile, realizing I was understanding the intricacies

---

*Blocks of crude sugar produced by boiling the juice of sugar canes.

of his still. "Ah, der's a half gourd fixed under de tit, and from dat a reed carries de nectar through a hole in de chimney to a bucket. Dat's where I blend."

"Blend?"

"Oh, most essential, sir. All de distillate be different. When de ferment be getting hot, I gets pure alcohol. When de ferment be boiling I gets mostly steam water. Dat's where de skill comes in. I mixes one wid de udder and adds aniseed till I gets two strengths dat seem nearly de same." Crisanto grinned. "De first pickle your guts but de second's as weak as angel piss. But oh man, dey both taste mighty fine."

"And then what happens?" I asked innocently.

"Well sir, I pour de nectar into bottles and plug de tops wid maize cobs. Den I takes wat's left in de bucket and we goes to take a rest in de shade." Crisanto sighed with contentment recalling the happiest hours of his life.

"You"d really like to make a still?"

"I surely would sir, I surely would."

We found a stretch of stream bank where thick woods concealed the still but where water could be easily carried to the condensation basin, and started production. Crisanto took pride in being a Master Distiller and perpetuating one of the oldest trades in recorded history.

Leading a donkey strapped with panniers, we hawked our wares down the two back streets of Poponte, which the growing village now boasted. Villagers commonly believed that if they started each day by swallowing half a glass of the water in which a shredded onion had steeped overnight, filled to the brim with our stronger elixir, their intestines would be kept free from parasites. They also maintained that a compote of herbs pickled in our elixir, applied topically, neutralized the venom of snakes, spiders and scorpions. Our weaker mixture gave greater stimulation than the same sum spent on beer and we seldom returned to Curucucú with unsold stock.

When I bought the farm I'd never envisaged keeping it solvent by peddling homemade gin from the back of a donkey. Selling Crisanto's hooch, however, had one unexpected bonus. It introduced me to the vocabulary of the coarser inhabitants of Poponte and I obtained a fluency in colloquial Spanish not found in standard dictionaries.

One evening Roland brought his sister, Teleri, and her husband, Cyril, to visit. They prided themselves on being serious drinkers and belittled those who couldn't hold their alcohol as socially unacceptable party-pooping-poofters. I had never been able to bring myself to buy a bottle of what, under the brand name of "Long John's Thomas," was sold as whisky in Poponte. Sampling one tot had convinced me that in some clandestine bottling plant amateur bootleggers had mixed metholated spirit with banana wine. The only drink I had to offer was the first undiluted distillate. I poured a round and we raised our glasses.

"Cheers, down the hatch." I was so delighted by the convulsive leaps of Adam's apples and the watering eyes of my guests that I burst out laughing and failed to drink.

"What the bloody hell have you served us, aviation gasoline?" gasped Cyril, clutching his throat.

"Just a local vintage brandy," I assured them. "Look, you can have some to light your Christmas pudding." I poured my drink down the middle of the table and lit it with a taper from the lantern. Leaping flames illuminated their figures hurrying down the pathway in an ungracious departure.

Crisanto must have known that if the crop of maize I'd planted after the sesame disaster was successful the still would be dismantled. Possibly he felt he had been in one place long enough and missed the freedom of the open road. One morning, before breakfast, he came to my room humming one of his emotive spirituals and asked for his wages. A utopian mirage of palm-fringed islands had stirred the wanderlust of his soul. I slipped a bottle of elixir into each of his loose-fitting rear trouser pockets and gave him a hug. He was a rouge but I was going to miss him. Halfway down the driveway he turned and gave me a farewell smile. As he'd stopped, he took a swig from one of the bottles then ambled out of sight swaying in time to the rhythm of his song.

Ranchers often pastured cows on peasant farms. In return for feeding the animals, the peasant was allowed to keep milk products. When a cow became dry, both it and its calf were returned to the owner. The deal was greatly to the advantage of the rancher but I accepted it. Foraging cows and calves would devour the palatable secondary growth which had sprouted in the fields where I had grown maize and convert it into fertilizer. Cutting the weeds that remained after the livestock had trampled about would then be easy and if I scattered a few more kilos of grass seed I'd soon have fields of luxuriant pasture. I decided to put together a corral and look for a rancher who would send me some cows.

In my mind's eye I had pictured myself tranquilly hand milking twenty

Friends join in a communal roofing activity in Poponte.

docile animals. That illusion vanished when, with much whooping and shout-ing, cowboys arrived driving in front of them a herd of wild and unruly first calf cows.

"Before ya try and milk any of 'em," a cowboy warned, "ya better lasso it by the horns and tie it to that *horqueta.*"* I could see things were going to be more complicated than I had imagined. I'd never lassoed a cow in my life and to have milk in Poponte in time for people's breakfast, I would have to light the corral with diesel flares and begin my day shortly after midnight.

After securing a cow to the *horqueta,* I had to recognise her calf, drag it out of an adjoining pen, and let it suckle. As soon as I saw the teats distended, the calf had to be pulled back and tied by its neck to its mother's right front leg. Most of the cows, tricked by the feel of her calf straining to reach her udder, tamely submitted to being hand milked. Others were less amenable. If their rear legs weren't hobbled they sometimes leapt into the air, knocking me back-wards, spilling the precious milk and nearly strangling the calf. My immedi-ate reaction was to thwack such a cow with a thick stick, but I soon learnt that didn't help. Only by patience can an animal be tamed. It took me weeks to

---

*A stout, Y-shaped post to which untamed animals can be secured.

acquire the knack of pressing my forehead into the hollow of a cow's thigh and relaxing her quivering muscles by transmitting the calming pulsating rhythm of my grip on her teats. Once I was rewarded by a rough lick on my ear but I wasn't sure if the cow had repented and kissed me or merely mistaken me for her calf. By dawn the churns on my mule drawn cart were usually in the main street and I was bawling my sales pitch.

"Ladies, leave your lovers, come and try my *leche*."

As the Spanish word "*leche*" usually means milk but can also mean semen, a yearning crowd of barefooted maidens and lustily cackling old crones soon surrounded me all wanting to barter whatever they had—even themselves—in exchange for a

Juan "Pescado" Molina, owner of the home on the previous page, doing the necessary job of splitting palm fronds.

dipper of milk. While bawdy repartee was more common than hard cash and milk sales were never going to make me a millionaire even in pesos, I was enjoying moments of pure hilarity. Villagers who had previously shunned me for peddling Crisanto's illicit gin, now greeted me with an amused and kindly twinkle in their eyes.

My rapport with homeowners in Poponte broadened to the point of helping one of them resurface the clay and wattle walls of his house with a mixture of trampled soil and donkey dung. Donkey dung, he explained, was highly esteemed because its high content of undigested cellulose fibres which formed a matrix preventing the soil from cracking when dry.

Only when I was actively pressing the mixture into the wall's fissures did I realize how cheaply and efficiently I was eliminating the places where vermin had been breeding. After a week in the sun the surface of the house had a smooth odourless finish which, when whitewashed, greatly improved the home's appearance.

Traditionally, thatching a roof with palm fronds was an unpaid, neighbourly activity. The owner of the house gave every helper a meal of chicken stew, known as *sancocho*, and provided jugs of lemonade for as long as the work lasted. Locally growing wine palms* supplied the fronds which before being placed in the roof had to be divided into two longitudinal halves. This was accomplished by grasping in each hand one side of a split in the tip and then ripping the entire length of the frond by pulling it past a sharp edged vertical stake. The split fronds were then tied in ascending tiers to the rafters with the "v" shape facing the sky and the overlapping leaflets forming channels to guide rain water over the eaves.

"One hand washes the other and together they wash the face," was a commonly heard expression which prompted me to offer my tractor and trailer to haul fronds. Before they had been dragged to the village tied to the sides of a wooden donkey saddle. My tractor wasn't always needed, or always available, but the knowledge that it had been offered created good will and I was elected President of Poponte's Communal Action Program.

My rapport with the villagers reaped unexpected benefits. Many years later when guerrillas established themselves in the hills behind the village—and began what they called a war of retribution against the rich enemies of society—everyone considered wealthy was scrutinised to determine how they should be treated. Should they be kidnapped and held to ransom or merely subjected to extortion by means of a revolutionary tax? *Campesinos* were sometimes consulted before a decision was made and I was favoured. While my background classed me as one of the rich enemies of society, my work ethic and unpretentious standard of living afforded me the description of "*de los malos, bueno* (Though "belonging" to a bad group, he's O.K.). I wasn't flattered but at least, initially, it made a dialogue with the guerrillas possible.

Small holders, disillusioned by scraping a meager income from the predominantly savannah soil in the valley on the other side of my river boundary came to ask if I'd buy their farms as they were packing up to start a new life in the hills behind Poponte. Their asking price was literally pennies per acre. I knew that the possessions had neither titles nor fences nor even clearly defined boundaries, but when put together comprised six thousand acres of woodlands, scrub and natural grassland. A mountain ridge rising to two thousand feet formed the eastern boundary and from it a dozen streams fed a river flowing through the middle of the property. Exit from the west was blocked by an immense stony hill. To the north was Curucucú. Only on the southern side was there need of a fence. I realised that the native pasture would only provide a holding capacity of acres to the cow but with thousands of acres

---

* *Acrocomia vinifera.*

A typical *campesino* kitchen.

that was of little concern. The area's potential, when sown with improved varieties of grass, was a ratio of cows to the acre. The chance to buy it was surely one of those unexpected opportunities mentioned by John Corner. After a week of frantic bargaining, Curucucú increased twelve-fold in size.

My letters to England describing my activities in Poponte met with mixed reactions. Accounts of distilling illicit gin did not amuse my relations. "Before," as one of them put it, "you are incarcerated in a Colombian prison as an undesirable immigrant engaged in illegal activities, I will see that you are sent funds to buy your own cattle."

That promise of help came at a pivotal moment. I could start a Curucucú herd of selected quality. When the transfer arrived I purchased seventeen heifers and a bull, used them as collateral for a bank loan, and was able to add another fifteen pregnant cows.

Gossip of my having a wealthy relative prompted a Chiriguana businessman to offer me fifty steers for fattening. They would be weighed and valued when I received them and any profit would be divided equally between us when they were ready to sell. As fifty steers would fatten on the same acreage of grass as was being eaten by the twenty cows and their calves I'd been given to milk, I decided to return the cows. I never regretted the decision. Being released from what for me had become an unprofitable, time consuming drudge allowed me to devote my energies to developing my new land.

FOUR

The General Intervenes

They who have nothing to trouble them, will be troubled at nothing.
—Benjamin Franklin, *Poor Richard's Almanac*

Major Gereral Alfredo Duarte Blum, the army`s representaive on the Military Junta that deposed the Colombian dictator, Gustavo Rojas Penilla, in May 1957, and who personally escorted him to the plane that flew him to his exile in Spain, owned a farm half way between Poponte and Chiriguana. The military DC-3 which customarily brought him from Bogotá for his monthly visit landed on Roland's airstrip, locally the only one long enough to accommodate a plane of that size. I'd been hesitant about meeting the General as the stream flowing through Curucucú, which I used for my ablutions, supplied his drinking water. Fortunately he was endowed with a robust constitution, and years of bivouacking in less than hygienic surroundings had inured him to the unsanitary hazards of frontier living. When Roland introduced me as a pioneer he decided that I was the sort of person Colombia needed and from then on whenever we met he would open his arms and clasp me to his chest in a great bear hug. Such an encounter if it happened in the long queue at the Chiriguana bank was both flattering and acutely embar-

---

*People of the Caribbean coastal provinces.

rassing for he would then express his impatience with the slowness of the service in a voice clearly audible throughout the building: "These *Costeño** bank tellers are an indolent disgrace. In the time you and I are obliged to waste here I could teach a donkey to play a xylophone."

On public holidays the General liked to take a troop of soldiers—doing their national service on his farm—through the local villages with a supply of spades and pickaxes. Groups of men seen drinking in the street or suspected of philandering would be brusquely rounded up and taken to mend one of the many stretches of road needing repair. The work was unpaid, complaints were ignored and there was no reprieve until the potholes in the selected section were leveled to the General's satisfaction.

The General was proud of his German ancestry and, even though his family had lived in Colombia for three generations, retained a degree of Teutonic disdain by pronouncing when irritated, "Colombia is a rich country. It appears to be poor only because the government, composed of avaricious *mestizos*, lavishes national holidays on an unskilled and only marginally productive work force. The Caribbean coast is dominated by lethargic Blacks and the rest of the country by Indians. None of them are culturally conditioned to work within a planned economic system, nor interested in anything but hunting, beauty queen contests, drink, football, and sex."

✄ ✄ ✄ ✄

Contractors wishing to supply quality sleepers for the new railway line connecting the Caribbean coast to Bogotá were constantly looking for hardwood trees. A woodcutter relative of Chiriguana's Mayoress thought he could disregard the respect due to private property and started to fell every suitable tree he could find in the woodlands on Roland's ranch. He collected the sleepers in a dump-truck, knocked down fences and allowed cattle to stray. When Roland forbade the work to continue the woodcutter complained to the Mayoress that Roland, by hindering the construction of the much-needed railway line, was causing grievous economic loss to the country. Ignoring Colombia's constitution, which explicitly states that nobody can be judged guilty before a defence is heard, she decided to make Roland an example of what anyone harassing woodcutters could expect and ordered the police to put him in the Chiriguana jail. The building, a filthy one-room lock-up provided with a bucket as the communal toilet, seemed specifically designed to deter prisoners from becoming second-time offenders. Inmates not wishing to sleep on bare concrete or go hungry provided their own rush mats and sent out for food. Roland's upbringing had not accustomed him to accept such conditions with equanimity and he sent an envoy on horseback to seek the General's assistance.

In spite of his penchant for keeping roads mended, the General's home was not easily accessible. In a previous century he undoubtedly would have had a moat and drawbridge to protect his privacy. However, not wishing to offend modern sensibilities, he used the stratagem of keeping casual visitors at bay by living at one end of an entrance track that was little more than a treacherous bog. Roland's envoy—and horse—arrived covered with sweat and mud.

The General read Roland's message. Pausing just long enough to tell his cook to expect a guest for lunch and, ordering his sergeant to take a sharpened axe and a contingent of soldiers on the double to his Unimog*, he strode into his bedroom to change his farming clothes for an ironed uniform and polished shoes. Minutes later the rescue party was on its way to the ramshackle municipal offices of Chiriguana to confront the Mayoress. Hearing herself summoned by a recognizable stentorian voice to present the key of the padlock securing the jail room door at once and in person, she fabricated a pressing engagement elsewhere and scuttled out of her office through a back door.

"Very well," intoned the General, "we will proceed without her." He pointed to a tree. "Sergeant, cut a battering ram."

"Yes, General, immediately."

The prospect of the jail's door being breached was met with popular enthusiasm. The Mayoress, realising the detriment to her political future should she further arouse the General's wrath, sent the key with a reluctant warder who sidled up to the General like a dog that has displeased his master and senses something unpleasant is about to happen.

"Open that door!" thundered the General.

Roland stepped out into the sunshine.

"Ah, my friend, how very nice to see you again," the General said, giving Roland one of his expansive embraces. "Come and join me for lunch. And you," he said, turning to the warder, "will scrub out that revolting bucket until it's clean enough to eat from. Mind that it is, because that is exactly where your meals will be served if I find reason to fault your conduct."

Before leaving Chiriguana, the General drove three times around the square facing the municipal offices announcing in a voice for all to hear that

---

*A high-axeled, four-wheel-drive, cross country vehicle made in Germany.

landowners—not politicians—ran the country. Politicians were but transient public servants, elected to enforce laws not to flout them. If anybody seeing Roland beside the General harbored any doubts about the truth of what they heard, they kept their reservations to themselves.

Roland's experience with the Mayoress convinced me that my ownership of Curucucú, based only on a notarized bill of sale, had to be reinforced with a government title. I asked the General how to proceed.

"You must have competent legal assistance for the paperwork." Expansively, he added, "Come to Bogotá with me next week in the plane and I'll give you a few introductions. You'll discover that it's easier to find a gold tooth in the mouth of a pig than an honest lawyer, but there, at least, they know how to get things done."

Rose Gaul and her parrot welcomed me back. The General gave me a list of lawyers and I set out to find the one most suited for my purpose. The first was undoubtedly effective. He had engineered the eviction of a sitting tenant from an apartment building due for demolition. The tenant had lived on its third floor for forty years and had obstinately refused offers of relocation or compensation for moving. The contractor waiting to begin work on the site was facing a financial crisis. One evening in a club, the lawyer overheard the contractor bemoaning his misfortune: "I'd give a million pesos to get that tenant out of there."

"Give me one and a half million and he'll be out in five days," the lawyer proposed.

"*Usted es un santo!* But I'll only pay after he's gone. You get nothing if he stays," the contractor warned.

"Agreed. But, as your lawyer, I recommend you to leave the country for a few days."

Two nights later the building was shaken by a series of detonations. The entire stairwell and elevator shaft for the first two stories were reduced to rubble, the water pipes broken and power cables severed. As the lawyer had anticipated, the authorities were obliged to order the evacuation of the weakened building. An extension ladder from a fire brigade truck was raised to the window of the distraught tenant, who gratefully scrambled down to safety. His furniture followed by winch.

I thought another practitioner with a less flamboyant *modus operandi* would be sufficient for my needs and went to make enquiries about Dr. X, the second name on the list. It was easy to find out where Dr. X's secretaries went for lunch and, engaging a brunette in conversation, I was soon listening to an account of her boss' latest triumph. It was plain she was proud of the astute manner in which he had managed the defence of a young man who, rushing to protect his sister from sexual assault, had fatally bashed in the head of a well known reprobate whom she referred to as Casanova. Thinking that by disposing of Casanova's body he would avoid both prosecution and scandal, the young man denuded the corpse, tipped it into the Bogotá river just above the Tequendama Falls and burnt the clothes.

However, Casanova's mysterious disappearance after being seen entering the home of the young man's sister, and the well known enmity between Casanova and her brother, caused the police to take the young man into custody. From the secretary's breathless comments I pieced together Dr. X's' movements after learning that a battered corpse, corresponding to a description of Casanova, had been retrieved from the Bogotá river in an eddy miles downstream. The corpse had been taken to the nearest morgue pending a coroner's report.

Leaving nothing to chance, the lawyer disguised himself as an elderly *campesino* woman and, equipped with a plastic shopping bag containing a meat cleaver, had gone under cover of night with two hired henchmen to the morgue's entrance. The night-watchman, hearing wailings and appeals of succor to the Holy Virgin, peered through the peephole of the door and saw a figure bent in anguish imploring to be allowed to see if the body recently brought in from the river might be her missing son. It was against the rules for unauthorized personnel to enter the morgue but the watchman was devoutly Catholic and to him it seemed both irreverent and callous to refuse such supplication. He slid back the bolts and was pushed backwards by the lawyer's henchmen bursting through the door. The watchman, a man of sensibility, preferred to be blindfolded, trussed and locked in a cupboard—with the promise of a reward if he behaved prudently—than be knocked unconscious. The corpse was indeed that of Casanova. His head and fingertips were chopped off and carried away in the plastic shopping bag. The following morning the judge received a writ of habeas corpus. As the remains in the morgue left no possibility of either of identifying the corpse or of ascertaining the cause of death, the young man was released from custody.

It was with considerable trepidation that I knocked on the outer office door of the third name on the General's list. A flunky glanced at the signature on my letter of introduction and ushered me into the inner sanctum. Possibly the lawyer suffered from dyspepsia or for whatever other reason was having an "off" day but he exhibited no sign of his colleagues' exuberant panache. Encouraged, I explained my business. Within half an hour we had agreed upon an all-inclusive fee to cover the costs of making a surveyor's plan of Curucucú, for the lawyer to be on hand on the day of the official on-site inspection of the ranch and for his office staff to prepare the paperwork necessary to obtain titles from the Ministry of Agriculture.

I returned to Poponte and waited for the surveyor to arrive. I had expected a request for a gang of workmen with machetes and axes to cut sight lines while he measured the distances and angles around the perimeter of the ranch. All he wanted, apart from a mule for his own use, was an assistant to push a wooden wheel which made a click at each revolution indicating that a linear distance of two metres had been traveled. They set off in the general direction of the far boundary counting clicks which the surveyor jotted down in a pocket-sized notebook. When the plan was shown to me I was convinced that the surveyor, while seated at his desk in Bogotá, had drawn the boundary lines with imaginary angles. Streams and rivers appeared in unlikely places and twice even flowed upwards but, as no Ministry of Agriculture official was likely to hike up the watercourses to check, I thought it unwise to jeopardize approval by pointing out these curious anomalies.

The General kindly flew the lawyer to Poponte on the day of the official on-site inspection. The blatant rapacity of the government representative still rankles. He arrived in a jeep with a cohort of cronies, and a nubile secretary, expecting whisky, chicken stew and a sum of money to sign the inspection's approval certificate greater than I had paid for the ranch. He decided that he didn't like me, an opinion which I heartily reciprocated, and although he and his companions continued drinking the decent whisky I had provided and eating my food, he made it abundantly clear that the price for his signature would not be lowered. It was an impasse I was not prepared for as I had imagined that the sum I had agreed to pay my lawyer for his services included every expense.

"You can think about it," I was told, "while we go and see another rancher also applying for titles."

"I'll deal with him," whispered my lawyer. "Quick. Give me another bottle of whisky." Beaming genially, he waved it merrily at the members of the commission and, climbing into their jeep, rode off with them to the next ranch.

I saw no more of my lawyer till the following day when he returned obviously pleased with himself. "I have his signature for you," he burbled. "All I had to do after he signed the other farmer's certificate was to get him drunk. We had quite a party."

"He signed a certificate for me?"

"No, not exactly. But it will do. After the secretary had to be driven home, I produced yet another bottle of whisky and made sure he had more to drink than anyone else. When I called his attention to a smudged document that I'd laid on the floor and told him it was the certificate he had just signed, he obligingly signed another. Do not worry, my friend. In Bogotá I'll make everything valid for your ranch."

I refrained from enquiring how. The General's lawyers were best left to their own devices.

When the General's messenger arrived to say that the DC-3 was ready to leave, I took the lawyer to the airstrip seated on a chair strapped to the three point hitch of my tractor. As I pulled the hydraulic lever which lifted him into the air, he twisted around in alarm and shouted over the noise of the motor, "Don't expect me back, and don't let the Commission question you. Go someplace for a month where you're unknown."

FIVE

Canoe Trip up the Kudiyari (1961)

My mind moves from its captivity towards
a freedom I've yet to understand.

—Stephen Graham

Having been told to make myself unavailable for questioning for a month, I'd gone to Bogotá and checked in at Mother Gaul's Hostel as a first step to going I knew not where. To my delight I found that Professor Richard Evans Schultes F.L.S., Director Emeritus of the Botanical Museum at Harvard University, was a fellow guest. We had written to him about botanizing in Colombia while planning our expedition as he was known for his sage advice to ambitious students and was a legendary authority on Amazonian travel. He'd arrived to arrange transport for an expedition of Harvard undergraduates to the Yapoboda Savannas at the headwaters of the Kudiyari, a river in the remote immensity of the Amazon watershed. That evening as we sat down to dinner I introduced myself. He remembered our correspondence and asked about my life in Colombia and what had persuaded me to stay. I mentioned John Corner's lecture and my surprise at discovering in myself a totally unexpected empathy with Colombian *campesinos*. While I was finding enormous satisfaction in homesteading Curucucú, I told him, there were drawbacks. During bouts of loneliness, for example, I longed for intellectual stimulation. He went off to his room shaking his head and the following morning offered me a place on his expedition, cost free. It was a privilege I hadn't dared ask for but one which I gratefully accepted.

Doors which were shut to others opened for Professor Schultes. The Air Force flew us to Mitu, the sprawling riverside capital of the Vaupés and there the gubernatorial residence, a board and bat affair resembling a grounded two-story Mississippi river boat, was put at our disposal. Most of the students found the change from Bogotá's cold early morning drizzle to the midday Amazon heat and humidity more than they could cope with and had a siesta. Finding myself alone I took the opportunity to stroll along a path that led to the Catholic Mission School for Indian children. Sitting on a cement bench at its entrance I came upon a priest fanning himself with a towel. With elaborate Latin courtesy he offered me a place next to him so I sat down and asked about the work of the Mision. Pleased by my interest, he described the surrounding Indian tribes who previously had lived in isolated tracts of jungle separated from their neighbours by boundaries of traditional delineation. Within a hundred mile radius, he told me, thirty distinct dialects were spoken. However, outboard motors and amphibious light aircraft were changing the lives of indigenous peoples. Priests helped young Indians from the scattered tribes to adapt to the modern world by bringing them to Mission School where they were baptised, converted to Catholicism and educated. Initially the programme sounded positive. What happened to children with emotional needs relating to their own culture was not explained. He proudly invited me to see the Mission buildings which were well kept, clean and orderly. Painted on a wall in a dormitory was a sign stating, "NO HABLA LENGUA" (CONVERSATION IN NATIVE DIALECTS, STRICTLY FORBIDDEN).

"Surely that denies children the means of maintaining contact with their roots," I protested.

"Yes," he replied, "but if they are to become modern Colombians, they must be made to use the Spanish language. When children converse in their dialects they are persisting in Indian expressions which conflict with the benefits of their being brought here by the Mother Church. It is our sacred duty to prevent ties with their heathen heritage from hindering their salvation."

With that comment it was time for me to leave. I was highly suspicious of cults which dictated to children what they must believe, like and do, but on my first introduction to Mitú I was hesitant to criticize the Mission's policy. Thanking the priest for his courtesy, I took a path to the river bank where a river taxi was waiting for passengers. Glad to have a captive audience, the garrulous boatman gave me his views on the Mission's shortcomings.

"Are you aware that most of the youngsters in that Mission were taken from their families by force? *Madre de Dios*! And the priests justify their actions by saying that if the kids aren't converted into the true faith the Evangelicals will grab them and they'll be damned for all eternity?" He pointed to a decapitated statue standing on a rock in the middle of the river. "Know who that is?"

"Tell me," I said.

"It's the Virgin Mary."

"Is it?"

"Well it was till a tree came down in the floodwater last month and knocked her head off. If you ask me, those heathen jungle spirits were sending a protest message."

That evening we were entertained by the Governor's secretary who invited us to gather on the second floor balcony of the residence. The Governor, he informed us in his stilted English, was in Bogotá, called there to answer charges of indecorous behaviour and lack of respect to ecclesiastical authorities. He obviously intended to tell us why and, with extravagant Latin gestures of eyes, shoulders, arms and hands, led us to the railings and explained the layout of Mitú.

"Look, I show you." He pointed to the church which dominated the far end of the central park and then with a sweep of his arms indicated the businesses on either side of the square where Indians exchanged their craft-work and crops for trade-goods. "In the streets behind are places of entertainment."

Mitú sounded very similar to Chiriguana. Bars and brothels were the principal meeting places for friends to drink and relax.

"The Governor, he is a sociable man and is happy in the company of beautiful women. He has his drinks and takes a lady. The Bishop? He is not allowed to openly enjoy such pleasures. He is jealous perhaps? I say nothing." The secretary shrugged his shoulders and rolled his eyes. "So, what happens? The Governor, he make love and the Bishop make a sermon on his loudspeaker. Of course the Bishop cannot mention the Governor by name, but all the people know who the Bishop refer to when he say, 'Oh sinner, debauchery will bar you from Christ. What will Saint Peter say when he calls you and you are in the arms of a lady of the street?' He talk like that for maybe half an hour, and the Governor hear every word but is *tranquillo*. Then, there is nothing he can do. But, when the light plant of the town is shut down for the night and the Bishop is made quiet, the Governor tell me, 'Start our light plant and turn our loudspeaker full.' *Qué maravilla*! All Mitú hear the song, 'I a man from Tolima'. The Governor has a strong voice and sings a verse that men with balls from Tolima, where he come from, wear trousers but men from Antioquia, where the Bishop come from, wear skirts."

"The implications of the comparison weren't exactly flattering," laughed Professor Schultes.

The secretary seemed unconcerned about the consequences of the outrage.

"The Governor is soon back from Bogotá. How can politicians there punish him for getting drunk when they are so often drunk themselves?"

✦ ✦ ✦ ✦

After breakfast Professor Schultes took us to see *Aganisia cyanaea*, one of the world's four blue orchids. He had discovered its habitat at the edge of a tributary to the Kudiyari River on a previous trip. We were fortunate that the river had flooded into the jungle allowing the canoe to glide under tree limbs laden with epiphytes. When the water level is low a particular species may only be possible to appreciate in detail if the tree on which it grows is cut down. Schultes sensed that this would be one of his last excursions into the Amazon with students and he wanted to pass on to them knowledge of the plants that for nearly thirty years had given him such joy. Standing up and steadying himself by grasping a branch, he pointed with reverence to an orchid flower whose column and wings of pure blue—though slightly tinged with streaks of scarlet—were surrounded with petals and sepals of slightly lighter hue. Pale veins ran through the lip. It was one of those rare and magical moments for a botanist, for *Aganisia cyanea*, first described by Von Humboldt and Aimi Bonpland in 1801, was only recorded twice again during the next one hundred and thirty-eight years. Richard Spruce mentioned seeing the plant in 1853 and José Cuatrecasas in 1939. Now Schultes was sharing their privilege with us. Undoubtedly much of the Amazon's attraction lies in seeing rare plants in their natural habitat.

By midday we were cramped from sitting in the canoe and ready to stretch our legs. A beach near an abandoned house seemed like a good place to stop but, before we dared have our lunch and a swim, we sought assurance from the Indian boatman that the owners absence was not due to anacondas, piranhas or crocodiles.

Rivers are the only highways in the Amazon. Roads tend to be short mud tracks between settlements. We had been told to assemble at 6:00 a.m. for our two-day trip up the Kudiyari River to the Yapoboda Savannas but the departure was delayed by a search for mislaid supplies, a frantic moment when the unattended craft was seen drifting from its moorings and people disappearing for a last chance to use a toilet. It was nearly seven o'clock before everyone was seated in the canoe. As we entered the mid-stream current, the hovering river mist lifted to reveal the beckoning jungle and there we were introduced to a breakfast of *fariña,** moistened with river water and sweetened with a few drops of condensed milk.

A few miles up the Kudiyari, Schultes drew our attention to a cluster of squalid Indian shacks encircling an abandoned Evangelical mission station and suggested that we stopped to have a closer look.

"This all looks very unsanitary," one of the students remarked. "With all the jungle to choose from, what on earth caused Indians to crowd together in such a dismal manner?"

"The stick and carrot method of Missionary conversion," Schultes replied. "The promise of eternal salvation if they did against the certainty of eternal hell fire if they didn't."

"And this is the result?"

"Sadly it is. Only Christians are considered '*civilisado.*' Missionary teaching is based on the concept of exclusivity meaning that only certain rites and prayers can be pleasing to or can influence God. Native chants and dances evolved over millennia deifying the birth of the sun, earth and water are pagan abominations to be stamped out. If you wish to see ceremonies sustaining Indians in their beliefs concerning creation or celebrating mystic spirits you have to go to remote jungle settlements."

"And these are the Indians who supposedly were saved? There's something very wrong," the student said.

"There is indeed. After the Colombian Concordat with the Vatican, Evangelical mission stations in the Amazon were shut down and their Indian converts were left to fend for themselves. They had been told that the white man's God was love but, as white man's diseases ravaged their community, I fear they found little evidence to support that proposition."

"Surely all Indian communities aren't as pitiful as this?" Schultes was asked.

"Fortunately not," he replied. "Many Indians living in jungle *malocas** maintain their spiritual integrity by a pragmatic practice. To placate prosely-

---

*A flat bread made from grated yucca.

---

*Large communal dwellings housing extended Indian families, common throughout the Amazon basin.

tizing missionaries who promise to save their souls, they go to Mitú and submit to baptism in both the Evangelical and Catholic Churches. For them it's more of a tongue-in-cheek double insurance ritual than a serious religious commitment. Around the first bend in the river on their homeward journey Indians commonly toss the amulets distributed during the baptism ceremonies into the river."

"It sure looks as though contacts between the '*civilisados*' and the natives haven't been very respectful," the student said.

"Too many '*civilisados*' entered the Amazon solely for personal gain. Explorers searching for El Dorado and traders wanting quick riches from tapping rubber trees used Indians as slaves. Even today companies prospecting for gold or oil are unconcerned that the crude morals of their supportive shanty towns corrupt native values. The ecological balance of square miles of jungle is upset by woodcutters using heavy equipment to extract valuable timber. Farmers and agro-industries taking advantage of being able to get virtually free land show scant regard for indigenous rights."

I had heard of occasional cases of missionaries being murdered by Indians and asked Professor Schultes why he thought this happened.

"It's not a case of how the cookie crumbles but of how one crumbles the cookie," he replied. "A few years ago I was with a group of botanists travelling in a remote area known to be unfriendly to visitors. We paddled our own canoe and at nightfall sought the hospitality of a *maloca* where we slept in our hammocks and ate *fariña*. The Indians accepted us as harmless and barely noticed when we continued on our way. A few months after my return to the States I read that this same tribe had massacred a group of missionaries who had arrived in an amphibious airplane, pitched tents, blown up air mattresses and unfolded camp beds, chairs and tables. Then they set up their radio-telephone, started their diesel generator and lit a portable gas stove. The Indians had never seen anything like it. They admired each new gadget in turn and thought them great. When the missionaries felt themselves sufficiently admired and tried to convert the pagans to Christianity, the elders saw that the whole structure of their authority was in danger and reacted in the only way they knew."

"The missionaries were overly endowed with zeal but deficient in psychology," I ventured.

"That would sum it up. When travelling amongst economically deprived people, maintain a low profile and keep your private life and thoughts to yourself. You'll be less likely to be mugged or murdered."

"Thanks, I'll try to remember!"

As we continued upstream, Schultes's ability to recognise plants of interest among the profusion of flora made us acutely aware of how little we knew and how much there was to learn.

"It's still there!" Professor Schultes suddenly shouted joyfully, his humour fully restored. "Cut the outboard and look under that *oropendola** nest hanging from those branches. Do you see that creeper with the obovate leaves? It's *Strychnos ericsonasae*, a plant you must see. For those of you with a notebook at hand jot down *toxifera* and *tomentosa*. They're the other two species of the

A family of Tucano Indians.

Menispermaceae we might find from which the Indians extract *curare*."

The canoe was scarcely tied to the branch of a tree before eager arms reached for the vine. Unfortunately there was no inflorescence, but Schultes's identification was absolute and the characteristic twists of the tendrils were noted.

"Hey Prof. If *curare* is a poison, how come the animal killed is fit to eat?" asked one of his students.

"Strictly speaking, *curare* isn't a poison. *Curare* affects the nervous system in a way that relaxes muscular tissue causing death from asphyxiation, but an injection of *curare* is not necessarily lethal. A rather eccentric English investigator-explorer named Charles Waterton proved this in 1812 by injecting *curare* into the shoulder of a donkey. When it was in its death throes, Waterton made a slit in its windpipe and, inserting the tip of a pair of bellows, applied artificial respiration to the stricken animal. He meticulously continued the treatment until the effect of the *curare* had worn off and the revived donkey was able to breathe normally by itself. Reportedly, the Indians who were waiting to eat it were very disappointed. Does that answer your question?"

---

*A group of South American birds known as the Icterids, which make pendulous nests of more than a metre in length.

A Tucano boy slides a canoe over a submerged tree trunk in the river.

"Suppose *curare* is injected via a blowgun dart, couldn't an animal, a monkey for example, pull it out before the *curare* takes effect?" the student asked.

"It could, but by cutting a notch with the razor-sharp tooth of a piranha just behind the ribbed point of a dart, the Indians ensure that if the dart is jerked backwards the *curare*-coated tip will break off and remain inside."

"Wow! The guy who said, 'know-how is American' should have travelled up the Amazon! And as we're on the subject of poisoned darts, what's the trick in making a blowpipe?"

"There's no trick in making a blowpipe," the professor said. "The trick is to blow a dart where you want it. Indians select a straight two-and-a-half-metre length of Macana palm stem, split it longitudinally, scrape and polish a narrow groove down the inside centre of each side and then rejoin them with a spirally bound vine. Beeswax is used to make an airtight seal and to mould the mouthpiece. Slivers of Macana with a twist of kapok fibres around the base make excellent darts. With a controlled puff of breath an Indian could kill you with a dart from thirty metres away."

"I bet you didn't tell that to my mother!" the student said.

"What else would have decided her to send you to the Amazon?" chortled Schultes. "But let's continue upriver and see what else we can find."

Each stretch of the river presented something of special interest, even the experience of leaping in to the water to push or pull the canoe up a rapid. Those whose feet found a firm purchase on a rock were able to heave the canoe onwards. Others whose feet slipped clung to the side of the canoe to save themselves from being swept away. Nobody shirked for we all knew that if the canoe rolled over, the loss of equipment would mean the end of our expedition.

Occasionally we glimpsed Indians intently scanning the water from boulders at the river's edge. A bow would snap, sending an arrow through a fish. Birds chattered and called warnings from the tops of trees as troops of monkeys swung past. Sometimes a danta—that amazing South American hoofed mammal of the tapir family resembling an imaginary cross between a pig and a donkey—would raise its head to sniff curiously in our direction. Aware at such times that the noise of our outboard motor disrupted the peace of their habitat, we reverted to the time-honoured use of the paddle, whose long silent strokes left the pulse of the jungle undisturbed.

"Hey Prof, are we going to sleep in a *maloca* tonight?" someone asked.

"We might if the one that was a few miles upriver is still there. If it's occupied and we arrive in time, you may see Indians preparing leaves collected during the morning from their plantation of *Erythroxylon coca*. It's a plant which has been part of South American culture for nearly four thousand years."

"Four thousand years!"

"That's what archaeologists believe. They've excavated figurines dated from that time in the ruins of the Chimu and Valdivia civilisations along Peru's Pacific coast that indicate use of the coca leaf."

"But how do Indians use the coca leaf, what's its importance?"

"Indian men of the Andean cordillera from Bolivia to Colombia express their social kinship on meeting by exchanging sun cured leaves taken from a finely woven bag which they carry slung over their shoulders."

"You mean it's like one of us exchanging a cigarette with a friend?"

"Exactly so. But instead of getting a nicotine boost Indians chew the leaves into a juicy wad which, when combined with lime, releases miniscule amounts of cocaine."

"Excuse me Prof, but where does the lime come from?"

"From the pulverized sea shells which Indian men carry in a bottle shaped gourd known as a *porporo*. By moistening the point of a special stick which slides through a hole in the top of the gourd with saliva and passing it from their mouths to the powdered shell and back again, Indians transfer bits of lime to the wad in their cheeks and the chemical reaction releasing cocaine occurs. In low-lying jungles, however, humidity would mildew sun dried leaves in a couple of days. Amazon Indians bake their coca leaves on the same day that they're picked in an earthenware pot till they're crisp. Having no supply of sea shells, charred leaves of a species from the genus *Cecropia* called *Yarumo* are used as a source of lime. Preparing and combining the leaves is an exacting process that I hope we'll be able to watch. If we are, remember we're uninvited guests and keep any criticisms until tomorrow when we'll be alone in our canoe."

Luck was with us. Outside their *maloca* Indians were putting coca and *yarumo* leaf ash into a bark cloth bag tied to one end of a long pole.

Inserting it into a hollow log and paddling the bag against the inside walls a mixture of the two leaves emerged in the form of an olive green dust which was carefully collected and divided into individual Indian bags and a communal gourd placed at the base of the *maloca's* central post. That evening, men of the *maloca* sat in a circle around it and using a spoon-shaped deer bone took turns to scoop the prepared dust into the hollow of a cheek.

"The circular movement of their jaws as they savour their coca is called *mambeando,*" murmured Schultes, as we ate the pieces of casava bread and fish he had arranged to have cooked for our supper. He grinned and added, "It's not unlike our granddaddies sitting around a spittoon after their day's work enjoying their plugs of tobacco. But observe, the Indians don't spit, they swallow their saliva."

"What's the point of that? It's disgusting," exclaimed a student.

"If you keep your voice down we can talk about it. Swallowed saliva containing traces of cocaine anesthetizes nerve endings in the stomach. By *mambeando,* Indians can go for days on hunting forays carrying little or no food. But there are other aspects of *mambeando* that intrigue me. Not only does one experience a slight hallucinogenic sensation, one feels as if one had benefited from a course of multi vitamin and mineral pills.*

"Prof, have you tried *mambeando?*"

"I have. Accounts of sixteenth century Spanish chroniclers from Peru persuaded me to experiment. According to what they wrote, coca was highly

---

*Schultes's intuition was confirmed by a nutritional assay of dried coca leaves evaluated by Tim Plowman of the Harvard Botany School and Jim Drake of the U.S. Dept of Agriculture (1974). One hundred grams of coca leaf contained the recommended dietary minimum of calcium, phosphorous, iron, vitamins A, E, and riboflavin, and was higher in calories, protein, carbohydrates and fibre than the same weight analyzed from fifty basic foods consumed in South America.

regarded by the Incas. With all the choice produce of an empire to choose from they must have found it gave them something that nothing else did."

"Did you discover what that was?"

"I could only guess. Perhaps shamans added hallucinogenic extracts from other plants for greater effect but, as the Inca civilization never evolved a written language, nobody will ever know for certain. Unconscious prejudices can so easily influence the results of studies evaluating the sensations of Indian tribes which have no words to express metaphysical concepts."

"So where does that leave you?"

"To understand why coca has been so important in the ritual life of indigenous South American Indians, I had to *mambear* with them. I'm more aware than any of you about the dangers of addiction, but compare the Indians in this *maloca* with drug addicts in the States. I trust it is obvious that coca leaf addiction is as harmless as crystalline cocaine addiction is degenerative."

"From your experiences, did you find that plants containing hallucinogenic agents can produce uplifting ethereal sensations?"

"Yes, I did. I'd even go so far as to say that some people achieve a peace of mind and sense of awe as nourishing to the soul as are Church sacraments to believers."

"But Prof, that upsets orthodox Christian teaching. What are you saying?"

"I'm saying that spiritual uplifts are neither the prerogative of, nor restricted to, participants in orthodox religious ceremonies. As temperaments differ, so do humans. Anodynes alleviate the fears and uncertainties of an ephemeral existence to people with differing temperaments. A musician finds rapture in music, a mathematician in pure maths, an aesthetic in a sun rise, lovers in an embrace, sportsmen in physical prowess, the mystically inclined in Gods, and South American Indians in coca and hallucinogenic plants."

"Am I correct in thinking that cocaine was once quite fashionable amongst respectable society?" a student enquired.

"Yes, indeed. Shortly after cocaine was isolated in 1855 by the German chemist, Friedrich Gaedcke, ophthalmic surgeons employed its anaesthetic properties for the painless removal of cataracts. A drink of mixed red Bordeaux and coca extract with the name of "Vin Tonique Mariani" was touted as beneficial by the French Academy of Medicine and endorsed by 3,000 physicians."

"And in the States?"

"At the turn of the century sniffing parlours were socially acceptable in

New York. In New Jersey the Stephan Chemical Company was authorised to import coca leaves and Parke-Davis marketed cocaine in a variety of its over-the-counter products. After cocaine was extracted for use in pharmaceuticals, an example would be as an antidote for morphine addiction, the residual essential oils and flavenoids were used to give Coca Cola its authentic flavour."

"So what happened when cocaine addiction became a serious problem?"

"Politicians in the States knew they'd be committing electoral suicide if they legislated against the millions of franchised addicts, so they passed the buck to the governments of producer countries with the request that they eradicate coca cultivations. They actually believed the fallacious argument that if a supply is reduced the demand will decrease. Not surprisingly their interference proved to be ineffective. South American Indians have never paid the slightest attention to government directives. In Peru, today, restaurants and roadside stalls openly sell an infusion of coca leaves called "*Mate de Coca.*" Try it if you go there. You'll not only find it refreshing, it's beneficial in counteracting symptoms of high altitude sickness. As with the laws to enforce Prohibition back home, government intervention proved to be nothing more than a boon for the Mafia."

"Oops! Don't let him get steamed up about the stupidity of governments," whispered one of Schultes's senior students. Quick somebody, ask him a question. He's totally convinced that most politicians are incompetent, mentally defective, or both!"

"Prof, please, how did the Indians discover which plants contained psychedelic or medicinal compounds? They couldn't have chewed, ground, or baked the leaves, bark, seeds and roots of every tree and shrub. Supposing there was some curative property in one of the plants. If the Indian wasn't ill how would he recognise what he had discovered? Is there some morphological characteristic to identify plants containing compounds of pharmaceutical value?"

"Those questions have always bothered ethnobotanists. It's possible that the properties of coca were found by pure chance. An Indian walking though the forest noticed an animal nibbling a coca leaf and wondered why. He plucked a leaf, chewed it idly and felt the better for it. But in other cases, for example the discovery of yagé from *Banisteriopsis caapiae*, intuition seems the most likely probability. *Banisteriopsis caapiae* is a seldom flowering, inedible, nondescript vine. An infusion from strips of bark is unpleasantly bitter. If you sampled a mouthful you'd soon find yourself vomiting with loose bowels. Would you experiment by drinking more?"

"Probably not."

"But the Indian who was experimenting did, and found himself transported into a visionary world of undulating blue and purple colours. Hallucinogenic compounds from other plants were possibly added and what is popularly called *yagé* became one of the most widely used drugs in Indian fiestas."

"Has *yagé* been analysed?"

"Thoroughly. The psychoactive compounds are the beta-carbolines, harmine and harmoline. It's uncanny that years ago Shamans discovered that harmol alkaloids are mutually potentiating or, as chemists would say, synogistic."

"Was that intuition, or luck?" interrupted a student.

"Certainly a lot of experimentation. One has to accept that much modern medical knowledge is the result of herbalist trial and error. Take the psychoactive elements called tryptamines found in *Psychotria viridis*, a shrub related to coffee or in *Diplopterys cabrerana*, a vine related to *Banisteriopsis caapiaei*. If snuffed or smoked tryptamines produce visual imagery. If taken orally they have no effect because tryptamines are denatured in the human stomach by an enzyme called monoamine oxidase. However if tryptamines are mixed with *yagé* before being swallowed the hallucinogenic effects are dramatically increased. Instead of undulating visions of blue and purple a kaleidoscopic tumult of every colour in the rainbow swirl around one's head. The chemical explanation for this is that the beta-carbolines of yagé are monoamine oxidase inhibitors."

Schultes yawned and scratched the back of his neck. "Botanising in the jungle can lead to some fascinating surprises but we've had enough for today. I'm off to my hammock. One never knows what one's going to discover tomorrow."

🖋 🖋 🖋 🖋

The water course above the *maloca* proved to be hazardous. Fallen trees blocked the stream-bed from bank to bank and the canoe had to be slid over horizontal trunks. Sometimes the shearing pin would break and we'd all have to leap quickly into the river to keep the canoe steady while a new pin was fitted.

As obstacle after obstacle was left behind, the vegetation became less dense and the raised open savannah of Yapoboda came into view. This area, studded with eroded Precambrian outcrops, is the remnant of an east-west mountain range that stretched from the Roraima plateau in Guyana through Venezuela and ended in the Macarena mountains in Colombia. As a result of Conan

Doyle's book describing an expedition's experiences in Roraima, the entire range is popularly called "The Lost World Mountains." Weird plants on archaic stems form a flora as strange as if one had stepped back a million years in time. It was the sort of environment where one would have been only mildly surprised to find a pterodactyl sitting on a clutch of eggs! Schultes occasionally stopped to collect herbarium specimens and showed us two species* new to science that he had previously discovered there. Observing our interest, Indians introduced us to plants they valued. At the end of the day they gave us leaves emitting a cleansing lather for bathing and at night lit tapers of balsa wood impregnated with a resin which burned with a bright light

After a week of botanizing we noticed activities in the *maloca*, where Professor Schultes had arranged for us to sleep, that suggested our hosts were preparing for one of their traditional fiestas. None of us had the anthropological knowledge to assess the significance of the occasion but it was plain that our continued presence was becoming unwelcome. How could the Indians celebrate naturally if observed by foreigners who might deride what they wore, sang, ate or drank? Professor Schultes's rapport would have allowed him to witness the fiesta but his students lacked his experience to blend unobtrusively into the background. Perhaps my feelings towards Curucucú had endowed me with a sensitivity that the tribal leaders recognized. I asked if I alone could stay and they let me on the understanding that I took no photographs. Saúl, one of our Indian guides, promised Professor Schultes that I would be in Mitú in time to catch the flight to Bogotá and remained to see me safely back.

After the others left I felt awkwardly out of place. As the Indians, busy unpacking feather crowns and other ritual ornaments from bark-cloth boxes stored in the *maloca* roof, neither desired my assistance nor sought my presence, I thought it best to leave them while they made their preparations and asked Saúl to accompany upstream in the small canoe borrowed for our use so that I could practice paddling. By the time we returned, the floor of the *maloca* had been swept and sprinkled with damp yucca waste. Children, gaudily daubed in red and blue-black markings, were running about excitedly while pairs of Indians, having no mirrors, trusted in their companion's artistic ability to paint traditional designs on each other. A group of musicians started playing panpipes and from the back of the *maloca* came the sonorous notes

---

Velozia lithophila R.E. Schultes and *Paepalanthus moldenkianus R.E. Schultes.*

from a long wooden horn with a curved end which rested on the floor. Men who had been sampling *chicha* from one of many wooden troughs began to dance six to eight abreast, each with his left hand on the next person's shoulder. They took six stamping strides forward, stopped, walked backwards two steps, forward four steps, stopped, about face, and took six stamping paces back. Women, sometimes carrying infants suspended in shawls on their backs, occasionally joined them for a few turns.

Canoes from neighbouring *malocas* arrived during the afternoon with entire households—babies, grannies, the lot—and the riverbank became a busy scene of families preparing for the fiesta. Some fortified themselves with food they had brought, others after bathing rubbed their bodies with aromatic herbs before donning arm bands and necklaces. Those wearing blue jeans and store-bought shirts and hats changed into breechcloths. When everyone was ready to start, I retired to my hammock slung in a corner of the *maloca* where I could watch without being in the way. In ordered measure guests carrying shotguns, bows, arrows and blowpipes ceremoniously approached the Elders gathered around the centre post to receive them. Each group chanted a chorus which seemed to both express and define traditions of cultural value. When formalized dancing began a delicately decorated earthenware pot of *yagé* was passed from person to person. It was expected that everybody should take a sip so, being curious, I swallowed a sample when it came my way. The bitterness made the gourd of *chicha* which Saúl brought me after each round of *yagé* very welcome. After several pints I was tempted to ask him to find me a loin cloth and head feathers so that I could join in the revelry, but feeling slightly giddy resigned myself to only observe. It would have been stupid to risk being thrown out.

Lying back in my hammock watching the Indians succumb to the spell of their tribal gathering, I recalled seeing a televised coverage of "Songs of Praise" sung by lovers of music in the Royal Albert Hall. I'd been deeply moved then without knowing why. Hymns had never brought tears to my eyes before. Only later did I realize that a shared cultural bond with the hymn singers had resulted in a collective unconscious emotion. The Indians in the *maloca* not only felt such a bond but, as expressed by their body language as they danced, were actively perpetuating it. Such traditional expressions of group cohesion had kept the tribal entity intact and for the Indians in front of me appeared to have a proven meaning greater than the promises of missionary imposed religion. Indeed, some celebrants seemed to have reached a state of ecstasy where communication with the spirit world was a reality.

Lines of bare-chested Indians, joined shoulder to shoulder, emerged from shadows into the flickering light of tapers in a stomping dance that rattled strings of nut shells tied around their ankles. As they passed by multicoloured feather headdresses nodded rhythmically in time to the repetitive tunes of panpipes and then moved on out of sight. A long drawn out wail—"ooh"— was answered with a shouted "baah" and a Conga line wound in and out of the *maloca*, the men shaking in their right hands pods which I wanted to identify. As I tried to sit up to see better, the unaccustomed effects of *yagé* combined with *chicha* overcame me and I lost consciousness.

The sun had long since risen when I opened my eyes. Oblivious to the smudged designs on their sweat-streaked bodies, a few resilient Indians were still dancing. There was an intensity about them that could not be confused with the antics of partygoers seeking to postpone the unwelcome reality of another day. They were sustained both by a feeling of belonging and of sharing. It struck me that all of us—Schultes in his relationship to the Amazon and his students, mine to Curucucú, the Indians to their fiesta and orthodox church-goers of any sect—experience similar emotions. Belonging and sharing fulfil an elemental human need to relate to something which in measured rapture enriches the quality of life.

By midday, heat and exhaustion took their toll and the dancers collapsed in disordered heaps to sleep among their families. Not till the following morning did they make their way to the river to bathe and wash away the after-effects of their indulgences. No one asked if I had enjoyed the fiesta. Suffering from a surfeit of *yagé* and alcohol, men gazed with vacant bleary-eyed contentment at their women who were rekindling dormant fires to reheat food. Being an outsider it was time for me to go. I would have liked to have left with some mutual expression of goodwill, a warm embrace, a thank you, a smile, something that showed a communion had been established between us. That is not the way of the Indian. Protestations of gratitude and displays of emotion are seldom publicly displayed. When it was time to leave, one simply left.

Saúl stowed our gear in the middle of the canoe and we took up our pad-dles. I glanced back and waved. There was no answering gesture.

Around the first bend we unexpectedly came upon a group of naked Indian children laughing and splashing happily as they leapt into the river from the branches of a fallen tree. I wanted to strip and share in their delight but I didn't. Aware that my intrusion might shatter the fragile bubble that protected the joy of their uninhibited freedom, I continued on my journey to Curucucú where I knew I belonged.

SIX

Potpourri

Ask questions for they are the keys that
open the storehouse of knowledge .

—Blaise Pascal

While my palm-leaf roofed shack with its familiar hand-made pieces of furniture gave me pleasure and suited my needs, sharing a coconut for breakfast with Crisanto made me aware of how I had neglected my garden. When Roland first showed me the homestead and I'd seen the lemons, oranges, grapefruit, guavas and coconuts, they'd seemed like a bounteous cornucopia. My diet had suffered from my ignorance and it was time to plant mangoes, maracuyas, avocados, zapotes, breadfruit, bananas, papayas, pineapples and sugar cane—all of which I could grow near the house with a minimum of care. I went scavenging for seedlings which I protected from iguanas with wire mesh cages. But rather than spray with pesticides I let my free range chickens deal with insects, bugs and snakes, for in such delicacies they found the protein lacking in my kitchen waste.

Roger, who had just been appointed Director of the Charles Darwin Research Station on the Galapagos Islands, treated the feathered creatures around him more graciously. In a letter he described how every morning a stork flew through the open French doors of his dining room and alighted on the table to join him for breakfast. He shared with it a piece of hot buttered toast, but in accordance with the principle that a hungry wild animal can be fed providing it is not pampered, only Roger's half was spread with marmalade.

Thinking it would give greater pleasure to read about what I enjoyed rather than be burdened with an account of my medieval amenities, I dwelt on the former in my letters. Friends told their friends until it was imagined that I was living in a tropical paradise. People I had never heard of wrote to ask if they might visit.

The charge for my hospitality was a pound jar of Marmite and reading material of eclectic interest. In order to deter termites who devoured the interior pages of my books while leaving the bindings intact, the shelves of my library were liberally coated with D.D.T.

Visitors who merely wanted to spend their days lying in a hammock drinking beer found their welcomes short lived. Guests with positive attitudes and interests were encouraged to stay. Zoologists recorded fifteen indigenous mammals and seven species of amphibians and reptiles in the vicinity of the ranch. Ornithologists sighted sixty–five species of birds. Some were leisured bird watchers, others were single minded. The husband of one newly-wed couple was an example of the latter. I'd taken them both—Paul and Dione—for a horseback ride high into the forested hills to see what new species could be seen. A rain storm in the afternoon forced us to take shelter in frontiersman's cabin. By the time the sky cleared darkness was falling and we had to accept the peasant's offer of sharing his floor to sleep on for the night. Paul arranged for Dione the saddle blankets between himself and the wall as rudimentary bedding and was soon gently snoring.

Sometime later we were aware of an agitated whisper.

"Paul."

There was no answer.

"*Paul.*"

People peered over their arms, expectantly.

"PAUL! Mice are running over my legs."

"Oh! For Heaven's sake woman, I'm not interested in rodents. I'm an ornithologist. Now go back to sleep"

On evenings when the night sky glittered through the shelter of branches that shaded the patio during the day, my guests often sat outside to exchange ideas about man's existence on the planet and his impact on the environment. I might be asked to justify my actions from destroying the termites that ate my books to encouraging my poultry to devour snakes—that one could only know were poisonous if one was bitten—or adding to the carbon dioxide levels of the atmosphere by burning scrub before planting grass for cattle. In turn

I might question the disproportionately high consumption of fossil fuels for generating electricity in my guests' own countries. Man's respect for the planet, we concluded, was determined by the lifestyle he wished to enjoy in the society he inhabited.

On one occasion, a huge and hairy tarantula appeared in the thatch of the dining room and stalked down a roof beam towards us. It was the size of a gorilla's outstretched hand and each leg seemed as thick as a thumb. Admiration for this splendid animal faltered when it stopped, just out of reach, and tensed its legs as if preparing to leap. I might have knocked it to the floor with a broom and swept it outside but if the spider returned it could crawl up the leg of a bed and under a sheet or creep down a rope into a hammock and bite one of my guests. The opportunity to make my visitors face up to the reality of living in a tropical environment seemed too good to be missed. I grabbed my shotgun and dismembered the approaching spider.

After a stunned silence a lady guest shook an accusing finger at me. "You despicable brute," she cried. "You've massacred an innocent animal."

"Don't talk soppy nonsense," I said. "Everyone does away with objectionable life forms whether they be flies and mosquitoes, cockroaches or rats. I bet you'd be happy if someone killed a scorpion about to crawl in to your nightgown."

"Oh dear, I had never imagined anything like that," she sheepishly responded. "I was taught that everyone should respect the right of wild animals to live."

The conversation was likely to continue with the following remarks: "That's a noble thought and one conservationists applaud. As it happens, not everyone is in agreement. Sportsmen enjoy collecting trophies of rare animals and peasants with hungry families hunt for food."

"Why, oh why is society so muddle headed and inconsistent about the sanctity of life? People raise money for The World Wildlife Fund to protect endangered species, but turn a blind eye on the armament industries which sell weapons to guerrilla groups or anyone else with money for the purpose of shooting fellow creatures."

"What's wrong with that? The human race isn't an endangered species? People have been killing each other for centuries."

I'm reminded of General Patton's remark that nobody won a war by dying for his country, he won a war by making the other fellow die for his."

"Oh, do shut up!"

"Images of basic civilised values aren't helped by television programmes of the Rambo type where people slaughter each other with impunity until only the hero is left standing. As long as the winner is a 'good guy,' violence is glorified and there's never any question of indicting him for human rights violations."

"We certainly ought to examine the criteria we use when it comes to terminating other lives. Homicidal acts of war such as the atom bombs on Hiroshima and Nagasaki committed by the victorious 'moral' side are exonerated, but if Ben kills a poisonous spider we make a fuss."

"As we're talking about spiders, endangered species and things that concern the environment, tell us what's happening in the hills behind Poponte, Ben. Are there any conservation projects there?"

"None that are effective. Land hungry peasants are still leaving springs and streams without protective bands of vegetation. Inspectors, who ought to be in the field ensuring that zones of woodland are left standing, prefer to be in air conditioned offices filling out forms and passing memoranda to each other. Office profile is a sign of prestige. It's safer to give orders seated behind a desk than on a mountainside to an obdurate peasant who resents interference in what he considers to be his private domain."

"Is there a solution?"

"Nowadays farmers realize that road access is essential for the efficient transport of bulk produce to market and the economic supply of the machinery, fuel and tools needed for modern husbandry. *Campesinos* walking to market over miles of rough track with harvests carried on the backs of mules lead a life of comparative poverty. I've noticed that the greater the distance from a road's end the fewer are the *campesino* farms. Approaching a fifteen kilometer distance into the jungle beyond a road terminal cultivations are so small their impact on ecosystems is negligible. If the politicians of the world's governments agreed to enforce a global ban on the construction of all weather access roads to wilderness areas the present indiscriminate felling of jungles would become economically unsustainable and the genetic pools of endemic species found there would be saved."

"Politicians would never agree to such a ban. They'd miss out on popular votes and the money passed around by big business corporations getting approval for mega development projects."

"I wouldn't care to have Saint Peter's job interviewing politicians trying to get into Heaven!"

⚓ ⚓ ⚓ ⚓

Accounts of the pioneering life in Curucucú caused many parents to ask if they could send their children to the ranch to experience conditions in the Third World. Usually I was requested to meet them at the airport in Barranquilla. One such plucky youngster was a lad I will call "Tom."

There was no official mail delivery service in the municipal area of Chiriguana. Village people picked up friends' letters or telegrams in the post office, stuffed them in their pockets and brought them back. Fortunately the message informing me of Tom's arrival date was still just legible as it had been inadvertently washed in a shirt pocket before I received it. To dispel any fanciful ideas that Barranquilla and its satellite towns were beautifully kept and inhabited by alluring girls—as portrayed by cleverly taken photographs during the annual Carnival Fiestas—when I met Tom I took him for a swim at Puerto Colombia.

At the beginning of the twentieth century Puerto Colombia had a railroad connection to Barranquilla and a pier where sea going vessels unloaded their cargo. Ocean currents had since altered the coast line. The silted up pier became an industrial archaeological remnant, the railway embankment crumbled into the sea and storms covered beaches and depressions between sand dunes with tree trunks. On working days Puerto Colombia was a respectable place for tourists to visit. At weekends and on national holidays the dunes swarm with randy city inhabitants liberating frustrated desires.

As an introduction to the odor of unwashed humanity and depths of urban poverty, I might even take Tom at night for a stroll through Boliche, the old centre of Barranquilla. To pause at a street corner invited the approach of destitute street dwellers soliciting the price of a meal or offering to share a bed. Only the tread of patrolling policemen returned them to the obscurity of recessed doorways.

After a day in Barranquilla Tom was usually eager to go to the bus station and buy a ticket for our two-day journey to the crossroads of Chiriguana. In those days intercity roads were unpaved and buses divided into two sections. The passenger section, in front, was wooden roofed, open-sided and traversed by rows of narrow wooden benches resembling austere church pews. In the rear was a section for cargo where baggage, farm produce and livestock were jammed together. The babble of conversation in front, mixed with the squealing of pigs, the squawking of poultry and the bleating of goats at the rear, turned the bus into something resembling a mobile social club accompanied

by a traveling circus. For the unwary, vendors hawked unlikely bargains ranging from locally made "Rolex" watches to evil-smelling cigars claimed to be
the finest Havana Coronas. First time visitors invariably found the first few
minutes a diverting, if somewhat alarming, novelty.

"This is GREAT. What a ball! Did you see the guy who just put a cage with
a live alligator into the back? My God, on a bus!"

As more people clambered aboard, the passengers were forced to sit closer
and closer together along the lumpy cotton padding on the bench. Tom felt one
buttock elevated on a ridge and the other sunk in a hollow. The proximity of
people on either side made it impossible to find a more comfortable stretch of
padding and, to add to the discomfort, our knees were rammed into the back of
the wooden pew in front.

"I hope we're not going to be stuck here all day," was Tom's reaction.

"That would be unusual. A good trip to Valledupar's only about six hours."

"Crikey! And what makes a good trip?"

"A quickly replaced punctured tyre. I noticed just now as we got on that
the tread on the rear wheel is badly worn. Short delays spent fixing the
mechanical failures of an old vehicle. Nuts loosen on worn studs, wheels fall
off, steering terminals come apart, dirty gasoline clogs up carburettors.
Anything that doesn't delay us more than a few hours makes a good run."

"Where does one go to the bathroom?"

"When we cross the river you can pee over the side of the ferry or, if you
want a loo, use the board with a hole that sticks out at the stern. It's messy if
you lose your balance but it's more private than asking the bus driver to stop
while you squat by the side of the road."

Appalling road conditions and maniacal bus drivers ensured that every time
there was an accident the carnage was spectacular. When one bus attempted to
pass another, it was obliged to enter the billowing cloud of dust churned up by
the wheels of the one in front. Swerving out into the lane of oncoming traffic
without being able to see if the road was clear, the overtaking driver accelerated
until his vehicle was alongside the other and he could judge if it was safe to continue. If no other traffic was coming, both buses would race down the road at
maximum speed, their drivers urged to suicidal risks by the supportive cries of
their passengers. Any advantage was spurious for after a few minutes of tearing
down the road neck and neck everyone was coated with dust. When at last one
bus pulled ahead, the vanquished driver paused at the next river fording and
allowed his passengers to rinse their arms and faces.

Nowhere along the route was there anything resembling a conventional restaurant. When the driver felt hungry he stopped at the next shack selling food.

"Ready to eat?" I asked Tom.

"What's on offer?"

"Fatty bone soup, tough, tasty meat, boiled green cooking bananas, yucca, and lemonade sweetened with panella."

"Thanks. I think I'll look for the candy counter."

"You'll go hungry then. There isn't one."

To make up for the time lost while the passengers ate, the driver continued with the accelerator pressed firmly to the floor. At every depression and hump—and there were many of each—passengers were lofted off their seats while the bus plunged wildly onwards. Having cracked his head twice on the roof beams, Tom hunched down and joined the mass of bodies grimly gripping the back of the benches in front for support. The noise of rushing air and the motor's roar kept conversational comments about the novelties to a minimum.

During one breakdown on a sun-baked stretch of road, a small boy appeared out of the bushes and watched us perspiring profusely as we tried to repair the damage. The driver straightened up, mopped his brow, and asked, "Hey, boy, could you find us something to drink?"

"There's some *guarapo** in the house. I can let you have if you give me two pesos."

"Bring it."

Presently the lad returned, carefully holding a bowl shaped calabash containing nearly two gallons of *guarapo* which was passed from mouth to mouth. Only overpowering thirst made Tom overcome his reservations about the unhygienic manner of sharing and it was not until someone tilted the calabash for the last drop that he noticed animal designs etched into the rind of the outer surface. His imagination flared. Perhaps he had discovered a South American equivalent of the cave paintings at Lascaux. "Would the boy sell it?" I asked, but the boy shook his head.

"What's the matter with you, boy?" chided the driver. "You sold the *guarapo*. Why don't you sell the calabash? The gringo's got lots of money."

"You got the *guarapo* because Mum found a mouse drowned in our vat this morning but I daren't sell the calabash. She uses it as a chamber pot when it's raining and she can't go outside."

---

*A naturally fermented *campesino* drink made from crushed pineapples.

When I translated, Tom looked as though he was about to be sick.

"He's a soft one," muttered the driver, as he collected his spanners. "Gringos get upset stomachs before they arrive in Colombia just thinking about what they'll have to eat or drink. Somebody ought to tell him, 'What doesn't kill, fattens.' That was good full-bodied *guarapo*. Pity it's finished."

Night had fallen when the bus finally dropped us on a street of cheap hotels on the outskirts of Valledupar. Between widely spaced street lamps, patches of darkness exuded an aura of danger and an odor of urine. In one pool of light, a table covered with plates of food was attracting hungry passengers. On closer inspection the greasy offal and fried chicken necks did more to kill hunger than whet appetite, but by now Tom was ravenous. He looked hopefully in an aluminum tub but there was only the dregs of a fruit drink. Although I assured Tom that the cracked glass used by customers was rinsed in a bucket of fresh water every morning, he decided to find some beer. Four bottles and two tepid chicken necks later we went in search of a room for the night. A hotel clerk led us along a corridor, past the basic bathroom facilities, up a flight of stairs, around a wash basin fastened to a post by a length of bailing wire and showed us a cubicle. It contained a double bed. The surrounding walls of two-by-two-inch struts were covered with sections of cardboard. Paper had been stuck over the cracks where the pieces didn't meet. Here and there, at strategic places, holes had been bored so that one could peer into the adjoining cubicle, or in turn, be observed. Squashed against these partitions was a collage of bugs whose burrows in the mattress had long since deprived it of any claim to integrity. The off-white sheet covering it bore the damp outline of previous perspiring occupants.

"The clerk's ruddy well mistaken if he thinks I'm going to sleep in here and on that," protested Tom. "Tell him we want a room with two single beds and clean sheets."

"This is all I have left," was the answer. "Take it or leave it."

"We could try and find something better elsewhere, but if we"re forced to come back and find this room taken, we'll have to sleep stretched out in the hall with our rucksacks as a pillow," I told him.

"How about the jail?" suggested Tom hopefully. "We could ask to be locked up there for the night."

"I hate to dissuade you, but there are rumours of mass rape occurring in the cells after dark. The town's electricity is about to be cut off, so we haven't much time if we're going to look around."

The decision where to sleep was made for us. The light bulb went dead and apart from a few hurriedly lit candles, the hotel was plunged into total darkness.

"Feel free to make yourself at home," I said.

"Are you kidding? With all those holes in the partition and after what you just told me, I don't even dare lie with my back to the wall."

"You can lie as you like. I'm going to get some sleep while I can. You never know what's going to happen in these hotels."

Tom woke later with a full bladder. Assuring me that he vaguely remembered where the bathroom was, he went off in total darkness to find it. Each creaking floor board allowed me to visualize his progress along the corridor, around the wash basin and down the stairs. I knew the windowless ground floor bedrooms were unbearably hot and stuffy. In the hope of catching a bit of ventilation from the night breeze which entered through a grill above the front entrance and passed along the hallway, many guests left their doors ajar. The consequences of Tom entering a bedroom instead of the bathroom and his outstretched arms—groping in search of somewhere to pee—stroking a bare midriff were too frightful to contemplate.

Tom told me on his return that the odor of stale urine had led him to his destination. A short while later I heard footsteps in the corridor which stopped at the top of the stairs. The wash basin was used improperly. I doubted if Tom's parents had envisioned this particular Third World experience and giggled till the bed squeaked.

"What the hell's so amusing?" growled Tom.

Before I could explain, the person in the cubicle on the right violently cleared his throat and spat on to the cardboard partition. Tom didn't know if he wanted to be sick or to laugh. He chose the latter and our bed shook till it rattled as we rolled around trying to suppress our mirth. "I can imagine people looking at us through the peepholes," I gasped. "They're bound to think we're on the job."

"Well I'm glad nobody knows me around here," Tom spluttered. "Let's get out of here before daylight."

The occupant of the cubicle on the left, who had twice woken us up by attacks of coughing, started to wheeze.

"I wish he'd shut up," said Tom. He lit one of the cigars bought as a bargain in the Barranquilla bus terminal and blew a lungful of smoke through a peephole on to the sick man's bed. After half a dozen more puffs the wheezing became a gurgled spasm and lapsed into silence. We went back to sleep.

Long before dawn a cock crowed and was answered by another. A portable radio was switched on and tuned for a time signal. An engine roared, back-fired and was revved noisily.

The first buses were ready to collect their passengers and begin their journey. Somebody entered the cubicle on the left.

"It's four-thirty, time to get up if you're going to catch your bus." There was the sound of a bed being shaken. "Come on! Wake up!" A violent shake and then a cry, "Oh God! He's dead."

There's nothing like a death to liven up a cheap South American hotel at that hour of a morning. Doors were flung open and the corridor filled with cries of macabre relish. "*Santa María! Qué horror! Donde está? Déjeme ver.*"

As we'd already decided to make an early start we tightened our belts, slipped into our sandals and, grabbing our bags, forced our way through the throng in the dark corridor. The clerk opened the front door for us and with a sigh of relief we stepped into the street.

"If I thought that guy had died because of my cigar smoke, I'd go back," said Tom as we walked towards the bus terminal. "But if smoke killed, all the old men who gather in the smoking lounge in my father's club back home would already be dead."

I agreed that the deceased must have suffered from a more serious complaint than six puffs of smoke blown into his cubicle

Arriving uneventfully at the Chiriguana crossroads we caught one of the collective taxis going to Poponte and got off at the entrance to Curucucú.

Before involving Tom in any ranch projects, I gave him a few days to recover from his trip and have time to practice his Spanish. In the village he was seen as a highly eligible young man. On Saturday nights inebriated *campesinos* would lurch towards him with a bottle of *aguardiente* in one hand and an unwed daughter or sister in the other. Firstly, they insisted he have a drink. Secondly, that he dance. To refuse, insulted both the peasant and the girl. To accept raised hopes of marriage—Tom might take his bride and her entire family to live in gringo-land where they would all become rich. Fortunately there were usually so many offers of marriageable girls that before Tom could be cornered into making a serious commitment, *aguardiente* had befuddled his brain and his answers were incoherent.

The lassitude of Poponte from Monday to Friday changes on Saturdays when *campesinos* buying their weekly provisions descend from hill-farms with their pack animals and give the village the appearance of a busy market town.

Apart from the business of buying and selling, Saturdays are a chance to socialise and drink beer with friends while deciding where to get a few hours sleep. Before dawn on Sundays butchers have sold their freshly slaughtered cattle to *campesinos* departing early so as to reach their farms before the meat they've bought spoils in the heat of the day.

Dances in José Chiquito's bar last all night and provide single *campesinos* with an opportunity to arrange amorous entanglements. A randy shopkeeper had been wanting to make love to a widow who lived on a farm in the high cordillera. Each week she walked for eight hours to Poponte, leading her donkey loaded with produce to be exchanged for what she needed. One Saturday she finished her errands early and decided to go to the dance. The shopkeeper met her and they arranged to rendezvous in an empty house just after midnight. "I'll be in the right-hand corner as you enter," she had told him. "If I'm asleep wake me with a kiss."

She arrived early but, finding a *campesino* snoring where she had thought to sit, settled herself in the left-hand corner. The day had been hot and the journey from the hills exhausting. She closed her eyes and was soon fast asleep. When the shopkeeper arrived, he made his way to the right-hand corner and very gently kissed the head of the snoring man. There was no response. He then decided to tickle what he thought was the widow's ear with his tongue. The startled *campesino* hearing a husky voice whispering, "Open your mouth, darling, so that I can taste some of your loveliness," lashed out furiously with his fist. Stories of how the shopkeeper got a black eye were hilariously exaggerated by village humorists and kept Tom amused for weeks. He found in the morals and mores of the village an endless source of entertainment and sometimes he stayed at the village dance long after I had gone to bed, recounting, between fits of laughter, over breakfast what he had observed.

Impromptu fiestas in Poponte were never subdued by the presence of police from Chiriguana, should they happen to arrive on patrol. On one such evening Lucho, a popular young man who worked on the ranch, was aroused by the lascivious dancing of one of Tom's partners. Quite clearly she was in the mood for love, so he asked for the next dance and held her in close embrace. Lucho's wife—the terms "wife" and "husband" are used here loosely—having had amorous affairs herself, sensed her husband's incipient infidelity. As her loutish brother was standing idly by, she gesticulated that he do something to separate the dancing couple. An empty beer bottle struck Lucho's shoulder. In the ensuing melee the police mistook Lucho as the instigator and locked him in a small room used as a temporary jail. It took half an hour for tempers to cool and Lucho to be released. He returned to the fiesta with undiminished desire and was soon dancing with his erstwhile partner to the rhythm of a Vallenato song that encouraged couples to engage their hips in erotic groin-grinding gyrations.

Lucho's wife grabbed the girl by the hair.

"Bitch."

"Whore."

"Slut."

Tearing each other's clothes and viciously scratching with their nails they were soon surrounded by crowd of leering men.

"Go on! Rip it off. Rip it right off! That's the way to do it! FIGHT!"

The sight of bloodied, sweat glistening breasts aroused the masculine concupiscence of the on-lookers and the welfare of the combatants received less concern than would have been given to a pair of roosters in a cock fight. Reluctantly aware of their duty, the police intervened before serious harm was done and escorted the two sobbing women to their respective homes.

During the wanton laughter which followed, Lucho threw a bottle which hit the forehead of his brother-in-law. This time the police, fed up with Poponte, and wishing to go back to bed in Chiriguana, told the Inspector to shut Lucho in the lock-up overnight. This time he didn't mind. His macho image had been upheld and, having consumed quantities of alcohol, he welcomed a place to sleep where he couldn't be disturbed.

✄ ✄ ✄ ✄

Ever since the days when, as a young lad, I had helped my neighbour in Laguna Beach make an extension to his home, I had dreamed of building a house of my own. Termites and weathering had ravaged my two cottages, putting them in a state of immanent collapse. I suggested to Tom that between us we ought to be able to overcome the construction problems of replacing them with something better. If we erred, it would be for exceeding specifications. Tom agreed and became assistant architect, mason, carpenter, plumber and electrician. The tractor driver brought sand, gravel and stones from the river. We dug ditches, mixed concrete and poured foundations while work-men trampled donkey dung, cement and soil in wooden moulds to make adobe bricks which were piled in the shade of a tree to harden. We selected hardwood trees needed for roof beams and, during the waning moon (no woodsman would cut trees at any other time), felled them. After the trunks had been chopped into the required lengths we tied them to the tractor, pulled them to the base of a ramp and then winched them to the top of a trestle where two men, one at each end of a 108-inch saw, cut them into timbers. In the two months he was at Curucucú, Tom discovered unexpected talents and worked with enthusiasm aware that his contribution to every well-done job made a sig-nificant difference to the finish of the new building. An admiration developed between him and the workmen who, unaccustomed to seeing visitors sweat alongside them as they toiled, stayed after laying down tools for the day to play scratch football.

If work was halted while waiting for cement to arrive, I paddled with Tom in a dugout canoe across the *cienagas** on the outskirts of Chiriguana. Forming an immense water maze studded with islets of vegetation every new view seems a repetition of the last. Water fowl thrive; tree sloths hang upside down from branches and blink sleepily as one passes underneath; giant iguanas sun themselves on mudflats; and macaws with scarlet, green and blue plumage make insulting noises as they fly overhead. After heavy rainstorms, colonies of stranded monkeys on half-submerged trees stare with round saucer eyes at distant forests on the mainland. It's a special world. As water levels rise, people fish from hammocks inside their houses and tie canoes in doorways. Observing the direction of water flow, people drink, wash and relieve themselves. Each kitchen has a raised hearth. Bundles of firewood are suspended from the rafters. For those partial to fish or tortoise for breakfast, lunch and supper, there is always plenty to eat and we found that providing we made a contribution of tomatoes, onions, plantains or oil we could arrive at any house and be made welcome.

There was never any likelihood that Tom would wish to live in an envi-ronment such as I had chosen, but as the time came for him to leave I realised we had both benefited in unforeseen ways from his visit. His companionship

---

*Lagoons that can flood over vast areas during the rainy season.

had made me aware of the selfish drawbacks of living alone. As for Tom, having been exposed to the full spectrum of my Walden*, from the vulgar to the sublime, much of the brash arrogance he had shown on arrival had been exchanged for a mature and informed tolerance.

---

*The Utopian country retreat of Henry David Thoreau, 1817–1862. American naturalist, philosopher and pacifist..

SEVEN

Rafael, Henry and Curry's Light Horse

Remember to so live that every word,
thought and deed might be your last.

—Anon

In the days when airport passengers were allowed to board aeroplanes without being electronically scanned, a visitor to the ranch smuggled out of Alaska and into Colombia a .38 magnum revolver in the voluminous pocket of his hunting jacket. At the end of his holiday he offered it to me as a parting gift. It was not something that I would have bought but thinking that it were better for me to keep it in an oil soaked rag on the top shelf of my cupboard than to let it fall into the hands of some enthusiastic local, I received it and told my foreman, Rafael, where it was in case of some night-time trouble.

I misjudged his sense of responsibility, for one Saturday night he tucked it in his waistband and took it to José Chiquito's bar. He had no sooner picked a girl and started to dance when what he had assumed was her previous partner pushed him to one side and snarled, "Get to the back of the queue buddy, she's still mine." Men behave reasonably during the week, but on a Saturday night beer and inflated egos cause macho tempers to flare. Rafael, although incensed by the manner in which his intention had been thwarted, curbed his anger when she mouthed, "Wait for me." Unfortunately she had already said that to several others and Rafael found himself surrounded by a group of drunken men who said they were also waiting their turn. One of the more inebriated gave Rafael a kick in the seat of the pants and advancing with clenched fists sneered, "You stuck up bastard. Think you're better than us?"

Whether to protect himself from the threatened attack or in a moment of panic I never knew, but Rafael pulled out the revolver, fired, and the approaching man fell dead.

I didn't know what I was supposed to do. Rafael went into hiding in a thicket at the far end of my valley and local opinion considered it my responsibility to provide a lawyer for his defence. Fortunately the dead man was buried on the following day and apparently had no relations in the area to start an immediate vendetta. It seemed irresponsible to wait until some tragedy I might have prevented happened. To blunder into some inappropriate course of action stupid. I went to see my doctor friend in the next village for advice. In the privacy of his consulting room he explained that as there was no district attorney in Chiriguana, if no interested party paid the costs of a lawyer to prosecute, the police would merely ask the Judge's secretary to record the details of the death in a ledger kept on a shelf at the back of her office. In time, he added, the case would be closed by termites shredding the entry. "But," he went on, "if Rafael went to Chiriguana and was identified, the police would feel obliged to put him in jail and then you'd find the process of extracting him expensive."

I looked at him disbelievingly. "Are you suggesting that freedom in Colombia is a negotiable commodity?"

"The laws of any country are only effective if applied impartially," he replied. "Judicially, Colombia is a Third World Country and negociating a favourable degree of latitude after committing a crime is not unusual. Rafael may have acted irresponsibly at the dance, but he wasn't disloyal to you. If you don't clear his name you'll never have employees or friends to help you should you ever need them."

"That's crazy. I told Rafael where the revolver was kept so he'd have something to protect himself with if he went to investigate some nighttime disturbance. If he hadn't taken it to the dance, all this would never have happened."

The doctor gave one of his worldly smiles. "If I remember correctly, in England you have the expression, 'if ifs and ands were pots and pans, where would the tinkers be?' But that, of course, doesn't help you solve your problems with Rafael. Here any judicial decision concerning the death of a drunkard in a whore house brawl will be influenced by bribery paid by the interested party's lawyer. The first law of survival in this community states 'stay alive.' The second states 'be loyal to your friends.' One day you may need friends who'll be loyal to you. My advice is to go and cheer up Rafael in his hiding place and tell him that you've decided to pay for a lawyer. Remember, lawyers in Chiriguana are unscrupulous Latinos. You'll need artifice to lower their fees."

Rafael spotted me coming towards his hideout. Seeing I was alone, he emerged from his cover, gave me an awkward embrace and blurted, "I didn't mean to kill that man. I only fired to scare him. He was attacking me and would have taken your gun. I've sat here and asked myself if I have ever behaved badly to you or the farm? I've always been loyal, but now I can't go anywhere without fear of being arrested."

"If the dead man's friends came to avenge him," I said, "then you'd really have something to fear. What would happen to your family? Do you imagine that they could look after themselves?"

"He was a bad man. He had no friends."

"Listen, Rafael, you knew that the revolver was ranch property. In taking it you assumed a responsibility that was entirely yours."

"You wouldn't have said anything if I'd gone to see why the dogs were barking in the middle of the night and I'd shot an opossum raiding your chicken house. You'd have thanked me. Thieves might come and steal if they didn't know that I sometimes carry a gun." Rafael concluded his case with the observation, "I took the revolver with me to José Chiquito's because I must maintain a position of respect."

"O.K., Rafael. I accept that Colombian customs differ from the English but, if what you call maintaining respect means that when you can carry a revolver you can shoot anybody who approaches you looking for a fight, the respect you seek is not based on who you are, but on the gun you carry. I'm not at all sure that it's the right thing for me to do but local opinion is unanimous that I should find a lawyer to help you." I waggled my index finger for emphasis. "Let me make one thing clear, if you commit any more murders I'll personally make sure that you go to jail."

There were only two lawyers in Chiriguana. I felt embarrassed to take Rafael's case to the first, who belonged to a colonial family of established respectability, and so went to see the other who, coming from wily peasant stock, had fewer professional scruples. Remembering the doctor's advice, I opened with the gambit that Rafael had very few savings. If his case could be given humanitarian consideration I would pay half of the defence. I was well aware that Rafael had no money at all and that I would have to foot the entire bill but when the lawyer smiled I felt better about my fib. He had obviously expected me to start with a lie and was pleased I had done so. Establishing fees was a game based on unprincipled bargaining. Thus it came as no surprise when he countered with a pompous spiel about the difficulties of reconstructing the crime, the logistic problem involved in transporting eye-witnesses from Poponte to Chiriguana for the Judge to cross-examine and the cost of bribes to ensure favourable declarations and a final acquittal. He toted up a column of figures and came to a sum which equalled seven months' salary for a farm hand. In a moment of inspiration I invented six children for Rafael and appealed to the lawyer to visualise the distended bellies and emaciated limbs of their starved bodies if he was obliged to exist on half pay for seven months. We haggled like two old gypsies negotiating the price of a horse, and finally settled on eight thousand pesos or four months' salary.

My doctor friend's surmise that the only official record of Rafael's crime would be a few lines jotted down in a ledger was corroborated by the lawyer when he asked the Judge's secretary if he could look at the record of recently committed local misdemeanours. Apologising for not bringing his spectacles, he took the ledger to the window where there was more light. Opening it on the sill, with his back to the secretary, the lawyer found the page containing the entry referring to Rafael and neatly sliced it out with a razor blade. Sliding the page up the sleeve of his formal jacket, he blew the dust off the ledger, returned it to the secretary, thanked her for her help and walked out of the office. A few days later the Judge received a request to issue an affidavit of good behaviour for Rafael. Nothing was found to disbar it. The Judge received a bottle of whisky, the secretary a bottle of scented shampoo and that, as far as I could determine, was the lawyer's only expense. While there was no longer any recorded reason for an arrest warrant to be issued, Rafael's wife lived in fear that at any moment a relation of the dead man might appear and seek a more down-to-earth justice. We agreed it would be prudent for Rafael and his family to leave the area.

✦ ✦ ✦ ✦

Shortly after their departure I found that the boundary fences at the end of my recently purchased valley had been cut into four-metre lengths by a roughneck called Roque. He was the leader of a group of avaricious Conservatives who turned cattle loose on other people's sparsely grazed ranch land with the object of gaining ownership by physical possession. A neighbour had recently lost his farm by being unable to throw Roque out and I sensed that, to avoid the same fate, I was going to need the help of someone with exceptional abilities.

Although I'd heard comments about Henry and noticed him in the street on various occasions, the first chance I had to closely observe him came one evening when playing billiards in José Chiquito's bar. Henry wasn't big physically but his features, framed with sideburns, were strong. His pale blue eyes, uncommon among the mestizo and black population, gazing around the room and the way he held his beer bottle implied a dangerous competence. My initial impression was that if he looked at a man and didn't smile it would be dangerous folly to try and stare him down. When I knew him better this was confirmed. At the time I was merely aware that he was a powerful leader among men, shrewdly sizing up the people around him and exuding the vitality of a man proud of his sexual conquests. Like many Latinos he dressed with style and was vain about his hat. The sides were curled up and the front curled down. From his belt hung a leather scabbard ornately decorated with plaited tassels in which, undoubtedly, he carried a razor-sharp, twenty-two-inch machete.

Village commentary buzzed with rumours that during "*la violencia*" Henry's family had been ousted from their lands in a Liberal village by a Conservative banditry. To avenge his sense of hurt he never missed an opportunity to heckle a Conservative bully, and that is exactly how he saw Roque: a puffed-up bully with influential backing.

Henry looked up as the swinging doors were pushed open. Roque entered, swaggered up to the counter and ordered an *aguardiente*. Ostentatiously displayed on his hip was a holster containing a .22 revolver.

"Why is it," said Henry in a voice which rose above the hum of talk, "that there is a certain Conservative who when he goes for a drink carries a gun as if that could make him a man?" There was a sudden silence. People stopped in mid-sentence and fixed Roque with their attention. The insult could only lead to a fight. Roque waited for his drink, swallowed it with one gulp and said, "I'd sure hate to kill a man who didn't even know what a gun was for."

"I know what a gun's for," answered Henry coolly. "But in your hands? You couldn't hit a barn door at ten paces."

"Why don't we step outside where your blood won't mess the floor?" countered Roque.

With the assurance of a poker player holding a royal flush, Henry withdrew his machete and waved it slowly in the line of sight between them. It was like a snake mesmerising its prey by the movement of its head—back and forth, back and forth. Henry must have guessed that Roque knew a .22 bullet that misses a vital organ is rarely a man-stopper. Seizing the initiative he grinned and stated, "I'm going to enjoy severing your cowardly head from your repulsive body."

They passed through the swinging doors into the silent street and faced each other with surreal intensity—Roque with his drawn revolver and Henry with a bare machete.

Drinks were deserted as everyone raced to the windows to witness the duel. "They're mad, they're going to kill each other," wailed the woman standing next to me.

Henry's eyes held Roque in their gaze. "Why don't you use your little gun, Roque?" he taunted. "You've got five shots, but as you fire the first one I'll slice through your neck. You won't have time to pull the trigger twice." And, like a tiger about to pounce on a mouse, he took a step forward.

"You're making me shoot you, Henry," blustered Roque. "If you come any closer I can't miss."

"Worried about missing are you Roque? You're nervous. Your hand, it's trembling and your grip's not steady. My machete's thirsting for your blood and it's going to get it." Henry raised the murderous blade and crouching on his toes prepared to leap. Roque leaned backwards and fired. The bullet twanged off a stone at Henry's feet. In panic Roque turned and ran wildly down the street.

On returning to his table in the saloon, Henry found his beer no longer cold enough for his liking and pushed it aside. I assumed he knew who I was and I seized the opportunity to approach him. "Henry, congratulations. I don't know if you are lucky, dumb, or a very shrewd judge of character. Undoubtedly you are the bravest man I've ever seen and I'm impressed. May I buy you a drink?

Henry motioned to another chair and I sat down. "Thank you," I said. "What will you have, beer or something stronger?"

"I'll stick to beer if it's cold."

I ordered two and ignored the usual crowd of well-wishers who flock like vultures around a dead cow when drinks are being bought. Henry was not in the mood for them either. He was gratified that they were offering their congratulations, but knew that had Roque's shot killed him, they would have sought free beer around Roque's table. Seeing that no drinks were forthcoming, they dispersed and I took advantage of the chance to interview Henry. "Tell me about yourself. What made you as you are? I'm interested."

Henry was not accustomed to talk fluently at length, so I have pieced together his story from what he told me over a period of months about growing up in a Liberal village in the Department of Caldas during "*la violencia.*"

"I must have been about eleven years old when I killed my first policeman. My father handed me a muzzle-loading shotgun which he had primed with pitted ball-bearings and told me, "If you miss we'll all be dead by morning." We were in a group gathered to ambush a column of Conservative police which had been seen approaching our village. My father explained how we must all fire at a separate target. He would shoot the first man, I the second and so on until each man knew whom he had to kill. This was during "*la violencia*" and for our Liberal village to sleep in peace our fusillade had to leave no survivors."

I couldn't resist asking, "How many policemen do you think you've killed?"

"Who knows? Some were shot dressed as civilians. At night, during a skirmish, one fired never knowing if one had been successful or not." Counting on his fingers, Henry estimated, "Probably more than twenty."

"But surely they must have known who you were and that you were…" I gave a non-committal swirl of my hand, hesitant to use the words "murdering them." "Did they never attempt to catch or pursue you by day?"

Henry gave a grim smile. "Yes they tried to catch me. Once, when I was walking through the hills to my cousin's farm, I realized that a Conservative vigilante group was following me. I was at the crest of a bluff when I spotted them fording a stream in the hollow I had just passed. At first I hoped that their presence might just be chance and then a voice echoed up the cliff wall, "Look, his footprints continue up the trail, come on, he's not far ahead." Well, I ran till I reached the next stream thinking to wade up it to hide my tracks when I reckoned that if I did, I would be showing the vigilantes that I knew I was being followed. I had a better idea. About a mile farther along on a ridge, above some waterfalls and bathing pools, lived a crusty old nurse who was known to sell food to travelers. She was a real character. Had a tart sense of humor." Henry grinned at some private memory. "Want to hear how she was thrown out of the hospital by threatening a nun in a disrespectful manner?"

"Is it amusing?"

"Well, I think so," he chuckled. "She believed that the nun was pretending to faint in order to avoid swallowing an unpleasant-tasting medicine. So she said in her no-nonsense way, 'I'll tell if the patient is really unconscious, bring me a greased candle and I'll shove it up her ass.'"

Before I could think of an appropriate comment, Henry had continued. "I hastened on to her house and mentioned that I was on holiday and wanted a relaxed afternoon. Would she please kill one of her fat hens and make me a *sancocho*? We haggled briefly over the price. I paid her, and said that while she was preparing the food I'd like to go to the river, find a pool and have a bath. Might I borrow a bar of soap? She fussed a bit, but provided a sliver of laundry soap and away I went. I don't know if I really fooled her or not, but I heard later that she convinced the vigilantes that if they were looking for me it would be easier for them to wait at her house as I would soon return. I think she was hankering to make a double profit."

"Double profit?"

"Sure, once they'd shot me, she'd sell them the chicken lunch I'd already paid for."

A cattle ranch normally employs cowboys, perhaps a tractor driver, some workmen to take care of fences, cut weeds, and plant grass, but not somebody as potentially dangerous as Henry. However my predicament gave me no option but to ask for his help. Without someone capable of leading a group of men willing to stand up to Roque and his Conservative clique, I would be ousted from Curucucú.

In spite of the *Frente Nacional* government's successes in establishing a civilized interchange between Liberal and Conservative enemies, due to the barbaric atrocities of "*la violencia*," when victims were fiendishly abused prior to being killed, many Liberals and Conservatives still loathed each other with passions difficult for anyone who had not experienced the mayhem first hand to comprehend. If Henry could find enough Liberals who hated Conservatives, I would have men to help me. Their loyalty could be counted on, not because I or my land meant anything to them, but because any opportunity to harass their political enemies would be enthusiastically welcomed.

"Henry, it would appear that you and Roque dislike each other intensely and he won't forget that he lost face when he missed shooting you just now. From what people say, you've got serious political differences. If you like the idea of getting the better of him, join forces with me and I'll give you the chance."

Henry looked up from examining the dregs of beer in his glass, which was once again nearly empty. "Roque been bothering you?"

"Yes, he's started to cut my fences and put his cattle to graze on my land."

Beckoning to the bartender to bring two more beers, I continued. "Choose your men and let's see what we can do with the bastard. I have a friend who could get us some guns."

Henry had been spoiling for action. He found four staunch Liberals and formed what came to be nicknamed "Curry's Light Horse." When Roque cut a hole in my boundary fence and herded cattle on to the ranch, Henry and his men would round them up and drive them off. I made it clear that I didn't want Curry's Light Horse to start shooting but to impress on Roque's gang of hoodlums that they were capable of doing so, I provided them with guns.

In a more civilized determination to defend Curucucú, I contracted a group of builders to make a two-story cement block house on the boundary threatened by Roque. Defective railway rails formed the skeletal framework for the concrete beams and made it obvious that the building was intended to be a permanent structure.

Roque attempted to frighten the contractors into leaving. At night they would see a cigarette lighter flashing or a dim torch waving. A little while later they would hear a deep-throated chuckle and whisperings. The report of gunfire and demoniacal laughter would shatter their sleep. Had Henry not bolstered their morale, they might have abandoned the work. One evening he crept out into the darkness and waited. Presently he was rewarded by the sound of soft footsteps from an approaching shadowy form just discernible in the starlight. Allowing Roque to come close, Henry suddenly bellowed, "Now men, now! Grab him, he's ours!"

Roque leapt into the air with a squeal of terror and scampered back to his side of the fence. After that fright he abandoned any further risk of meeting Henry alone, and accompanied by his cowboys, resumed driving cattle on to Curucucú It was easier for him to cut a fence than it was for me to mend it.

I seemed to be getting nowhere, Henry's patience was wearing thin and my cavalry were getting bored. It was time for a face to face encounter. We put men to work reinforcing Curucucú's boundary fence at two of the three likeliest places where Roque might enter his cattle and left the third apparently abandoned. If Roque took the bait and cut the wire there, his herd would have to pass a declivity between two hills.

I posted lookouts on top of them and we waited. The day was hot and there was nothing to do but seek the shade of scattered trees on the hillside and be patient. I had found a comfortable nook and was leaning back with my eyes shut when I heard the whisper, "Here they come."

We crawled to the top of the ridge where clumps of spiky savannah grass hid our prostrate bodies from view. In the valley below swirls of dust raised by the trampling hooves of cattle nearly obscured Roque and his companions urging the herd on from behind. In front a lone cowboy was calling them onwards with the repetitive call, "Ho ho ho ho ho hooo."

"It looks good to me," I said. "As soon as the cattle begin to bunch up at the entrance to the defile, I'll run out with the farm hands whooping and yelling. Henry, you take the cavalry and charge down the hillside firing your guns. Between us we shouldn't have any trouble making the whole lot stampede back where they came from. Please remember that if you kill Roque you'll have to kill his cowboys as well and I don't want a lot of dead bodies found in a mass grave on Curucucú. They won't shoot back but even if they do, in all the chaos, they won't be able to take decent aim. When they see you coming with your guns blazing they'll turn and run."

I thought it prudent to remind my cavalry about the danger of people who live in glass houses throwing stones.

I was lucky. Roque led his men in a disorderly retreat to his side of the fence and didn't even stop to help us mend the cut boundary wires after the last of his cattle had followed.

After a week of peace Roque tried a new tactic. He used the name of one of Colombia's most feared and successful guerrilla leaders, Manuel Marulanda alias Tiro Fijo (Sure Shot), as if he were the person with whom I had to contend. Tiro Fijo was the totally ruthless boss of the F.A.R.C. (*Fuerzas Armadas Revolutionarios de Colombia*) and had he in fact been in any way involved in my dispute with Roque using force against him would have been foolhardy. The army had been trying to capture or shoot him for years. Each failure had increased his image as an invincible folk hero protected by a network of campesino supporters. One morning an agitated messenger arrived from the block house on the boundary to report that a hundred meters of boundary wires had been cut into pieces. Pinned to a fence post was the notice he handed me to read: "Collect your fence or suffer, (signed) Tiro Fijo."

The notice was crudely written in pencil on a piece of lined paper. I couldn't believe that Tiro Fijo would sign his name to such a banal warning. Nevertheless a paper with his signature, if genuine, was not to be torn into shreds and trampled into the ground. I folded the paper thoughtfully.

"Henry, spread the story that I've taken Tiro Fijo's message between two pieces of glass to the Secret Police for fingerprint identification. I'm fairly confident that Tiro Fijo has nothing to do with this, but if the fingerprints are Roque's we could denounce him to Tiro Fijo for forging his name."

"That note's horse shit. Why not keep things simple? Show it to the Mayor, it'll give us a reason for carrying guns."

The Mayor, as I expected, was neither impartial nor friendly. He was a career Conservative politician who had acquired a certain notoriety by conceiving a child with his mother-in-law. When I complained that my fences were being cut either by Tiro Fijo or by my neighbours masquerading as Tiro Fijo, the Mayor glanced at the message unsympathetically. Looking up, he brusquely demanded, "Is it true that your cowboys are armed with guns?"

"Yes," I replied. I knew he could prove that they were.

"Have your cowboys fired these guns recently, causing the disruption of Roque's cowboys in their work?"

"Yes." But before I could explain where they had fired their guns and why, he stood up shaking with anger and accused me of being one of Castro's guerrillas.

"Colombia," he raged, "will not tolerate the presence of foreigners who organise mounted thugs to terrorise campesinos in their work."

I pointed out that the mounted thugs to whom he referred were the neighbours who were harassing me.

"Take my advice," he retorted, "Let *campesinos* graze their cattle on land traditionally theirs or I shall indict you with obstructing their rights."

Henry's uncle had told me that the officials in Chiriguana had been bribed by Roque and offered a share of any farms successfully taken. After my interview with the Mayor, I had no doubt that there would be more trouble.

In the valley that Roque coveted I had left virgin stands of woodlands unfelled as wandering among the majestic trees was a tonic that always restored my calm. A week after my visit to the Mayor, Henry reported that a group of men with axes sent by Roque, were working there in an attempt to claim squatters' rights. As far as I was concerned they might have been desecrating a cathedral. I issued Curry's Light Horse with spades and we galloped off to save the woodlands that were left. In case the squatters had posted a look-out, we dismounted at some distance from where the cutters were working.

"I'm going on alone," I said, "to see if I can get them to leave peacefully. If I can't, I'll need you so keep me in sight. If I wave come running."

I found the would-be squatters taking turns to sharpen their axes on a stone in the stream bed. Tucking my revolver at the back of my belt, I made myself seen at the top of the embankment.

"Buenos días," I said loudly. They stopped what they were doing and stared at me in surprise. "Señores," I continued, "I fear there is a misunderstanding about the ownership of this land. The government gave me titles to it in 1961 and I have neither authorised nor requested that this woodland be cut down."

I was answered by their leader. "Woodlands belong to those who fell them. You have more land than you need and we have nothing. By the law of the axe and machete we claim these woods as ours."

He was supported by cries of "Well spoken" and "That's right!" from his companions.

"The law of the axe and machete only applies to untitled land," I answered when the hubbub died down. "All of you know that once land has been titled it becomes private property, and that's the case here. Look for free jungle up in the hills. I believe Roque sent you here, but whether he did or didn't you need your daily wage to feed your families. If you agree to stop work now and not start another clearing on this ranch, I'll pay you for yesterday and today's work."

"Why do you want so much land?" one of the cutters cried. "It offends us to see the rich with land they don't use."

"That's a very good question," I replied. "But look around you and what you see is woodland that was here before any of us were born. Here Indians hunted wild animals for food or harvested medicinal plants or cut vines for making baskets or shelters. It's been a centuries old storehouse which nature always replenished. We should think of this forest as a trust to preserve. I keep it for all our children and grandchildren to enjoy."

I noticed that two of the older men nodded their heads, but the younger ones were clearly unimpressed.

"Agh, what do you know of hunger or our needs?" muttered one of them. "You talk from a full belly."

"I have also been hungry. I have told you where there is free jungle. I have offered to pay you. These trees must remain as they are."

"And what if we decide to ignore you, gringo? What are you going to do then?"

"I'll show you." I waved and Henry and his men came running. "You see they each carry a spade. If you wish to receive your money you can walk away freely. If you don't, a pit will be dug and you will remain as fertiliser to renew the forest that you thought to destroy. Dead men tell no tales."

I withdrew my revolver and cocked it. Henry pointed delightedly at a new pair of boots that one of the cutters was wearing and wondered out loud if they would fit his feet. Probably that comment, more than my revolver or the spades, persuaded them to leave. They picked up their axes and machetes and queued for their money.

Smarting from this defeat, Roque tried political pressure to oust me. I was warned by a friend that Chiriguana's mayor had formally asked the Governor of the department for help in eliminating Castro guerrillas—meaning me and my Light Horse—from Poponte. In the middle of the night a group of policemen forced their way into the *campamento** where Henry and his family slept. Henry barely had time to slip his revolver and box of bullets high up between his pregnant wife's thighs before the bedroom was invaded and searched for arms. The members of Curry's Light Horse were less fortunate and were left with only their machetes.

I played my trump card.

In the 1920s my mother, Ena Isherwood, had taught at Bedales School in Hampshire. She was an exceptionally gifted teacher and had helped a young pupil, John, through a troublesome period. They became lifelong friends and John eventually became chairman of an influential international tea company. When he married and occasionally had problems with his own children, he consulted my mother for her advice. As a result of the confidence established between them, he adopted an avuncular interest in my adventures which, as he put it, "provided entertaining light relief without involving him in their absurdities." I sent John an express letter stating my difficulties and asked him to please intervene with the Colombian Chargé d'Affaires in London, who was at that time the son of Colombia's President. Would it be possible to infer that his company had been researching a project for growing tea in Colombia and had commissioned me to find suitable land? However, a disturbing report had been received that officials in Chiriguana were aiding and abetting squatters who invaded land legally titled by Colombia's Ministry of Agriculture. Unless the Colombian government could assure his company that this injustice had been remedied, his company would regretfully be obliged to invest in another country. John wrote such a letter, had it checked by the company lawyer and delivered it. The results were highly satisfactory. A presidential investigator was despatched to Chiriguana. Within days a new mayor was appointed and Roque and his friends vanished.

---

*Outlying buildings constructed at a strategic location to house workmen.

After "Curry's Light Horse" was disbanded Henry brought his wife, a young son named Wilson and a baby daughter to Curucucú and worked as my foreman. A year of routine cattle management was enough. He felt the need of something more exciting. One evening in Jose Chiquito's bar he met an old friend who confided that he was looking for a partner to plant marijuana on land he owned in the hills behind a neighboring town. They drank a few beers and fired their imaginations with the money to be made if they pooled their resources and worked together.

I was sorry to see Henry go, but friends should never stand in each other's way when one of them has chosen a path to his destiny.

EIGHT

Mincho

*For know rash youth, that in this star crossed world fate drives us all to find
our chiefest good in what we can and not in which we would.*

—George Bernard Shaw

O f the many cooks and cleaning ladies I employed on the ranch, the one I
remember most was a jolly, roly-poly woman with the name of Goya. She
initially endeared herself by laughing at my jokes till tears ran down her
cheeks and by wiping her bare feet against the calves of her legs when entering my room so as not to leave dirty foot-prints on the new cement floor.
Experience had taught me that the women of Poponte lacked the finesse to
produce culinary treats, and this she confirmed on her first day by placing in
front of me a bowl of fish head soup filled to the brim with scales, bits of bone
and melancholy eyes. She boiled vegetables to a mush. She fried meat, especially pork, to a crisp—a necessity she informed me to destroy embedded cysts
of tapeworm eggs. When I stopped buying meat, she started killing my fat
hens. Her children looking for a free meal began to appear at mealtimes, hoping to be fed. There were over a dozen of them and it wasn't their fault if they
were always hungry. One day I overheard two of them discussing their
mother.

"I wonder. Do you think Mama's a whore?"

"That's not nice. You shouldn't even think like that."

"I know, but there're thirteen of us and we all have different fathers."

The badinage of the resident workmen in the cookhouse after tools had been put away flowed over my head. There were evenings when I'd be asked to describe England, why I had left and what I was looking for in life, but otherwise it was a time when I rested in my hammock, wrote letters by the light of a paraffin lantern, or when I wound up my ancient gramophone and listened to classical music with Heraclitis.

One evening, however, the men began grumbling about the hygiene in the kitchen and I felt it my duty to investigate. After some embarrassed protestations of ignorance as to what the men were complaining about, the cook broke down and confessed. She had been torn between loving the children she produced and the thought that she should have no more. Compromising her conflicting and confused emotions, she had buried an induced miscarriage in the earth floor of the kitchen where it could be near her.

✦ ✦ ✦ ✦

My second cook came with a husband whom I employed to get up at four in the morning to milk the cows. He then took the milk in two churns, strapped on either side of a donkey's saddle, to sell in the village. He was a strong lad with a ready smile and was soon a popular figure as he made his rounds to the homes of regular clients. On his return to the farm his wife, mistrustful of how he had spent his time, would demand, "Where did you stop? Who did you see? Why were you so long?" and to reassure herself of his fidelity, would put her hand down the front of his trousers.

Being happy in his work, he tolerated the ignominy for a month. Then one morning, as was bound to happen, he rebelled and stayed in the village. His wife became consumed with suspicion. Finally, grabbing a machete, she hitched up her voluminous skirts and strode off into Poponte to find where he was dallying. She traced him to José Chiquito's bar where he was drinking with a friend. Brandishing her machete she barged in and accused him of being unfaithful. He downed his drink in one gulp and did the accepted thing in the circumstances. With one hand he seized her by the hair and dragged her out into the street. With the other he untied the waiting donkey and started pulling them both back to the ranch.

"You filthy, drunken, whoring son of a bitch," she screeched and thwacked him across his shoulders with the flat side of her machete.

Such behaviour, in public, was an unforgivable affront to his macho image. Letting go of the donkey and her hair, he opened both arms and in one continuous sweep grabbed the hems of her skirt at foot level. Lifting them upwards, he joined the hems tightly above the top of her head which immobilized the upper half of her body and left the lower half bare. The cheers and whistles from the village idlers—who have a miraculous knack of always being on hand to witness such events—caused the embarrassed woman to sink to the ground in an effort to hide her nakedness. Men would strip and wash themselves in any river but women were obsessed with modesty. Humiliated and disgraced by having her vagina exposed to the entire village, on returning to the ranch, she packed her bags and left.

I remained without a cook for several weeks. The men arranged to be fed from the village and I prepared my own food. Washing dirty crockery and pots was never a chore for me. I put them in the stream. There was a special stone for sitting on where I relaxed and watched scavenger fish break the reflections of overhanging boughs with streaks of silver as they darted about vying for morsels of food. If there was anything left to clean, I made a quick wipe around with a lump of moss or a handful of sand. Sometimes, if there was nothing urgent to be done, I would strip and have a swim in the pool. Afterwards, I'd stand at the edge of my newly planted field and let the sun dry me while I watched the breeze chase itself in ripples through the spikes of sprouting grass. Going to the stream to wash up became a time to philosophise on my relationship with the environment and the community where I had come to live. In deference to my university degree, members of the "respectable" elements of village society often asked me to join them in censuring someone whose behaviour they deemed inappropriate. When I considered how scandalised my orthodox grandparents would have been by the behaviour considered respectable in Poponte, I was reluctant to take sides in disagreements about what was socially acceptable.

My next cook brought a nephew named Mincho and I learned through him what I was missing by not having a son of my own. He couldn't have been more than eleven years old when he arrived—a winsome tropical forest elf attired in a pair of faded red shorts that set off his glistening brown skin and long black Indian hair. He looked at me uncertainly, much as a mischievous monkey might have done, and his eyes, which gave special meaning to his expression, darted over me anxiously. I said something welcoming to his aunt and added that I hoped Mincho and I would be friends. That must have been reassuring, for his whole countenance burst into a smile of such radiance that I felt strangely purified just to observe him.

Mincho was supposed to help his aunt by bringing firewood, yucca, water and plantains to the kitchen and sweeping the patio with a broom she made from palm leaf fibres, but he was often found by the stream, fishing. He fitted into the bounty of the ranch like an Indian Tom Sawyer for he possessed the rare gift of finding in nature everything he needed to create a child's paradise where realities and fantasies intertwine and beckon to be investigated. He had apparently seen very little of his father, a compulsive cattle thief whose life oscillated between time in jail and stealing more cattle. From what Mincho told me, he sounded like the reincarnation of some medieval poacher. Mincho's mother, facing up to the realities of her matrimonial state, had gone to live with the butcher who, being a widower with six dependant children, was glad to have her. Between them they had more children than they could afford to raise decently and Mincho had been farmed out as a companion for his maiden aunt who became my cook.

The opportunity to act as surrogate father to Mincho was not displeasing when he, tired by unchartered freedoms and the weight of chance desires, came to me for guidance. Initially I was amused and touched by his smiles offered as a tentative overture of friendship. Gradually a bond of affection and trust developed between us and we came to count on and enjoy each other's company.

His first big gesture in accepting me as more than the boss occurred one evening after I had finished eating. I was gently scratching the side of Heraclitis's head when Mincho joined us.

"Want to go fishing?" he asked.

"When, now?"

"Yes, if you get your torch and machete, I'll take you."

He led the way to the edge of the stream chattering happily about his technique of fishing. "Slide your feet along the bottom of the stream carefully so you don't step on a ray. I've seen people cry from the pain when they're stung. We'll wade upstream so the cloud of silt raised by our feet'll be behind us. Move your torch slowly back and forth till you see a fish. I'll show you how to cut it with my machete. If the water's shallow you can chop it with a swipe from the air, but if the water's deep you've got to gently lower the blade till it's under the surface and then suddenly cut downwards. Grasp the fish behind the gills and drop it in my sack. Oh, and look out for water snakes. They're all poisonous."

"What do I do if I meet a snake?" I asked him.

"Chop its head off," he replied nonchalantly.

We reached a stretch where Mincho had previously noticed some large fish and began to wade upstream. The water seldom reached above our knees except in pools fringed with ferns and curtained with intertwined roots that camouflaged the mouths of mysterious burrows in the bank. Bent forward, with all our senses concentrated on the hunt, we waded stealthily side by side like two atavistic figures hidden from the rest of the world by walls of dense foliage that occasionally crossed above us. A raised torch beam would send weird shadows of drooping branches fleeing up the tunnel. Only a machete blade cutting through the surface of the water or the agonised cry of some creature caught by a nocturnal predator broke the murmured whispers and secret rustlings of the night.

When we'd caught enough for breakfast, we scaled and gutted our catch at the edge of a pool where scavenger fish left the water clean. Returning to the buildings by starlight, we agreed that the evening's excursion should be the first of many.

A few nights later Mincho introduced me to the art of catching caymans, a species of alligator which occasionally grew to a length of two metres. Small boys caught and skinned these animals for a dealer in Chiriguana, who sent the skins to Barranquilla where they were stuffed and sold to tourists as souvenirs. Before sniffer dogs made their appearance at customs control, it was not unusual for the customary straw filling to be replaced with marijuana.

For me, caymans were a pestilential nuisance. They wreaked havoc among my ducks and chickens and I kept their numbers down with a shotgun. Mincho grappled with them in a way that didn't damage their skin. He shone a torch along the stream banks until the fiery eye of a cayman was caught in the beam of light. This hypnotised the reptile and allowed Mincho to approach slowly. Some hunters used a pole with a two-forked prong to pin a cayman to the ground by its neck but branches of low trees and the nature of river banks often made this method of capture impractical. Mincho preferred to use a short stout stick sharpened to a point at both ends. As soon as the cayman opened its jaws to snap, he thrust the stick vertically into its mouth. The closing jaws impaled themselves on the two sharpened ends and the cayman, instead of letting go, bore down on the offending stick as if to kill it. When this happened, and not before, Mincho withdrew his hand. Then, wrapping string around the snout, he pulled the writhing creature on to the bank where it was further trussed prior to being skinned. It made me nervous just to watch. When the trade in cayman skins was finally banned, the reason was not, as one might have imagined, to protect little boys but to save the reptiles!

In return for educating me in native lore, I taught Mincho how to read, write and do simple sums. Finding him eager to learn, I bought some adventure stories in Spanish and read them aloud at the end of each lesson. These kindled in him a desire to leave home. One day shortly after his thirteenth birthday, he went to explore the Spanish Main.

Mincho returned to Poponte about a year later. He was now a young man, fond of using the word "yup" but no longer interested in helping his aunt in the kitchen. As he hadn't developed the physique necessary to wield a machete in a work crew, he found employment as a gardener-handyman with Roland's sister, Doña Teleri. She often invited society guests from Bogotá to their ranch and was planning a gala Christmas and New Year's Eve party. With the intention of guaranteeing the hygiene in the elevated concrete tank used to store drinking water, she sent Mincho with a scrubbing brush, bucket, soap and disinfectant to scour the interior walls. She wanted none of the stomach disorders that plague visitors to the tropics in her house. Apparently Mincho had enjoyed the job, for after the guests arrived he offered to clean the tank again. "Don't be silly," she replied, "you've already done that. Now go along and weed the flowerbeds."

Part of the entertainment designed for the visitors was a series of practical jokes. To appreciate them required a singular sense of humour, several hours of drinking and a stout heart. One evening Mincho was sent to capture the largest alligator he could find and bring it back to the house secretly. There it was trussed in a manner which allowed it to writhe but not snap and put between the sheets of one of the guests' beds. The evening's conversation was animated with ribald accounts of the snakes, spiders and scorpions found on the premises. Just as the guests were beginning to say goodnight, but before they could reach their bedrooms, the light plant was turned off.

Every day was enlivened by some such prank, and every day Mincho suggested that the tank needed cleaning again. One day Doña Teleri lost her temper.

"What's wrong with you boy? Why do you think you're here?" she ranted. "You just want to be in the water tank because it's the easiest job. Well you can't, it's perfect, and while my guests are here I will not have it contaminated by you sploshing around. I think perhaps you're just lazy."

"Señora," he replied, "I'm not lazy, it's just…"

"Just what?" she demanded crossly.

"It's just that when I was up there scrubbing the tank it got so hot I took off all my clothes. When you called me down, I left my soaped underpants up there, thinking I'd get them later. They may be old and dirty but they cost me what I earn in a day."

When Mincho asked me for work, explaining indignantly why Doña Teleri had fired him, I was too amused to say no. He was growing up and in the evenings more inclined to go into Poponte and flirt than go fishing or practice reading and writing. One night I was woken by an insistent whisper at my window.

"Don Ben! Don Ben!" It was Mincho's voice.

"Yes," I yawned, "what do you want?"

"Soyla and I have just eloped. Can we have the key to the spare room behind the barn?" There was a hurried whispering and he added, "We'd like a coverlet."

"And what are you going to use as a bed?"

"We'll manage on my hammock, but a pillow would be nice."

Rummaging about in a cupboard for the requested articles, I was aware that Soyla's parents might think I was being irresponsible. However, I rationalised that Mincho and Soyla's intended nocturnal activities were not going to alter because they did or didn't have a coverlet and pillow. Following the custom of young lovers in Poponte they would undoubtedly face her parents in the morning and work out some arrangement. To ease my conscience, I also passed Mincho a packet of condoms, urged him to use them and went back to sleep.

I was not unduly surprised when Mincho returned from his interview with Soyla's parents looking glum. Among the *campesino* community it was not the girl's father who provided a dowry, but the groom who bought the bride. A wealthy rancher had recently offered to give a peasant twenty heifers for one of his daughters on the condition that the cattle would only be handed over in the morning after he was satisfied as to the girl's virginity. Soyla's parents had presented a list of household goods and kitchen utensils which Mincho had been forced into agreeing to buy if he wished their union to continue. It wasn't an excessive request and, from their point of view, preferable to pursuing the dubious benefits to be derived from a charge of statutory rape. Soyla was under the age of legal consent but, as she was older than Mincho, her parents feared that a Chiriguana Judge might decide that she had seduced him.

I went through the list with Mincho, noted separately what was mere wishful thinking and totalled the rest. The bare essentials would cost about two months' salary.

"I plan to go to Santa Marta this week," I said. "You can come with me if you like. You'll have a better selection and what you buy will be much cheaper."

Mincho was reluctant to leave Soyla so soon but, when I offered to advance him a month's wages, he saw it was to his advantage to accept. I was becoming worried about the reliability of my old jeep and was quite pleased to have Mincho as a companion in case it broke down on the journey. Three days later we set off. The road, full of potholes and protruding stones, was more hazardous to traverse than the open country on either side. I had heard that the top of the railway embankment, then under construction, was better surfaced. Knowing that Mincho liked to explore, I followed the next set of car tracks disappearing across the open country in the general direction of the proposed railway. After several false turnings that led to isolated cattle farms, we were directed to the embankment which, due to flooding in the rainy season, was a raised earth ramp in places three metres above the level of the savanna. We found a place where the jeep could climb to the top and, taking our direction from the setting sun, headed towards Santa Marta.

"I'm not sure this idea was too clever," I remarked. "Fortunately we have some sardines and salt biscuits because I doubt we're going to find a hotel up here."

"Our luck's been good in the past," observed Mincho. "Why should it change now?"

"We'll soon find out."

Twilight in the tropics is short-lived. When the sun goes down darkness drops like a curtain. Not knowing what lay in front I drove cautiously, which was fortunate as the embankment we were on ended abruptly at a river's edge. There was no bridge. The headlights illuminated a continuing embankment on the other side merging into darkness.

"What do we do now?" inquired Mincho.

"Let's eat, then we'll rinse out our sweaty clothes in the river and look for a fording place. It'll be safer to cross in the light of day so we'll spend the night here. In case anybody comes along thinking to steal something, you sleep at the front and I'll guard the rear."

I spread my wet clothes over the jeep's door frame to dry and handing Mincho one of the conveniently movable seat paddings to use as a pillow, took the other and lying down naked in the back was soon asleep. I don't remember if as dawn broke I'd been dreaming of having a Soyla of my own but as I arched my back and stretched I was brought to my senses by titters and the sound "ooee." Staring at me goggle eyed were two young girls carrying bundles of dirty clothes on their heads. I was lying across their pathway to the river.

Before the other washer women I could see approaching—whom I feared might be the young girl's mothers—had a chance either to upbraid or use me as butt for ribald witticisms, I'd grabbed my clothes, woken Mincho, crossed the fording and disappeared in the cloud of dust left by the jeep as it bounced along the uneven surface of the embankment leading to Santa Marta.

When Mincho remarked, "You didn't make much of your opportunity," I answered primly, "There's a lot of easy sex by the river but it's a venereal disease trap. I wasn't in the mood to risk the latter."

At that moment a rear half shaft snapped and the jeep glided to a halt. By engaging the four-wheel drive we reached the shade of a thorn tree in the patio of a nearby ranch house but as the splines on the front drive shaft were worn it seemed best not to risk going further. If we economised, our budget might allow us to return with the needed spare part. Having accepted the rancher's offer to take us to the main road on his tractor, we continued our journey in the back of a truck which took passengers and reached Santa Marta at nightfall without having eaten anything all day.

On the side of the street a gaggle of women were cooking food over five-gallon tins filled with glowing charcoal. We stopped to see what there was and in one meal ate our breakfast, lunch and supper. When, finally, we could eat no more, Mincho hoisted the overnight bag to his shoulder. "We can stay at the Beach Hotel for nothing," he said. "I used to have a friend there."

"What if he's not there now?" I said.

"It won't really matter. I'll arrange things."

"Excellent! Let's go."

As we walked along the ocean front, I realised that we were moving away from the hotel area and towards the edge of town. "Where's this Beach Hotel?" I asked.

"In front of us," Mincho waved his arm towards the shore. "Lots of fishermen use it regularly. Put your valuables in one shoe and bury it, use the other shoe as a pillow, turn your pockets inside out, and lie down on the sand and sleep."

'Why all the complications?"

"Well, if muggers come along and find you barefoot, your pockets turned out and guarding a shoe under your head, they'll think you've already been rolled and leave you alone."

"In the year you spent travelling you received quite an education."

"Yup."

Darkness concealed us as we skirted three beached dugout canoes where fishermen, seated around a drift wood fire, were mending nets. Crude jokes followed by guffaws of laughter floated across the sand as a bottle of *aguardiente* passed from one mouth to the next.

We buried the overnight bag further along and marked the spot with a discarded plastic bottle half full of sea water. Another marked our shoes. We turned our pockets inside out, scooped hollows in the sand and wriggled our shoulders until we were comfortable. The gentle sound of the surf and kindly twinkle of the stars eased me to sleep. If muggers came searching for victims in the night they left us alone.

I opened my eyes as the sun began to rise above the horizon and noticed Mincho observing wisps of cloud turning in colour from grey to scarlet.

"Did you know that the dawn had religious significance for our ancestors?" I asked. "They believed that every sunrise gave men another chance to be true to life."

"Yup, I can understand that. When I was very young I saw more of my grandfather than my dad. I loved that old man. He'd carry me outside on his shoulder just as the sky was clearing and whisper that people who found the time to watch the sunrise together would always be friends. Can I tell you my good news?"

"Of course."

"Soyla thinks she's pregnant."

"That was quick work."

"Well I'd had her before she decided to elope with me."

I was highly tempted to voice my reservations about the suitability of starting a family before being economically secure but Mincho had so often trusted me with matters of importance for him, and now wanted me to share his happiness, that I left such comments for later.

"Have you decided what name to give it?"

"If it's a son I'll christen him Hyder. It's a really warm greeting I heard when I was travelling by myself. If it's a daughter, Soyla would like to call her Ladidaee."

"Ladidaee?"

"Why not? Soyla likes it for its class. Says it's a name used by one of your British royalty."

"I can't fault her originality. After a swim lets celebrate by finding something to eat. I'm ravenous."

There was nobody in sight save the fishermen casting nets in graceful swirls from their canoes far out to sea. We took off our clothes to shake out the sand and plunged into the sea. By the time we had dried ourselves with our shirts it was nearly 6:30, an hour when cheap restaurants open for early customers. Retrieving our buried possessions, we headed into town in search of breakfast. The benefits of Beach Hotel had renewed my belief in a benevolent providence.

Our route happened to pass in front of the bank that had a branch in Chiriguana and I wondered if they would help me with an overdraft. As long as the manager didn't know where I had slept for the past two nights, he might be amenable. Shortly before the opening hour I used the plate glass window as a mirror to comb my hair and beard and then strode up to the cashier's booth and asked if I might speak with the Director. To my joy I learned that he was a man who had once been the secretary in the Chiriguana Bank. He had been promoted and transferred to Santa Marta. We greeted each other affably and he sympathised with my predicament. Within minutes I'd signed an I.O.U. and had the money I needed to buy a new half shaft tucked safely in my pocket.

* * * *

While I liked Mincho for his good qualities, I was not prepared to help him with all his financial and matrimonial difficulties. At the end of the month Mincho and Soyla moved into Poponte where he apprenticed himself to a carpenter. Soyla imagined that she would have greater control over Mincho if he worked nearby. As so often happens when one partner tries to dominate the other, the union, instead of being strengthened, deteriorates. Mincho's salary was insufficient to purchase all the missing items on the agreed list and nobody felt it their duty to lend him the money needed. A virgin señorita, by local custom, was worth a considerable amount to her parents if the right suitor could be found, but a young pregnant girl had to take what she could get should her first lover leave her. Soyla's parents asked if I would guarantee Mincho's outstanding debt to themselves as they sensed that things were not going well and might worsen. I felt that with their decision to be independent Mincho and Soyla had to solve their own problems and refused.

Though Catholic teaching to generations of the faithful in Chiriguana had taught that marriage was for procreation, sex for pleasure a sin, and contraception a plot of the rich to decimate the working classes, such tenets were beginning to be ignored. Modern technology and Family Planning offered everyone a better standard of living. Any feeling of guilt for having sinned metamorphosed into contented indifference as couples, after a care-free bedroom romp, cooled themselves with their own electric fan while watching a program on their own television set.

Soyla, having been raised in Poponte, must have known how babies were conceived and how a child altered a woman's life. Mincho had yet to evaluate his economic situation, assess his commitments and determine his personal aspirations.

I feigned indifference when Mincho attempted to drink away his worries in José Chiquito's bar. If Mincho needed my help I would listen, but he had to contact me.

Contract work for my tractor increased. Farmers who had planted maize or yucca by hand found that mechanisation increased yields and I was offered more work than I could handle by myself. I hired an experienced relief driver and offered a service which nobody else provided. Taking turns, one of us was either driving the tractor, sleeping or cooking some basic food over a wood fire. If the contract required several working days to complete, we could usually find a convenient clump of trees where we could sling our hammocks. By the end of the season we were worn out, but happy. Profits from the tractor work enabled me to buy professional tools and a light plant producing enough power for electric welding.

I found the light plant as a single unit too heavy for me to place over the vertically placed studs in the newly poured concrete base, and to reduce the weight I separated the motor from the dynamo. During the night somebody broke into the barn and stole it. Everyone agreed that the thief must have seen it disconnected. If I made a list of all those people who had been in the barn on the previous day it would include the guilty party. I started with my five ranch hands, all of whom I trusted, then added Mincho who had been sent by his boss to borrow a plank of wood. Lastly I wrote down José, an ex-bandit and member of the disbanded Curry's Light Horse. José was quite capable of stealing anything or killing anybody if he thought it was to his advantage, but he had been loyal to me and more than once appeared at my side with his shotgun when he thought I needed a body guard. On leaving my cavalry he had settled on land bordering Curucucú and had passed by for a kilo of staples to repair a common boundary fence. On entering the barn he had commented on the size of the dynamo.

Much to my relief, for I had been worried that if his name was on the list he would take umbrage and slit my throat in a fit of pique, José agreed that if it was included he would be in a better position to help me identify the thief.

After days of transporting people back and forth to Chiriguana for cross examinations, there was no indication who was guilty. Everyone on the list had been embarrassed by the experience and were upset that their honesty was in question. I decided the official investigation was getting nowhere and took matters into my own hands.

I offered a reward of five thousand pesos—the equivalent, with a devaluating peso, of two months' wages— for information leading to the return of the dynamo. I questioned various shopkeepers in neighbouring villages who might have been approached as possible buyers, and asked friends to advise me if they heard of any dynamos for sale. There was no response, not a single lead. Everybody was sympathetic and promised their co-operation, and then someone suggested that I go to see José Chiquito. In spite of his reputation for lacking scruples, I had felt that he was too much of a public figure to be able to steal anything as cumbersome as my dynamo so close to his business.

"Hola, Don Ben, what can I do for you? A cold beer? I have a new girl you might like. All the clients rave about her." José Chiquito gave me his special pimp's smile, grabbed my elbow and ushered me into his emporium.

"I"m glad to see you bear me no grudge for dropping that lighted cigarette into your trouser pocket last time I was here," I said as we approached a table." Let me buy you a beer."

"I am at your orders."

We drew up two chairs and we sat down to talk.

"You know that my dynamo was stolen and that there is a reward? I'd appreciate your help in finding it."

José Chiquito gave a worried frown. "There are so many bad people about. Things are not as they used to be. However, I'll remember the reward and if I hear of anything I will let you know at once. Thieves are dangerous. Want me to lend you a revolver?"

"It's not necessary." I leant forward conspiratorially and said in a whisper, "The secret police are also helping."

That was pure fantasy, but knowing that he would spread the rumour throughout the unsavoury members of the community, somebody might decide to claim the reward while they thought there was still a chance to do so. What seemed so odd was that nobody appeared to be spending more money than they could justify. These people were not the sort to save, nor did they possess strong personal discipline where money was concerned. If one of them had the dynamo, which he couldn't use, it was extraordinary that he hadn't tried to sell it. We finished our beers and, once again turning down his offer to sample his latest acquisition, I left to further my investigations.

My cook suggested, "Why don't you try a witch doctor, Don Ben? They know things that are hidden from us."

I had heard of ranchers who employed faith healers to kill blow fly maggots eating into the flesh of their animals. Cattle passing between thorn bushes often emerge with bleeding scratches. Blow flies lay eggs around such wounds. If the stricken animal can reach hatching larvae with its tongue and lick them away, the wound soon heals. If not, maggots make an ever widening sore and the debilitated animal dies. The traditional cure required lassoing the wounded animal, felling it, tying its legs together so it couldn't kick, and pouring a creoline based antiseptic. Reinfection was prevented by applying a fly repellent powder or spray. Faith healers, who never touched an afflicted animal, purportedly achieved the same result by spiritually willing the larvae to die. Had this not been successful, faith healers would never have been employed. I had kept an open mind on the subject but saw that now, if I was seen to be consulting soothsayers, someone afraid of the supernatural who knew where the dynamo was would be so alarmed that he would tell me where to find it.

The first two mystics I went to see might have sent off breakfast cereal box tops for a junior magic set as their antics did not impress me. However, a neighbour, hearing that I was dabbling in the occult, mentioned an uncanny experience with a clairvoyant in the neighbouring village who had told him where to find a lost set of keys. Being desperate to find them, he had gone to see her. They had no friends in common and it was difficult to imagine how she could possibly have known his daily movements. He had described the key ring to her and she had spread out her tarot cards.

"Last Thursday you were going around your fields on horseback and came to a tall tree," she said. "As you lent down from your saddle to open a wire gate the keys fell out of your shirt pocket. Look on the ground at that spot and there you will find them."

"What impressed me," he said, "was her conviction. She was absolutely correct, but wouldn't receive more than a pittance."

I recalled reading in a book on mysticism that Professor Henry Sidgwick, founder of the Psychical Research Society, had shown that some people possess powers of perception beyond our five senses. I had no intention of abandoning intellectual scepticism but, if the clairvoyant in the neighbouring village was genuine, the opportunity of observing her first hand was not to be missed. After all, if science had found that matter is a form of energy, couldn't mystics be receptive to vibrations not understood?

I went to see her. Strands of white hair falling from an untidy bun on the top of her head framed a face etched by age into serene wrinkles. Her gaze seemed to pass through me as if discerning some hidden reality behind. The simplicity of her sparsely furnished room, with its crumbling mud and wattle walls and a palm thatch roof that needed repair, showed she was indifferent to worldly wealth. She invited me to enter and motioned me to a chair. I explained why I had come. She "looked through me" and began to lay out her much-used tarot cards.

"The person who has your dynamo is a man. The dynamo is hidden in a thicket on the far side of a stream from a path." She seemed discontented with what she saw, collected her cards and laid them out again. Studying them she continued, "Within three days the dynamo will be returned to you."

Her assurance was astounding. There were no vague generalities that could be interpreted in different ways. If what she said proved to be correct, few doubts would remain in my mind about the truth of psychic phenomena.

"Will the person who brings back the dynamo be the same as the person who stole it?"

She looked at her cards again and replied, "No, he is not the one. The one who stole the dynamo is of good heart."

"What should I do till the dynamo is returned?"

"Do nothing, the man of good heart will make himself known to you."

She had finished. Picking up her cards she put them aside and then laid her head on the back of her chair and half closed her eyes. Sensing that she wished to rest, I rose to go and asked what I owed. Her worldly needs were many, but she would only accept enough money to buy her daily ration of food. It was clear that any payment beyond that put a commercial value on a supernatural power; however, I resolved that should her forecast be correct I would send men to fix her cottage. Nearly two months had elapsed since the theft and I had been depressed, but now I felt a strange optimism. Two mornings later I was woken at dawn by a familiar voice at my window.

"Don Ben, Don Ben, I must speak to you."

I pulled on my shorts and opened the door. "Hello, Mincho. You're up early. What can I do for you?"

"I have your dynamo."

I hesitated, hardly knowing how to phrase the questions that rushed into my head. "Where is it?" and "Did you bring it?"

"It's hidden, but tonight after dark we can go and get it."

"Why don't we go and fetch it now?"

"I don't want people to know that I'm involved. In the daylight they'll see me."

"Why did you come now then?"

"So you'll wait for me tonight."

The words of the curious old lady rang in my head. Was Mincho the thief of good heart?

During breakfast I wondered how Mincho was going to explain his behaviour and what part he had played. As I pushed my chair away from the table, I looked up and saw José Chiquito and his assistant coming towards the house carrying between them a dynamo slung from a pole. José Chiquito was clearly satisfied with himself. "Buenos días, Don Ben. To prove that I am your true friend, look what I have brought you."

He set his end of the pole on the ground and with an elaborate wave of his hand indicated the dynamo. I identified it as mine, but before I could say anything he continued.

"You have an enemy: Mincho. It was Mincho who stole your dynamo."

"But how did you get it?"

"He tried to sell it to me, so I seized it and brought it here."

"When did he try to sell it?"

"He offered it to me last night, so this morning I went and took it away."

There was clearly more to the story than that, but being heartily relieved to have the dynamo once more in my possession, I wrote out a cheque for the reward money. José Chiquito folded it carefully and put it in his pocket.

"Well, Don Ben, thank you. I must be going. I have many things to do today, perhaps your driver...?"

"But of course, with pleasure." I told my tractor driver to take José Chiquito and his assistant to the village, find Mincho and bring him back.

I dragged the dynamo into a cupboard where I hoped it would be momentarily safe and sat down to sort out my thoughts. The old lady had said the person who brought back the dynamo would not be the person who stole it. If that were the case, how did Mincho fit in as he had offered to return it first? How could he tell me we could go and bring it if he was trying to sell it in the village? The pieces didn't fit together.

When my driver returned, I invited Mincho to come in and sit down. I wanted a moment to observe him without making accusations and offered him a *tinto*. I had initiated a penal investigation and knew that in Colombian law this could not be retracted. In any case the innocent suspects mentioned on my list would rightly expect to have their names cleared. The guilty person would have to be identified and go to jail.

"Mincho, I think you owe me an explanation. José Chiquito has just brought my dynamo and says you tried to sell it to him. If you wish to say something to me privately we can go to the bridge and talk there, but if you are involved you can't expect that fact to be hidden."

He looked at me resignedly, stood up and I opened the door. From the bridge a view opened across the meadow and up into the Andes where swiftly blown clouds swept among the peaks in games of hide and seek. Rather like life I thought, one moment things seem startlingly clear and the next they're lost in shadow. We sat and dangled our feet in the stream where he had taught me to fish. If he had stolen the dynamo, restoring my confidence was not going to be easy. "What happened?" I asked gently.

Bowing his head in confused emotion he started to explain that after our trip to Santa Marta his relationship with Soyla, in spite of the purchases, had deteriorated.

"A couple of months ago we had a fight, well, no, it wasn't a real fight, but we just got fed up with each other. She was mad at me because, apart from the list, she wanted new shoes and another dress and accused me of spending my money in the bar. Her chickens had died of some contagious disease and I blamed her for not having any money if she couldn't look after them properly. We shouted at each other till she flew into a rage and told me to get out of the house. I got drunk and spent the weekend in José Chiquito's place. On Monday morning he said I owed him two thousand four hundred and twenty pesos. Imagine! With what I earn, there was no way I could pay."

"Why didn't you tell me?" I asked

"You know what you would have said, "Drunk again, Mincho? You can't expect to buy clothes and beer."

I had to admit he was right.

"Well, José Chiquito kept pressing me for money and I kept putting him off, and Soyla kept giving me hell. One day he suggested that I steal something and he would send whatever I brought hidden in a load of timber he had ready to send to send to Barranquilla. He could sell anything in the thieves' market there and would give me half after deducting what I owed him. I told him he was crazy. I asked my boss for a loan but he turned me down. And so it went on for a week. When I was sent here to borrow a plank of wood and saw the dynamo dismantled, it seemed so easy." He bent forward to hide his tears.

We were silent for a while, but I knew it was important, now that Mincho had started, for him to continue, and prompted, "So you took the dynamo to José Chiquito?"

"Yes, that night I caught a donkey on the savannah and used it to carry the dynamo to José Chiquito's bar. When you told him the secret police were investigating, he had such a fright that he made me take it away. He tied it in a waterproof plastic fertiliser sack and I hid it on the other side of the stream from the road that goes to Poponte so that it could be loaded on to the timber truck."

"What happened? That pile of wood is still there."

"I think the truck must have broken down, because it never came."

"You were lucky in that, or at least I am. And then?"

"To begin with I thought I would have money to go to Venezuela and start a new life, but when that didn't happen I had time to think. One night two of your workmen were talking in the bar about the robbery. One said he wouldn't mind stealing from a politician if he had the chance, because they stole from everybody, but he wouldn't steal from a friend. The other agreed and said what he valued after his health wasn't money but friendship, real friendship, the conviction that he could count on another person never to act dishonestly or cause him shame or harm. To have a companion who would be there when needed. I hadn't thought like that since my grandfather died. It was all I could do to finish my beer and leave before they saw in my face that I was guilty. Am I cursed not to have friends because I don't give what I'd like to receive?"

Perhaps my occasional philosophic ramblings with the workmen had come home to roost. If suffering the inconvenience of not having a dynamo for two months would always achieve such maturity of insight in the thief, I would willingly forego its use. Mincho broke my reverie.

"Last night I confronted José Chiquito and said I was going to give myself up. He told me I was just nervous. If I stole more things I'd soon become hardened. He simply didn't understand what I felt."

"No, I don't suppose he would."

"He must have gone to the hiding place this morning to take the dynamo and gain the reward money for himself." Mincho gave a deep sigh. "Will I have to go to jail?"

"Probably. I must tell the Judge that the dynamo has been returned before he hears about it from street gossip. Your companions deserve to have their names cleared of suspicion and they're entitled to know the details. But it's not my duty to turn you in. You could disappear now and find a warrant for your arrest should you ever return. Or you could come with me now and face the music."

"What would you do?"

"I don't know. Being punished doesn't necessarily reform. I guess it depends on the sort of image you want people to have of you. You could become the sort of friend the men you were mentioning just now would be proud to have, or you can run away."

"You mean I can go away with my guilt, or give myself up and have respect?"

"Yes, something like that. Choosing isn't easy. It's so damned tempting to think oneself perfect. We all criticise others and find fault with whatever they do, as if we were Gods. We're not. Most of us have secrets we would rather weren't made public. When you first came to Curucucú you had charm, imagination and a capacity for companionship. You went off and experienced life by yourself. Then, finding that lonely, you started a family. That was natural and Soyla provided a part of what you wanted. Regretably your relationship with her doesn't appear to have worked out very well. But if the companionship and trust that you find with male friends is important, you must show that their good opinion of you matters."

The sun had risen, sending the shade which had earlier sheltered the bridge into the undergrowth. I stood up. I was hot.

"Will you really come with me to the Judge?" Mincho asked in a subdued voice.

"Of course I will, Mincho. Let's go and get it over."

As I expected, the Judge, after taking Mincho's statement, sentenced him to a term in the Chiriguana jail which had been enlarged and modernised since Roland's brief visit. The Judge was also interested in cross-examining José Chiquito, who appeared as both instigator and accessory. With a prudence probably gained from previous skirmishes with the law he was no longer in Poponte and the Judge was obliged to summon José's companion and question her. She confirmed what Mincho had said but, as she was José's common law wife, her evidence was officially inadmissible.

At that time the Judge was kindly disposed in my favour. I took advantage of that state of affairs and went to his office the following week, ostensibly to discuss the morality of the case. I knew enough not to immediately state the real purpose of my visit and bided my time till we had finished sipping our *tintos* and commenting on the weather. When I sensed an appropriate moment I remarked, "It's scandalous that José Chiquito isn't in jail. 'Justice,'" I quoted, "'would not only be done but be seen to be done' if he joined Mincho inside."

"That's very well put," said the Judge, nodding his head sagely. He had left me an opening and before he thought to close it I asked ingeniously, "Would it be possible to look for, arrest and bring back José Chiquito if an unofficial contribution covered the expenses?"

The Judge didn't actually commit himself in words but I noticed that in stretching his neck he nodded his head again. Upon leaving I placed a magazine—on which I'd scrawled "see article on page eleven" where there were some bank notes—on the corner of his desk. At the time he studiously ignored it. Within the week José Chiquito was locked up.

While many approved, José Chiquito was not among them. It was not the first time that he had seen a jail from the inside and he was mortified about losing face. There he was in the same jail and on the same charge as the person he had accused of being the thief. Using his reward money he secured the services of a lawyer of few scruples and, as the witnesses who could have proved his guilt would not testify against him, was released two weeks later. When he returned to his bar I professed sympathy for the way he had been treated after his friendly and honest act of returning my dynamo. Life was far too amusing to have it terminated by a bullet in the back fired by a crook like him.

The Judge, having released José Chiquito whom he knew to be guilty, gave Mincho a suspended sentence for good behaviour so that, as he put it, "Justice was seen to be done." I was pleased with his interpretation.

★ ★ ★ ★

I was sitting down to an early supper when I saw Mincho coming up the driveway towards the house. I had thought it best not to be a visitor while he was in jail and didn't know how much resentment he might have been building up. I'd heard accounts of convicts harbouring such grievances against those responsible for their imprisonment that on release they'd murdered their accusers. There wasn't time to speculate, he was at the door.

"Hello, Mincho." I paused uncertainly and then, in the hope of diffusing tension added, "Have you eaten?"

He came in and we shook hands awkwardly.

"Thank you. No, I haven't. I'd like to."

I told the cook to fry a couple of plantains and eggs and bring them to the table.

"Well, I"m glad to see you out of jail. Was it awful?"

"Yes."

"And how did you find Soyla?"

"Oh, about the same. She seemed flustered when I entered the house so I don't know if she really missed me or not. People over-react now when they see me as if they had forgotten how to be normal."

"I can understand that. When you came up just now I wasn't sure what to do. It is embarrassing. When you've finished eating let's go to the stream where we can talk by ourselves."

Night was falling when Mincho finished his meal. The tuneless rasping of the cicadas' evening concert grew silent and over the meadow thousands of fireflies twinkled as if in response to the emerging stars. We sat on the bridge and dangled our legs over the edge in remembered companionship and listened to the soft gurgles of the stream.

"Are we OK? I mean are we still friends?" Mincho asked timidly.

"I hope so."

I knew this was the time to define our relationship. In the culture of Poponte people excused the purloining of other people's assets when money was needed by saying, "Things don't belong to their owners, they belong to those that need them." Moral standards were no more than flexible theoretical guidelines and yet here was Mincho displaying an underlying decency that made him ask if we were still friends. Human relationships in Poponte were guided by gut instinct and I felt Mincho should express his feelings before I uttered mine.

"Tell me about your time in jail. I understand the Warder is a remarkable fellow."

"He made us think why we were there."

"Tell me what he said."

"That all humans are driven by emotions. Love, trust and respect are good. Hate, greed and violence are bad. As he didn't want to lock any of us up again, he would take it as a personal favour if we would regulate our bad ones."

I laughed delightedly. "What a marvelous man."

"Listening to him made me decide to see you when I got out to find out if..." he struggled with himself before stammering, "Will you, will you please forgive me for what I did?"

"Oh Mincho, I forgave you long ago. I should ask if you can forgive me."

"Forgive you?"

"Yes, let me try to explain. When we first met you regarded me as an authority whom you respected and I found in you the child I was missing by not having a son. Perhaps we were both seeking an unrealistic perfection and so were disappointed when our imagined ideal fell short of expectations. If I failed you as you thought I had when you needed me, that made it possible for you to take the dynamo but you, not I, went to jail."

I wasn't sure how to continue for neither in English nor Spanish are there the array of words which the classical Greeks had at their disposal to identify the many facets of love. It was a word I wanted to use to express my fondness for Mincho but as it also conveyed feelings about a favourite food, one's country, a horse or sex, I needed to define and apply the word carefully.

"Sincere forgiveness implies the presence of love and that, I think, is only truly felt when it wells up inside one and is freely given. Unselfish love is the most powerful force on earth. I'd like to think we've both learned that human relationships are more important than possessions. If we really forgive each other, we may find ourselves more receptive to the spirit of what one calls "God.""

"During my first year here when I went off by myself to play by the river instead of helping my aunt," Mincho said, "and she smiled and forgave me, I'd feel something like that. There was a happiness inside me."

"Only then?"

"Yup." He paused to reflect and then added, "When I grew up life became too complicated."

I recalled Mincho's gift of finding joy in the environment of Curucucú and the tenderness in my heart and pride in his achievements when he allowed me to witness his childhood skills. Were all those emotions meaningless?

The feeling we'd shared from the day we'd first met of having found someone with whom it might be possible to have a special friendship demanded expression.

Impulsively we reached out gave each other a hug.

NINE

The Quest

*You can't always sit in your corner of the forest and wait for
people to come to you...you have to go to them sometimes.*

—From *Winnie the Pooh*, by A.A. Milne

Mincho had often asked me why I didn't have a wife. Photographs of
myself at the time show a thin, tanned, tousled young man in ragged
dungarees standing proudly on the porch of an adobe-brick house. It was
whitewashed inside and out and had an office, two bedrooms, a living room,
larder, and a kitchen with piped water fed from a cement tank filled by a John
Blake hydram water pump. The floors, tiled with polished squares of baked
red clay which were cool underfoot, and the ceiling of slender bamboo canes
helped to modulate the heat coming from the asbestos tiles in the roof. Breezes
blew unhindered through the mosquito netting in the windows and if squalls
made puddles on the floor I dried them with a mop.

I had spent eleven bachelor years building up Curucucú. It was time I married and had children. The wife I was looking for wouldn't just accept me and
live on the ranch but would be an active partner sharing the hardships and the
joys. Some local girls would have made excellent companions in many ways,
but I feared the dissimilarity of our backgrounds would prevent a successful
long term union. Our schooling, interests, tastes, friends and habits were different. Educated Colombian girls tended to shy away from returning to agrar-
ian origins, considering it a step backwards, and those I met who liked ranch
life already had husbands. I decided to return to England. I might find the perfect wife there.

With the sophisticated computerization of today it seems incredible that in 1969 I could have been seated in a London marriage bureau being questioned by a fusty secretary with a flip-top wooden file box. She seemed distressed that I hadn't filled in the questionnaire as she would have liked.

"Now then, Mr. Curry, you work in Colombia I see."

"Yes, that is correct, I have a cattle ranch."

"And you're here to find a wife. How charming. Now in order for us to be able to cross-reference in our index, you really must answer these questions. Colour of hair, Mr. Curry, what is your preference?"

"I don't think it matters, as long as it's natural and not dyed."

"Ah, I see. Well then, colour of eyes?"

"I left that blank because the expression of a person's eyes matters more to me than their colour."

"Height then, how tall would you like your wife to be in her stockings?"

"Well, if she's reasonably proportioned, neither a pygmy nor a giant, I suppose somewhere between five and six feet tall."

"Good, now at least we have something. I'll just write that down, five to six feet tall. Now then, the next question, also left blank. Dear, oh dear! Weight, what is your preference for weight?"

"As I said, anybody who is reasonably proportioned between five and six feet tall. But I left these questions blank because the answers just don't matter. It's the attitude of the girl, her sense of adventure and ability for hard work and fun that interests me."

"Hard work, did I hear you say, Mr. Curry? We don't usually consider that aspect. Most of the young ladies on our lists are working now, of course, but upon marrying they rather expect that the husband will take the hardness out of their lives. Well now, let's continue with the questionnaire. Religion, that's so important. What religion do you prefer?"

"A religion that doesn't profess to know all the answers to life, that lives in harmony with nature and is free from pompous pretensions."

"Mr. Curry, this is most irregular. I really don't see how we can help you. To register your card will cost five guineas, but as your answers to the vital statistics seem to be 'no preference,' I really don't see…"

"Well, let me ask you a question. Do you ever get a girl in here saying she would like to go and live abroad on a primitive cattle ranch, put up with occasional bats, saucer-sized spiders and snakes in her bedroom, wash in a river and ride on horseback into town once a week to do her shopping among Spanish speaking *mestisos*?"

"Mr. Curry, I think it would be misleading of us to take your five guineas. Good afternoon."

I had an almost identical interview with their competitors farther down the street.

What does a young eligible bachelor, with a ranch in the middle of nowhere in South America, do in London when his quest for a wife has been turned down by the two leading marriage introduction offices? A friend suggested the agony column of *The Times*, but I doubted if my country girl would see the advertisement. Just be receptive when fate puts you both on the same path, was the advice.

I was spending the weekend with my uncle and aunt on their farm near Hitchin. Having asked for some exercise, as vacations in England play havoc with my waistline, I was busy weeding their extensive greenhouse when my aunt called me to meet two local journalists. My uncle, who had spent most of his working life in the tropics employed by the Colonial Service, genially announced that as the clock had struck eleven it was time to have a drink. We carried our gin and tonics to the living room where, sitting on a stuffed rhinoceros, I answered questions about my life in Colombia. I slightly exaggerated to keep the party amused and joked about my problems in finding a wife.

My aunt turned to the journalists and asked, "Do you think there's a story?"

"If your nephew doesn't mind."

By that time I had downed sufficient gin not to mind about anything. One of the newspaper chaps took my photograph. The other scribbled down a few notes. We all had another drink, and they left.

A few days later my aunt telephoned me in London. Between shrieks of laughter she told me that her telephone had never stopped ringing with calls from lonely hearts who wished to twine their fates with mine in the backwoods of Colombia. The July 12, 1970 edition of *The Letchworth Evening Post* had devoted a full page to my appeal for a wife. Half the page carried a photo of me on the rhinoceros. The rest was a script inspired by gin.

My aunt was jubilant, "What a scoop, darling. Just imagine, when the Queen Mother came to visit Hitchin, she was only given two columns."

"She probably wasn't advertising for a mate. Winnow the grain from the chaff and I'll come as soon as I can."

With a mixture of eagerness and trepidation at what I might find, I returned to Hitchin and the mound of letters, photographs and telephone messages waiting for me.

Headline and photo of author appearing in the July 12, 1970 edition of *The Letchworth Evening Post.*

Some girls were tall and slinky, fair and suave. Others were squat and dark. Some had faces free from cosmetics. Others, thin or plump, pretty or plain, had smiles and expressions which were stereotyped copies from fashion magazine covers. Some were virtually illiterate and others quoted Keats. There were invitations to dinner and requests to be taken out.

I began sorting them out into categories on the kitchen table like a game of solitaire. My uncle looked disapprovingly over my shoulder and snorted, "You'd never be asked to judge heifers at a cattle fair. It's no use sitting there like a love-sick adolescent. What you have to do, my boy, is go out and prod them. Begad! I wish I was forty years younger with such opportunities. I'd show them a thing or two."

My aunt told him to shut up and, adding that he was lucky never to have been booked for indecent exposure, handed me the keys of their vintage Bentley. I grabbed a handful of names at random and sallied forth to sample Hertfordshire beer and beauty. By the end of the weekend I was exhausted but no nearer finding the girl who was "IT."

I was obliged to spend the next few days in London but returned at the end of the week, rested and ready to renew my quest. There were even more messages and letters. The telephone rang. One of the more persistent young ladies was enquiring if I had arrived.

My aunt pushed me out of the door and told me to go and meet her.

The pace was too hectic, the circumstances unreal. Was I infatuated with an illusion that the next girl on the list might be better than the one I was with and I should hurry on to meet her, or were the maidens confusing me in my uncle's white Bentley with the Prince Charming and stallion of their fantasies? The magic spark that elicits "that certain feeling" just didn't happen. By Sunday night an excess of drink and exposure to damsels who had tried too hard to please had befuddled my brain and drained my body. Names, faces and addresses were jumbled in a purple alcoholic haze. All the girls had been fun to be with but not one of them was special.

Before leaving the ranch for England, I had received a letter from Jill Lance who had been a contemporary pupil in school at Dartington. She had four children, her husband had deserted her and she wanted my advice about starting life abroad. As she lived in Totnes, Devon, near other aunts whom I always enjoyed visiting, I decided to give myself a change and go and see them all.

My first visit to Jill's home was less than a total success. I took a block of ice cream as a present for the children and finding that the front door was open stuck my head in and called, "Hello."

Four young faces peered at me curiously over and through the banister railings of the upstairs landing. "Is your Mummy home?" I asked cheerily.

"No, and you can't come in because one of us had mumps and we've been quarantined till next week," one of them replied.

"I'm very sorry about that."

"We're not. There's a horrible teacher in our school whom we haven't had to see."

"Oh, I see. May I ask what you're called?"

"I'm Rachel, this is Marcus, that's Barnaby and Felix is sucking his thumb. Now, what do you want?"

I didn't have much experience in talking to young children for I remember saying inanely, "I've come all the way from South America and I've brought you some ice cream."

"What flavour?"

"Chocolate."

"We prefer vanilla."

I attempted another line of conversation."Will Mummy be home soon?"

"Don't know."

"Ah, well, I see. Um, yes, shall I leave you the ice cream?'

"Leave it on the door-step and we'll collect it after you've gone."

I was made to feel that I was the person in quarantine who had to be avoided. However, I left my present as instructed and heard as I turned to go, "I'm not sure I liked that strange man. What a funny ginger beard."

Jill was more effusive in her welcome. I found her self assured, creative and stimulating company. She had become a member of the Guild of Devon Craftsmen where her pottery was frequently displayed. Her energy amazed me; she made her children's clothes, cooked and cleaned and was the accordionist in the Wild Oats Band, which played at country dances in villages throughout Devon. She managed this by putting her children to sleep in the back of her mini-van in the guest parking lot and going out between dances to check that all was well. On returning to her home, she made wholemeal bread for their breakfast before going to bed.

One market day in Newton Abbot she persuaded me to accompany her to auction a van-load of her pottery seconds that she needed to sell. I was put on my mettle. Seizing a pot, I leapt to the top of a tea chest and improvised a torrent of blarney that would have made any Irishman's grandmother blush with pride. I sold the first few pots cheaply but as a crowd gathered around I pointed out that what we were selling was not mass produced in a Midlands factory but hand thrown by a master craftsman and raised the price. Within half an hour every pot had been sold. The market manager was so impressed that he asked us to come and sell every week. Celebrating over a ploughman's lunch, the friendship established when we were pupils in Dartington fell back into place and we found that it was fun to do things together.

On the strength of the Newton Abbot Market success, I agreed to go camping for a week with Jill and her children. She hoped that they and I could improve on our first impressions of each other. We strapped a canoe on the roof of her mini-van and drove to a surfing beach on the north Cornish coast where we pitched an old six-man tent. On wet mornings we squatted around a paraffin stove and took turns to fry pancakes in our one and only frying pan. Jill had forgotten to pack a spatula and our attempts to flip half-browned rounds of batter to cook on the other side were hilarious. They landed in the frying pan edgeways, stuck to the canvas roof or fell to the muddy groundsheet. We stacked our dirty plates in the rain to be washed and while our stomachs recovered, played Monopoly. I was never sorry when the game finished for then we'd race down to the sea for a swim. Afterwards, while Jill brewed hot chocolate, I read stories to the children or described roundups on the ranch during an inventory when everyone's help was welcome. Barnaby had always pictured himself as a cowboy and his enthusiasm, imagining himself on horseback herding cattle to a corral for branding was infectious. The tent walls shook with laughter and imitated bawling of calves as, astride our rolled up sleeping bags, we whooped and twirled imaginary lassoes.

At the end of the month Jill and I were ready to make a serious commitment, our relationship had gone way beyond a casual infatuation. Realising that a successful lifetime partnership didn't thrive on taking, it required a willingness to give, we came to the following agreement: She would leave her children in the care of her parents for a month while she visited the ranch. Not wanting to feel indebted to me, she would pay her own fare if I would return first and install a bathroom. That agreement marked the beginning of our life together.

🍂 🍂 🍂 🍂

It took two days of acclimatizing to the heat of Poponte before Jill announced, "I'm ready to be shown the ranch." We set off for a two hour horseback ride to a river sculptured with sink-holes, underground tunnels and bathing pools. Jill tore off her clothes and would have splashed about happily for hours had small hungry fish with sharp teeth not treated her white bottom as manna from Heaven. That evening I had to apply calamine lotion where she was saddle sore, sunburned and bitten. She knew those discomforts were avoidable and didn't complain, but the wild native animals living in and around the homestead—giving Curucucú the aspect of an open zoo—were more difficult to accept with equanimity. Giant iguanas, resembling archaic savage beasts with raised tails, scuttled on tiptoe from one tree to another. Small green iguanas crept along branches of flowering bushes and ate emerging buds. Cockroaches, snakes, rats, spiders and frogs strode, slithered, ran and hopped over the floor of the house. Bats swooped from rafter to rafter in the roof. Thousands of flying insects swarmed around the Lister motor-powered light bulbs after a rain storm and beat themselves to death in mating dances. Large toads gorged themselves on their fallen bodies and burped contentedly.

Jill watched their antics with a brave smile by imagining how strange her habits must seem to them and, barring one or two exceptions, managed to co-exist peacefully.

However, the breakfasts my cook prepared of boiled yucca and plantains surmounted with a fried egg was something she was determined to improve.

"Darling, instead of those rather dreary pieces of yucca and plantain wouldn't you rather have hot buttered toast spread with marmalade?"

"Most certainly."

"Well then, where do I find bread, butter, oranges and sugar?"

"That, my dear, presents various problems. There are no bakeries within a hundred miles and, as in this environment flour quickly becomes infested with maggots, storekeepers don't stock it."

"If you're the pioneer you told me about in England who was moulding his environment, I think you ought be able to do something about it."

I was neatly caught. Either I came up with a solution or I was a braggart.

"I believe there's an abandoned mill started by some crank who went bankrupt where there might still be stone grinding wheels. If I can get them, I'll ask the chap who drives the vegetable truck to bring some wheat and dried yeast on his next trip. We could churn cream from our own milk into butter and there're oranges in the garden for marmalade. Refined white sugar can be bought in Poponte but if you really want to do the pioneer thing, squeeze sugar canes and boil the juice till it sets."

A team of men, intrigued to see me make flour, accompanied me to the mill. The bottom grinding wheel had to be freed from masonry, the top one was fitted with a handle for rotating it and in the middle had a hole where one poured in grain. We brought both of them back to the ranch and reassembled them outside the kitchen door.

Jill had never had any problems baking bread in England. She knew the properties of the ingredients and could finely tune the heat of her oven. It would have been a gross understatement had a health food store described the flour which emerged when I turned the handle of the top mill stone to start grinding as "high in natural roughage," it was more like commercial corn-cake for cattle. Nobody had ever tried to bake bread in my wood fired brick oven and the first attempts to do so were experimental disasters. An incautious neighbor boasting that he could eat anything ate a whole loaf and suffered from constipation for days afterwards. It took many re-grindings and several further trials before Jill produced a loaf that people trusted. She then turned her attention to making butter. She poured the morning's pail of milk, brought straight from the corral, into a hand- operated centrifuge with two spouts. The herdsman's son turned the handle and from one emerged low fat milk used to make cheese and from the other cream which was put in the refrigerator to thicken. When it was of the right consistency she ladled it into a bucket and churned it with a paddle inserted vertically through a hole in the lid until the cream solidified. The whey she gave to the herdsman's son to fatten his pig but the butter, kneaded under cool water and sprinkled with a pinch of salt for taste, she kept for ourselves.

Oranges grew in the garden, but nowhere could I find glass jars. Dry goods in Poponte came wrapped in banana leaves, liquids in bottles, sardines in tins. Jill suggested searching through a rubbish tip but, in that non-throw-away society, there wasn't one. Everybody prized jars. Small ones were used as table glasses, larger sizes protected food from rats and cockroaches. Our orange, lemon and grapefruit marmalade was stored in dry calabashes and sealed with melted candle wax.

Before Jill came to the ranch, I'd seldom stayed in bed at dawn to listen to the variety of bird call in Curucucú's dawn chorus. I'd certainly never dawdled there admiring the cattle egrets waking on the branches of a giant dead tree in the front field. With Jill at my side, time passed pleasantly doing both. Egrets in orderly sequence would lift themselves into the air with a beat of brilliant white wings and soar in graceful circles before joining others to fly away. As evening shadows stretched across the fields they returned and, descending like spiraling confetti, alighted on familiar branches.

On afternoons, when the sky was slightly overcast, I'd take Jill on horseback to the top of a ridge where we'd watch the sunset. To the west shimmered flood plains of the Magdalena river. Behind us in the east, ridges of the Andes rose in undulating tiers till they disappeared among clouds. For a few brief moments, rays from the descending sun would bathe the lagoons, clouds, mountain tops and ourselves in glowing scarlet. Aware of the transient insignificance of our lives we promised to make the most of our time together.

Neither of us were accustomed to the use of flattery to show affection. Engaging in a bit of friendly rivalry was our way of showing how much we enjoyed each other's company. When Jill got the better of me, I devised a come-back.

"Have you always slept in the nude?" she asked me one night as we were getting into bed.

"Ever since coming to the tropics. Sleeping nude is both cool and economical. I don't have to buy or wash pyjamas."

Jill pursed her lips in mock disapproval, blew out the kerosene lantern—which provided us with light after the light plant was turned off for the night—and was soon asleep. Some time later we were woken by an agonised squawking which, as I leapt out of bed, I knew from experience was the cry of a chicken in the jaws of an opossum. Ignoring Jill's cry to wait for her, I stuck my feet into the Wellington boots that always stood ready by the bedroom door to protect my feet from being bitten by a snake, grabbed my torch and a machete, and rushed out into the night. I despatched the opossum with a swipe of my machete and had just picked it up by the tail ready to throw it to the dogs, when I was dazzled by the light of a flashbulb from Jill's camera.

"I'm thinking about writing an article for *Field and Stream* on big game hunting in Colombia and illustrating it with this photograph captioned, 'What the well-equipped cattle baron wears while stalking game at night.'"

On the following day I drove Jill to a restaurant which I knew had a curious custom. This time *I* had the camera. We sat down and, while waiting for our food, drank several beers. It was not long before Jill was looking for a sign to the toilet. As there was none, I suggested this was a suitable opportunity for her to practise her Spanish. She approached the owner and asked quite correctly for the *sanitarios*. He nodded, handed her a truncheon and a short stick on to which was nailed a square piece of cardboard, and then pointed to the yard behind the house.

"*No! No! Necesito los sanitarios*," she cried. He said something I missed and once again handed her the stick and club and led her to the back door. "*Por alla, Señora*," he said indicating the yard. Jill looked to see if there were any outhouse buildings. There was nothing except a few weeds, one or two scraggly trees and the owner's pigs and chickens. She looked appealingly towards me. "Lord, I'm hopeless at learning Spanish," she sighed. "I was so pleased when I thought that he understood me, and then he handed me these. I've no idea what they're for and what he said didn't make any sense."

"You probably did understand him but perhaps I should have told you that you must do what every other woman does here: go out and try and find an unused bush and squat behind it."

"But what do I want with these?"

"Oh, the cardboard fan is to give you some privacy while you perform, and the truncheon is to beat off scavenging pigs. Incidentally, I'm thinking of sending an article to *Country Life* on 'Wining and Dining in the Wayside Inns of Colombia' and thought a photograph of your squatting form being lifted into the air on the snout of a pig would be a stunning illustration."

ᵃ ᵃ ᵃ ᵃ

By adopting low profiles we immersed ourselves in the mainstream of rural Colombian life and accepted situations which others might have found intolerable. The sameness of the sanitised accommodation in brand-name hotels and their predictably aseptic food was not for us. We joked that if guests never went outside they wouldn't be able to tell if they were in Bogotá, Bangkok, Beirut or Boston.

As her thirty-day stay neared its end, Jill said that she would like to visit the Sierra Nevada de Santa Marta, whose snow-capped peaks were visible from the ranch. At that stage she had no intention of trekking high into the mountains but thought a change from the tropical heat of Poponte for the cool climate village of Atanques would be pleasant. She also wished to see the homespun garments that Sierra Indians wore when going about their daily chores. A trip would give her an inkling of the amazing diversity to be found in Colombia should she ever return.

Atanques, built on an ancient glacial moraine littered with massive boulders, has the rather charming distinction that no street is either level or straight and houses perch where and as they can, often abutting against each other unevenly. When rains fall the streets become rushing torrents and the refuse, which would otherwise make the village sordid, is washed away.

Higher in the mountains mule tracks lead to Indian communities where, without a special permit, "civilised" visitors are not allowed to tread.

A bus dropped us at nightfall on the only nearly flat piece of ground and turned around, ready for its outward journey in the morning. Peals of thunder crackling across the sky indicating imminent rain so we hurried to what we were told was the best hotel. Lighting the way with a paraffin lantern the clerk led us down a dark corridor and showed us the predictable communal bathroom. Squares of newspaper dangled from a nail conveniently in reach of a hole in the floor. For those desirous of bathing, a gourd dipper hung over the side of an upright, fifty-five-gallon fuel drum filled with water. There was no room available with a double bed so we accepted one where two cots supported a three-legged chair wedged between them. Even I had hoped to find something better.

The clerk lit a stub of a candle, stuck it into the neck of a wax streaked bottle and placed it on the chair with a box of matches. Satisfied that we had everything any guest could possibly need, he mumbled "Have a good night's rest" and returned to the recess of his office.

I had not expected orthopaedic mattresses, but those on the cots defied description. We tried them from one end and then from the other and even turned them over. Only a contortionist could have slept comfortably between the lumps and the hollows. The candle spluttered and went out. A tentative patter of rain on the corrugated iron roof sounded an overture to the abandoned frenzy of a tropical thunderstorm. Worried that our clothes, where we'd piled them on the unused cot might be getting wet, I ran my hand over them and felt drops of water falling from the ceiling. I tipped the cot on its side. The chair fell over and the bottle shattered on the cement floor. Our thoughts of a romantic night were dispelled by swarms of starving bed bugs—or fleas—crawling above, below and between us. Not until Jill reached England could she find a delousing solution strong enough to kill whatever they were, while I, on my return to the ranch, had to wash myself with gasoline.

"Did you get any sleep?"

"Sleep! How does a place like this stay in business?"

"I guess some people are just thicker skinned than others."

We leapt over the rivulet draining the rain-washed street in front of the hotel's entrance and went in search of a place that sold food. On the flat where the bus had left us we saw a tarpaulin stretched between two trees. Under it was a trestle table flanked by two benches. By the side of an open hearth someone was attempting to light a fire by pouring diesel fuel over damp wood. Clouds of oily smoke with little flame indicated there was ample time to take a stroll before breakfast.

Our future together was in balance and the omens that morning were scarcely auspicious. Jill had to make up her mind whether, on returning to England, she would collect her children and come back to the ranch, or remember her time with me as an ephemeral episode stolen from the routine of her daily life. Immersed in our own thoughts, we walked hand in hand down the road that led out of the village.

"I could apologize for the fiasco of last night, but it's pointless as we both know that if you come back something similar will happen again. I'm sorry it's a lousy ending to your trip. Even I can think that it might have been more idyllic." We walked on in silence and then I looked at her and grinned. "It was unusual, though. Think you'll remember it?"

"Yes, it was certainly bizarre. I think when I return to England and look back on last night I shall find it rather funny, and then I shall miss all the crazy things we've done together and life there will seem dull and insipid by comparison."

"Could your children adapt to this life?"

"I think they'd like the freedom and adventure. Rachel would enjoy the ranch and the horses. Marcus likes tractors and machinery. Barnaby has always wanted to be a cowboy and as long as little Felix is with me he'll adapt to wherever I make a home."

"Then you'll come back with them?" I breathed hopefully.

She gazed at me with one of her quizzical expressions and then flung her arms around me pressing her face against my chest, but I managed to hear, "If you accept all of us, yes."

I was too choked up with happiness to speak and gave her a squeeze as an answer.

Later when friends in Poponte joshed me that my days of freedom were numbered, I didn't mind. After all, the children were human beings and the ranch was a fairly big place—large enough to go off for a day's ride by oneself if one needed to be alone for a change. And when I got back there would be Jill.

In England Jill's photographs and tapes were eagerly awaited and her parents had a family gathering to enjoy them. The tapes began with a few introductory remarks by Jill and then the sounds of tropical birds welcoming another sunrise filled their living room. "Heavenly, simply heavenly," sighed her aunt.

"Yes, isn't it?" agreed her mother.

Suddenly the peace was shattered by a raucous noise as though a boa constrictor had wrapped itself around the neck of a crowing cockerel.

"Good God in Heaven!" exclaimed her father. "Whatever was that?"

"Oh, that was just Ben clearing his throat in the bathroom," explained Jill. "He has his share of disgusting habits."

I have always thought it a sign of her family's breeding that they never inquired about the others.

✦ ✦ ✦ ✦

Jill's return to Colombia as a betrothed immigrant was an opportunity to import many things from England which otherwise would have been subjected to exorbitantly expensive customs and excise taxes. One of my Devonian aunts, Margaret Isherwood, gave us a long wheel base Land Rover. Into, on to, and behind that versatile vehicle Jill packed her camping gear, a three-point hitch cement mixer—described as part of her potter's equipment—a sewing machine and an upright piano. The latter was a disappointment as it was impossible to keep it in tune due to the frequent changes of humidity on the ranch. There was scarcely any space left for herself, her children and their clothes.

There were travel documents to obtain, farewell parties full of tears and laughter to attend and give, and last minute things to buy. When her money gave out, friends in Totnes replenished her funds with the proceeds of an impromptu auction.

On arriving at Liverpool, she discovered that the boat's date of departure had been postponed for a week. Without enough money either to return to Devon or stay in a hotel, Jill persuaded the captain to let them live on board. Once there, each of her children adopted a member of the crew. Barnaby, ever the businessman, even managed to earn money by polishing the ship's brass fittings.

Meanwhile I was finishing the chores on the ranch to have everything ready for their arrival. I'd whitewashed the house, cut and raked the garden and chosen saddles and suitably tame horses for the children to ride. Even the water pump was overhauled. The last item on my list were new carbon brushes for the dynamo and to buy them I had to go to Valledupar.

My trip was delayed by a strange dream in which an aunt, who had died five years previously, told me to move the steers I had been given to fatten from the lush pasture bordering the river to an upland field on the savannah. It was an outrageous thing to suggest, contrary to all the tenets of good cattle management, but she appeared so vividly and was so insistent that the following morning I moved them. For many years she had felt emanations from friends who had died and during her final months these had become visions of certitude. After the physical body had been absorbed by the earth, she believed it possible to become a free spirit. "I'll always help you," she'd said. "You'll know when I'm near by the song of a bird."

It is easy to dismiss such remarks as the delusion of a deranged mind, but I believe that during meditation she experienced a paraconscious knowledge of what mystics call "the God immanent" (that which is divine at the centre of one's being). Even H.H. Price, formerly Wykeham Professor of Logic at Oxford, once observed, "Telepathy is something which ought not to happen at all if the materialistic theory were true. But it does happen. So there must be something seriously wrong with the materialistic theory however numerous and imposing the normal facts which support it may be."*

Hitching a ride in the back of a truck taking sacks of rice to Valledupar, I found a comfortable spot and lay back trying to remember if there was anything else I had to buy or needed my attention. Two days later I returned with my shopping and the spare parts for the dynamo. As I walked into Poponte from the main road where the bus had dropped me, I had a strange feeling that people were looking at me as if they wanted to say something comforting, but didn't know how. Odd, I thought, I wonder what's happened.

"You know about the flood?" a woman riding a donkey asked me.

"No. Where was it?"

"Oh, Don Ben," she choked, "I am so sorry." Overcome by emotion, she rode on.

I saw no reason to be alarmed until I reached a rise on my entrance driveway. On the night I had left for Valledupar the river, which flows about three hundred yards in front of the house, had flash flooded across the fields depositing a metre of mud and debris. Animals up to their bellies in glutinous sludge ineffectively struggled to free themselves. I wanted to go and help them but on leaving the raised road-bed I sank up to my waist myself and was lucky to get out. Over the next few days many of my herd died of thirst and exhaustion.

Thirteen people caught on the flood plain had been drowned. Pecking and

---

The Hibbert Journal, Volume 47, p.291. 1949.

squabbling vultures indicated where they lay but only when the mud had hardened could their families collect the scattered bones for burial.

On that first day I saved very little. Tucking my trousers, shirt and shoes under my arm, I slopped into the dank and forlorn house. The caretakers had abandoned it on the night of the flood and not returned. The back door leading from the kitchen into the garden leaned drunkenly on one hinge and the walls and roof of the garage and fuel store were either buried or had been swept away. In the house everything lower than a metre—bedding, clothes, and books—was a sodden, muddy mess. I didn't know where to begin until I remembered a treasured pair of handmade shoes made for me by Thrussels, the old family firm of Sidney Street, Cambridge. Thrussels had gone out of business as cheaper mass produced footwear swamped the market but, for me, those shoes had a quality of craftsmanship that distinguished them from expendable footwear. They should be in the bottom of my cupboard with a tin of Propert's saddle soap, I thought. I found them and waded through knee-deep sludge to the stream where I could wash off the mud. Sitting on a stone in my underpants—which fortunately I was still wearing—and engrossed in rubbing saddle soap into the leather of the shoe held between my knees, I was unaware that a delegation from the Mayor's office in Chiriguana had arrived to assess the extent of the damage. The Mayor's position excused him from taking off his shoes and rolling up his trousers but his assistants had been ordered to follow my tracks to the stream. A scandalized voice made me turn around.

"Don Ben! What ARE you're doing?"

"Oh, hello! I'm washing my shoes."

As I held up my half cleaned footwear their leering expectancy turned to chagrin. "The Mayor wishes to know if you managed to save the account books and receipts from your office?"

"No, not yet. They can wait."

As I stood up to greet the delegation, a reporter took my photograph which, two days later appeared with a garbled write-up on the front page of the leading Colombian newspapers. There was no offer to help with anything. They waded back through the slush to their car and drove away, no doubt feeling virtuous for having made a call of duty. I was left in peace to continue cleaning my shoes.

Lying on a makeshift bed of boards in the rafters that night, I had an idea of how I might make the chore of cleaning up the house enjoyable; children sometimes played in mud for fun. With that thought in mind, on the following morning I went to the village. By promising to give each child a new pair of shoes, I collected a group of urchins who gleefully paraded back to the ranch with me, willing to help till the job was done. Stripped to their underwear they began to scoop mud out of doors and windows or into a wheelbarrow which I managed to push out of the house and empty. Occasionally the kids "accidentally" dumped mud on each other and in the afternoon when the walls and floors were ready to be washed the house became the scene of a riotous friendly water fight. Buckets filled from the water tank were occasionally emptied over unsuspecting victims with shouts of laughter but enough were aimed at the walls so that by the end of the day most of the debris left by the flood had been washed away and the house was relatively clean.

Only with the help of loyal villagers who came to work with me every daylight hour was I able to put the house and machinery in order before Jill and her children arrived. Cupboards had to be emptied and their contents sorted and scrubbed. Bedding and clothes were saved by being washed twice but mattresses had to be thrown away. All the wiring and fuel pipes on the tractor had to be checked and the motor serviced. Anything made of paper needed special care. Mud clogged bank notes and printed pages could be soaked, carefully separated and then hung over a clothes line in the shade to dry, but most things written in ink were irretrievably smudged. Day by day the acrid stench of putrefying carcasses lessened as vultures tore into the dead cattle in the surrounding fields. When I received the telegram from the shipping agent in Barranquilla informing me that Jill and the children were due in port in two days, the house was nearly ready. I engaged a stalwart friend called María to be in charge of a final wash down with lemon smelling disinfectant and went to meet them.

The boat was already at the wharf when I arrived and the disembarked passengers gathered in front of the Customs Shed. The mass of Jill's second-hand possessions guarded by four determined young children was like a scene from "The Grapes of Wrath." The immigration inspectors must have seen Jill and her children as part of a similar saga, for upon receiving the import papers for the Land Rover—with my signature forged by the shipping agent—they were allowed to enter Colombia with a minimum of hassle. When I later asked if she forged the signatures of all her clients, I received the wounded reply, "Certainly not. I only forge the signatures of friends"

Before leaving Barranquilla I bought two, one hundred pound propane gas bottles and a new stove for Jill's kitchen and lashed them on top of the already laden roof rack. It broke five times on our fourteen hour journey to the ranch. Luckily most wayside garages in Colombia have electric welding equipment, a metal scrap heap from broken implements and a mechanic accustomed to improvise. Jill kept the children entertained by turning the breakdowns into a game of guessing when the next one might be and they remained good-humored till lunchtime. None of them were accustomed to the taste of boiled yucca, green plantains and meat. The bottled soft drinks were strange and unappetizing. They picked at the food and left it. There was nothing else on offer except water and with that in their stomachs we continued. The break-downs ceased to be amusing and I feared that the children were going to find adjusting to this new way of life difficult.

Luckily, the ranch's dismal mud flats were shrouded in darkness when we arrived. The day's drive had been exhausting both physically and emotionally and the children were desperately hungry. Unfortunately, María's bone soup, which I considered both delicious and nourishing, was also strange. They were too young to enjoy experimenting with new tastes and too tired to make the effort to try. One by one they asked to be excused from the table and went unhappily to bed dreading, no doubt, what the morning would bring. Determined to allay my premonition of impending failure and Maria's distress that her meal had been a failure, Jill started to play her accordion. The music came uncertainly at first but as I beckoned to the curious farm hands appearing at the window to come in their friendly smiles of welcome gave Jill confidence and her playing filled the house with toe-tapping rhythm. It changed what might have been a disastrous beginning into one of celebration and, for the children dropping off to sleep, one of familiar comfort and security.

After a suitable breakfast of porridge and boiled eggs I took my new family for a walk where the mud had hardened to show them the damage. There was still much to be done and work where everyone could help. Nobody had begun to dig out buried fences to retrieve the barbed wire. Half submerged hardwood trees brought by the flood were waiting to be uncovered for splitting into posts. Luckily the children found it a wild playground beyond expectations and ran off to explore. Soon they came rushing back dizzy with excitement at having seen markings in a depression where a large snake had slithered into a copse. From that day onwards it was always respectfully referred to as Anaconda Wood.

I had sent a message to Alfonso Angel Gutierrez, the owner of the cattle which I had moved, informing him that they had survived the flood, as from the newspaper reports he might well have imagined that all were lost. He was one of a breed of tough, self-made cattle men who respected honest work without pretensions, and came to inspect the damage himself. He knocked on the door just as Jill had removed loaves of her whole meal bread from the oven. Sniffing the aroma, Alfonso headed straight for the kitchen to introduce himself. With the charm of a man who had wooed his way into the favor of many women, he smiled admiringly and pronounced, "I haven't felt such a mouth-watering sensation since my mother baked bread thirty years ago."

Jill waited until she thought a loaf cool enough to eat and offered him a slice. He stayed to lunch and ate several more. Afterwards I told him what had caused me to move his cattle. He listened gravely, and looking out of the window at what might have been their graveyard, accepted that my dream was inspired.

"I'm glad I came," he said. "You could have told me my cattle were drowned, as many of yours were, and I might never have known the truth." He looked at our glum faces. "Don't despair over what has happened. The flood has given you a meter of fertile silt and rotten vegetable matter which will make your fields even better than they were. Some farmers pay thousands of pesos for chemical fertilizers to improve their fields, but they'll never see the results you're going to have. As soon as the grass is up again, I'll send you more cattle. You manage them; we will split the profits fifty-fifty, and you'll soon be independent."

Later that evening Jill remarked, "The flood was really a good thing for me and the children. By helping you put the ranch together again, we'll feel we have a right to be here. That's so much better than accepting something already made."

Once again I was made aware of how lucky I was that Jill had chosen to share my life.

TEN

An Idyllic Interlude

*How good is man's life, the mere living, how fit to employ
all the heart and the soul and the senses for ever in joy.*

—Robert Browning

The news of Jill's reappearance with four lively young children caused much excited gossip in Poponte.

"Why has Don Ben taken on a ready made family?" people asked each other. "Do you think they'll stay? I wonder if he's sterile? I hope Curucucú won't become stand-offish."

Concerns changed to relief and criticisms to admiration as the children quickly learned Spanish and made friends in the community.

Jill's qualities as a parent and teacher were soon apparent. She redesigned one end of the barn into a school room but her classes were not restricted to the confines of four walls—they took place wherever there was something happening which might stimulate an interest or lead to a hands-on competence. These ranged from collecting honey combs from bee hives to planting tufts of rooted grass in a ploughed field.

Activities in the arts included a weekly reading of poems that we had to compose on a given topic and singing folk songs accompanied by Jill on her accordion. The discovery of a vein of clay, which was found to be of excellent quality, encouraged sculpturing. I made a wheel on which everyone tested their ability to throw pots and Jill built a kiln. The tableware she made using a glaze containing ashes of various hardwoods was greatly admired, but she was

Top: Justa Sanches, a local artisan, straightens out fibers from dwarf palm leaves. *Right*: Enis Simanca weaves the fibers into an *estera* or sleeping mat.

emphatic that her dishes were not treasures to be saved, they were there for us to use and enjoy.

Jill's appreciation of craftwork led her to visit the homes of local artisans who wove sleeping mats on primitive looms. The fibers used as weft were stripped from the leaves of dwarf palms growing locally. Dyed with fruit and earth pigments and strung in the sun to dry they made a cheerful sight. Jill considered some of the finished mats to be works of art and hung a selection of them on the walls of our house. Not to be outdone, the children tie-dyed old white sheets and made curtains for their bedroom windows.

As letters to England or America mailed from Chiriguana took at least a month to arrive, in the first few days of November Jill turned the school room into a Christmas card workshop. Each child depicted a line from a carol in a drawing. One was chosen, etched into a linoleum block and printed using the silk screen method. Ranch Christmas cards were fun to make and their originality made them greatly appreciated.

Jill and I wanted to get married but discovered that, as her marriage in England to a practicing Catholic had never been officially annulled, she would have been guilty of bigamy had we done so. I found the delay in receiving a decree nisi damnable for having waited to have children, I wanted mine, when I had them, to be legitimate. On the day that the ecclesiastical notice of separation arrived from England, I bundled Jill and the family into the Land Rover and drove to San Antonio's registry office in Venezuela to legalize our union. Worried that her limited Spanish would prevent her from following the ceremony, Jill told me to nudge her in the ribs when the clerk asked the vital question. She answered "*Si*" and we sallied forth happily man and wife. While the secretary typed out our certificate the children chose to celebrate by buying ice cream cones from a vendor's cart in the town square.

Although we lived as one family, Jill's first four children, as a gesture of their independence, decided to retain the surname of their father. When asked if I found taking on four half-grown children difficult, I always replied that there were advantages: mealtimes were never dull, the children were indisputably showing competence in a variety of practical skills and their criticisms prevented me from becoming complacent. Jill's impartiality to the rare but inevitable disputes that occurred between the children and myself was that of a tree to the birds that flock around it. She provided support, was always there for comfort and presided over our larking-about with an admirable mixture of discipline and tolerance.

My clumsy attempts at being a gaucho cowboy and my habit of using a pommel as something to cling on to when I felt myself about to fall—or as a convenient peg on which to hang my picnic lunch—sent the disappointed children to Adriano, my foreman, for instruction in horsemanship. He soon became their confidant for he not only taught the boys the art of lassoing and the proper use of a pommel but with his love for the horses in his care imparted to them all an ability to feel at one with the horses they rode. When not restricted by disciplined cattle work they were soon chasing each other on their galloping mounts for fun .

To celebrate their first ranch Christmas the children all received new saddles and chose a horse for their exclusive use. Barnaby tamed a grey stallion, "Hippy," that he alone could ride. Rachel took two mares: one with loose lips that she christened "Flaberlilly" and another which suffered the prosaic name of "Favorite." Marcus liked an aged white mule called "Simón Bolivar," because he could rely on it not to buck when he vaulted into the saddle. Felix was happy with a chestnut gelding, "Potro," on which he often rode bare-back.

When Alfonso Angel returned to the ranch for a friendly visit and saw the luxuriant pasture sprouted through the alluvium deposited during the flood he sent us one hundred steers for fattening.

I shall never forget November 13, 1972. On that day Jill, attended by Poponte's midwife and myself, gave birth to our son, Diccon. Elatedly, I'd dashed off to the sitting room intending to put a record of the chorus, "For unto us a child is born" from Handel's *Messiah* on the gramophone when a shriek of dismay from the midwife sent me racing back. She'd dropped the scissors for cutting Diccon's umbilical cord on the floor! Remembering Poponte's erstwhile nurse, but resolved to improve on her sterilization technique, I picked them up and raced to the kitchen where I had boiling water ready for washing. The joyful birth of our daughter Antigone, on the 19th of March 1975, was uneventful by comparison.

Jill and I tried to keep evenings as a family time to read a story to the children. Books ranged from *The House at Pooh Corner* to *A Story Like the Wind*. If a change was desired we played "animal, vegetable or mineral," charades or any other game in which we all took part.

Rachel, being the eldest child, liked to make sure that nobody escaped their turn with the chores and nailed a chart detailing the daily jobs each of us had to do on the kitchen door. The boys had to hand milk a certain number of cows before breakfast, take a pail of milk to Jill in the kitchen and separate what was left in the centrifuge.

She would take enough low fat milk mixed with ground maize to feed Marcus's pig and her hens. The consideration lavished on the imagined sensibilities of the animals in her care knew no bounds. Each chicken was given a name and the only ones eaten were those devoured by opossums, snakes or alligators. The rest died of old age and were buried in a tearful ceremony. She even pampered an orphan donkey—whom she named "Michael"—by feeding him a litre of milk every morning at the dining room door. He wouldn't drink from a bowl because he knew that by nuzzling up to Rachel she'd let him suckle a rubber teat fixed to the end of a baby's bottle.

Marcus, when he wasn't helping to round up cattle, devoted his free hours to the maintenance of machinery. By studying service manuals he developed an uncanny ability to diagnose mechanical failures and rectify faults. Jill had not been mistaken in Barnaby's desires. He was more interested in being a cowboy than in book learning. Felix's capacity to adapt sensibly to his new

Photo of the family taken in 1975. L*eft to right*: Tiggy, Ben, Jill, Diccon, Barnaby, Marcus, Rachel, Felix and Heraclitis.

environment and still find fun in spending weekends with a group of village friends fishing in the river made him a very popular young man.

✍ ✍ ✍ ✍

Ever since Jill's first trip to Colombia, when she and I had spent that uncomfortable night in Atanques, she had wanted to return to the Sierra Nevada. This was not an easy thing to do as the attempts of peasants to colonise Indian lands had resulted in the Institute of Indian Affairs in Bogotá declaring the upper reaches of the Massif a restricted zone. Ika Indians believed the snow-capped peaks to be sacred and requests to enter the area were routinely denied to all but the most highly accredited applicants. Our chance to visit came in 1974 when the Royal Air Force Mountaineering Association, having been granted access for a climbing expedition, asked me to organise ground transport from Barranquilla airport to the snow line. I assured them I could make

Marcus rounding up cattle on the savannas of Curucucú.

Diccon learning how to lasso and paddle.

Rachel, on her horse "Favorite," crossing the river that flash flooded.

Barnaby (*below*) on his stallion "Hippy" in the main street of Poponte. Felix (*bottom*) providing a pail of milk for breakfast.

Barnaby (*left*) and Felix on the lake behind the dam.

Felix dragging a poisonous snake that he'd killed in the roadway to show his brothers.

Top: Tiggy at eighteen months being given a horseback ride.

Bottom: Tiggy at nine years leaning against a friendly bull.

An Ika Indian in traditional homespun clothing surveys his homeland.

the necessary arrangements but added that my wife and family, for whom I would be solely responsible, would be very grateful for permission to accompany me into the peak area.

Jill, the children and the Ika guides with their bullocks were gathered at the road head in Atanques when I arrived with the lorry bringing the expedition from Barranquilla. Introductions were made and we set off. Each Air Force climber, so as to condition himself to the altitude, carried a backpack of his personal gear. The bulky equipment was carried on either side of wooden cargo saddles strapped to tame bullocks. On one of them, in a gap between two duffel bags, rode Jill with two-year-old Diccon in her arms. For the first hour we journeyed through countryside that bore signs of "*civilizados*" but at the settlement of Chemiscamena we were stopped by an official of the Institute of Indian Affairs who demanded to see proof of our identity and our permits. Satisfied, he allowed us to pass through the portal marking the entrance to the Indian Reserve. The trail passed through settlements of conical roofed houses where families of Indians in homespun garments cast watchful eyes as we skirted gardens of peas, potatoes, pumpkins, sugar cane and onions. Late that afternoon we reached a low stone-walled round-house backed by two sheep pens and found a friendly shepherd. The expedition leader struck a bargain with him. If we could sleep on the uneven dirt floor of his home for the night, he could share our evening and breakfast meals.

We slept, if that is the appropriate word, like the spokes of a wheel around the central fire pit, our feet roasted by burning embers and our heads exposed to icy draughts blowing around the circular wall. Our leathery host was apparently impervious to discomfort. He disappeared under his homespun blanket and only emerged once in the night to add more wood to the fire. Morning light found most of us needing the warmth of the rising sun to limber our joints before we were interested in breakfast. The friendly shepherd, glad to earn solid money in an area where bartering was more common, agreed to supply us every third day with mutton from his flock, potatoes and onions from his garden and *curuba* fruits from the vines growing up the walls of his house. Meeting an Indian one day's march from our destination willing to supply fresh food to vary what otherwise would have been a restricted diet of concentrates was an unexpected boon. Nothing edible for humans grows at four thousand five

Our friendly Ika shepherd holding a *porporo.*

hundred metres near the Naboba lakes where we planned to make our base camp.

Altitude slowed our progress on the second day and when, panting for breath, we reached the lakes, our only desire was to rest. It took a supreme effort to pitch the tents and open a tin of pemican and beans before the intense cold drove everyone to their sleeping bags. I was thinking how very acceptable a tot of whisky would be when I heard a voice say, "Please accept this with the Group Captain's compliments." I unzipped the flap and was handed a bottle of Glenfiddich. It was a drink that Jill didn't care for but a few sips of that exquisite elixir fortified me against the spine chilling uncertainties of the night.

The following morning, to repay the Group Captain's kindness, I demonstrated another way of keeping warm by giving a lesson in practical botany. The Air Force climbers were quick to learn and before lunch every dry *frailejón* leaf in the vicinity of the lakes had been gathered and spread as a soft insulation to separate the ground sheets of each tent from the frozen ground.

The only sign of life among the five to six thousand meter, snow-covered peaks were a pair of condors that glided through the capricious winds with consummate skill. A crashed helicopter near the lakes afforded a sheltered playhouse for the younger children, while the older ones were taken on minor ascents by members of the expedition.

On his second visit the faithful Indian who supplied us with provisions was sighted approaching the camp using a long pointed stick, usually used to coax his reluctant bullock up the trail, on a weary visitor who turned out to be Louis de Bernièrs. Jill had hired him as a tutor to prepare Rachel and Marcus for their "O" level exams. Louis's arrival in Barranquilla had coincided with our trip to the Naboba lakes and she had arranged for him to be brought along to join us. He taught the children for a year and recalled his experiences of Poponte in his book, *The War of Don Emanuel's Nether Parts*. While flattered that it was dedicated to me, I often thought that accounts of his exploits would have been differently phrased had he remembered Robert Burns's line, "O wad somebody the giftie gie us, to see ourselves as others see us."

Nobody washed properly in Naboba. The lakes were too cold. Even had one splashed enough water to be able to soap oneself the unapealing prospect of immersing oneself afterwards to get rid of the lather kept most of us dirty. By the end of the second week I was not only desiccated but convinced that proximity to the peaks lacked long term appeal. They might provide a challenge to talented climbers as a place to hone their prowess but, for me, Curucucú provided all the excitement I needed for everyday living. The expedition had been a wonderful experience but when the time came to escort the R.A.F. climbers to their plane in Barranquilla, I was happy to say goodbye and return to my stream for a blissful bathe.

Other than the hour before dusk when the children played football, croquet or miniature golf on an obstacle course, little time was given to sport. Exercise, team spirit and competence came from participating in projects which benefitted us all. One such project was to derive free electric power from the stream. The children were keen to help for although I started the diesel powered light plant for two hours every evening—or for obviously justifiable daytime needs—the cost of fuel made me reluctant to run it all night for the luxury of turning fans.

I'd heard of an ingenious Frenchman named Roland LeCoutre who had a workshop equipped for designing and founding pieces of machinery in Codazzi, a town some fifty miles away. I went to visit him and explained what we wanted to do. The idea of applying his expertise to a project in the country appealed to him and he eagerly accepted my invitation to join us for lunch on the following Sunday when he would have time to study the terrain and explain what we had to do. He showed us where, if we built a dam to form a lake, water could be diverted along an elevated leat to give an approximate two metre fall near the house. If the survey we were to make confirmed his estimates, he promised to design and make an efficient water-driven turbine.

I borrowed the surveyor's theodolite which the Spanish rice growers had left on Hacienda Poponte, and for the next few days the children joined me in the work of cutting sight lines, marking levels and measuring the gallons-per-second flow of water in the stream bed. Our calculations showed that the elevated water behind the dam could not only fill a leat ending with a vertical drop of two and one half metres but the energy produced by the volume of falling water would power a water turbine driven dynamo of a four kilowatt capacity. The prospect of an electric refrigerator, ceiling fans at any hour of the day or night and a boating lake behind the dam spurred the children to master the necessary maths.

The lake was "out of bounds" to adults. It was a children's sanctuary where the route through the maze of channels and walls of rushes leading to the haunts of dragons and underwater monsters was a secret kept by themselves.

When Jill or I asked the children for their help on the ranch we firmly believed that by learning a variety of skills they would develop the confidence to tackle jobs that many pay others to do. Occasionally, wealthy neighbors criticized us for our attitude. However, when a project was successfully completed in which every member of the family had the satisfaction of having taken part, we felt that parents who protected their children from developing a hands-on competence were the ones who were at fault.

✦ ✦ ✦ ✦

I had learned to mistrust the quality control of expensive chemical compounds sold to farmers, for if Colombian forgers could produce passable banknotes within weeks of a new issue, counterfeiting the seals of industrial containers and adulterating the contents was child's play. Cyril, Roland's brother-in-law, thinking to concoct a mineral mix for his cattle, ordered two tons of calcium bi-phosphate from an established chemical firm. Doubting its purity when it arrived, he had it analyzed. A third of the consignment turned out to be floor sweepings. Unwilling to risk a legal wrangle with a multinational chemical company—which whatever the rights one would be unlikely to win—I decided to process bone meal on the farm. The Frenchman put together the necessary machinery and little boys scoured the countryside for skeletons picked clean by vultures and whitened by rain and sun. Grinning with delight at what that crazy Don Ben would buy, kids arrived with their donkeys staggering under bulging sacks of bones. They were converted into brittle shards in my autoclave and then put through a mill which ground them

into powder. By adding trace elements, I produced a variety of highly satisfactory mineral supplements. Any specific deficiency of the soil—such as
found in parts of my valley—could be rectified by adding the missing element
to the salt permanently available in roofed troughs built in every field.
Curucucú steers fattened on grass and were ready for market at two and a half
years of age averaging four hundred eighty kilos.

Once a year the ranch made a gift of a calf to Jill, to each of the children and
to the permanent workmen. As a special perk for faithful long time service,
Adriano was allowed to graze up to fifty head. This practice ensured that during the four monthly inventory everybody worked overtime with a will. Before
daybreak Adriano and the boys had saddled horses needed for the day's work
and by breakfast time selected lots of cattle were in the corral ready to be
injected with preventive vaccines, branded, castrated or checked for pregnancy.

This work usually took from three to four days and there was time to see
whose animals had grown the most. Barnaby's always seemed to have made the
most progress, Jill's—if they hadn't already died—the least. Her bad luck with
animals seemed grossly unfair as, out of all of us, she was the only vegetarian.
However, she never railed against her ill-fortune and, when I gave her a replacement, always hoped it would do better. When the inventory was completed, and
if the results had been satisfactory, we invited the entire village to a ranch party.

I replaced Crisanto's use of anise for flavouring alcoholic brew with sliced
pineapples and citrus fruits and produced fifty-five-gallon drums of palatable
non-distilled *guarapo*. Guests arrived early in the afternoon and, after imbib-
ing liberally, gathered around the corral where all who wanted—and some
who didn't—took part in playing toreador for year-old stock. Young children
and their mothers were given a perch on the corral's upper railings where they
could safely cheer and squeal when somebody—usually a man who had misjudged the strength of my *guarapo*—was dragged into the arena between two
roisterers and used in place of a toreador's cape. It was taken as good fun if he
was knocked into the dirt by a bullock. By local tradition, law suits resulting
from bull-fighting injuries were never pursued. Both litigant and lawyer would
have been hounded out of the community had any such action been attempted.

When at dusk the bull-fighting finished, we severed the barren heifer that
had been roasting on a spit into pieces, dipped them into a mixture of beer,
mashed spring onions and garlic and glazed them over a charcoal grill. The
guests gathered round the trestle tables laid with freshly cut banana leaves and
used their hands to help themselves to as much meat, potatoes and yucca as

they could eat. *Guarapo* was served in paper cups. Buckets of water, bars of soap and towels were always ready for guests to "tidy up." When guests had eaten, Jill put records on the gramophone and the paving stones under the arches of flowering bougainvillea became a dance floor for happily gyrating couples. If the party showed signs of faltering, Jill organised obstacle and elimination competitions and gave prizes to the winning couples.

Insensate bodies of inebriated guests were lifted onto the tractor's trailer by the boys and, when filled to capacity, driven to the village and tipped off in front of their respective houses. Nobody complained, for in the tropics people often sleep out-of-doors by preference.

Celebrations to mark children's birthdays were slightly less boisterous. Kids were never expected to bring presents. They were invited for their company. Advised to wear old clothes, they arrived shortly after lunch ready to participate in the afternoon's games: obstacle races, climbing to the top of greased poles, pillow fights while balancing on a narrow log straddling the stream, encoded treasure hunts and paper chases. Jill served an early supper with fresh lemonade and afterwards played her accordion. I, creating more laughter than finesse, attempted to teach square and long set dancing.

They were happy times for us all. The ranch was reaping benefits from the hard work that had gone into it and each year we took a month's holiday either in England or America. Then, having had a change, we returned to the life we preferred and the home that Jill had made.

It would be untrue to say that the relationship between Jill and myself was always on a high. We were both strong willed and our unorthodox lives had accustomed us to make decisions on our own. On the ranch she ruled in what she considered her domain, and I in mine. While we often discussed issues, and were usually in accord in matters affecting our relationship with the community, when something cropped up needing immediate attention which my experience told me had only one solution, I occasionally had to say, "I'm sorry, my dear, but my decision of the way it's going to be is final." Jill never felt put down for long. Quite apart from her sewing machine or tub of kneaded clay there were just too many things where she excelled for her to lose self-confidence.

In one aspect, however, Jill was at a decided disadvantage in never discovering a woman nearby with similar interests and outlooks with whom she could exchange intimacies. Understandably, accumulated frustrations sometimes boiled over and in the middle of the night I might be jabbed in the ribs by her elbow and subjected to a torrent of woes. These outpourings were often repeated for, if Jill realized that I had dozed off to sleep in the middle of her tirade, she would jab me in the ribs once again and start afresh! At some appropriate moment on the following day she would meekly fling her arms around me and touchingly explain that I was the only person she had on whom to unburden her soul.

Of course, she could describe her feelings, and a typical day of her life, better than I and did so in a letter to her parents:

May 15, 1978

Dear Mum and Dad,

This is a joint birthday letter. I've been wondering what I could write about and have decided that what impresses me on an ordinary uneventful day might give you another picture to put with the many photographs and slides that you have seen over the years.

I lie in bed feeling sure that it is time to get up but not wanting to confirm the fact. But as the birds are singing away I open my eyes and look out of the window and see a brilliant cascade of yellow Cassia fistula *flowers. Beyond them lies a wide expanse of mountainous scenery under a gently pinking pale blue sky and I can't help feeling how fortunate I am to be able to witness so much beauty, not just now but every day. I get out of bed, where Ben is just beginning to waken, and stand at the window. It has rained in the night and everything is new and fresh looking. There is all the profusion of salmon pink lilies. I think how much I might admire one of these clumps in anyone else's garden, and here I am looking at twenty or more. The 'Pride of Barbados' are looking their best too, with their orange, yellow, or pink flowers. The lawn needs cutting. It is the only thing that spoils the otherwise perfect picture.*

Chickens cackle and it is obviously time to get on with the day's doings. I wash and dress quickly and pass through Diccon and Tiggy's (Antigone has decided she prefers to be called Tiggy) bedroom where they are still fast asleep and draw their curtains. Then grabbing a basket from the kitchen I walk down to the avocado trees which are in the middle of the cooking banana plantation (the platanera) *All the banana trees are a light emerald green in the morning light and their large leaves are dripping after the rain. Between some of the trunks spiders have made their webs, which I break, unaware that they are there. There are lots of avocados on the ground. Cats and dogs have arrived*

Jill and her garden
at Curucucú.

*before me and several fruits are partly eaten. I never cease to be
amazed by the size of these avocados, they are so much bigger than
any you see in England. Some weigh a kilo! I fill my basket with the
best and struggle back to the house.*

*Mangos have fallen during the night and I return to collect some for
breakfast. I notice it is nearly six o'clock, just in time for the BBC World
Service news which Ben and I enjoy listening to while preparing our
usual breakfast of toasted home baked bread, farm marmalade and
butter, free range scrambled eggs, and a bowl of sliced fruit. There is
just time to make the bucket of fresh lemonade for people to help themselves from throughout the day. When it's very hot, the bucket has to be
filled twice.*

*I ring a bell to announce breakfast and as the children appear they
remark that they would rather not do school today, which is what they*

say every morning! From the table is a marvellous view of mountains rising behind a field of contentedly grazing horses and cattle.

As we finish eating the workmen begin to arrive on their bicycles, on donkeys or on foot. Ben tells them what they should do for the day and everyone goes about their chores. Diccon goes out to the corral where he helps Domingo milk eight or nine cows to supply our needs. Tiggy feeds the cats and dogs and then does a round of the lemon trees. We use dozens of lemons every day. I wash the dishes, clear up the kitchen and sometimes prepare lunch which is left to simmer in the crock pot. There is the ground up maize mixed with sour milk to cook for the young chickens, ducks, and turkeys. The hens, fed a pan of whole maize and the vegetable kitchen waste, are kept in their pens till midday in the hope that most of the eggs will be laid there.

As soon as the milking is finished the children take the cows back to their field and I decide what is to be done with the milk. Two or three times a week I separate it for butter, the others are cheese days. When the children return it is usually eight o'clock and time for school. By then I may just have had time to sweep the floor of the kitchen. Going over to the schoolroom, I can't help but gasp at the fantastic sight of the huge lush bundles of blossoms of the cassia which arch over the gate. Beyond it towers a 'flamboyant tree' with large bright red flowers, while overhead on the trellis the 'bougainvillea' is a blaze of apricot and cerise coloured 'petals' (Ben says they're not really petals, but I think that describes them best), some of which have fallen covering the paving stones in an extravagant confetti. If all that isn't enough, white clusters of 'frangipani' flowers fill the air with their powerful scent. What surroundings to live in!

School time and the children take out their books. It is a lovely little room, always fairly cool, with a view to the garden and the stream which runs through it, lined with red hot poker lilies which grow to about two metres high. I have them planted all along the edges as their roots form thick clumps which help to control erosion. The school lasts from eight until three-thirty with a half hour break at ten-thirty, and an hour at twelve. During the morning my time is mostly spent enjoyably teaching, though sometimes I can write a few letters while the children are studying. They are quick and if necessary can be left to get on with project work while I finish preparing lunch or do other odd things in the house. *Often I have to feed the cowboys or the lady who comes three days a week from the village to do all the heavy cleaning.*

Two villagers shout 'Buenos días' as they go looking for firewood with their donkeys--most of the village people cook on three stones. There is a fairly constant stream of passers-by: cyclists who rush by for a swim, boys going to the river to fish, ladies with bowls of washing on their heads and children carrying cooking pots full of yucca and platano to eat with the fish at lunch time.

There is a cattle call in the front field, another one a bit louder and then the sloshing, splashing of many feet as mooing cows and their calves are herded by Adriano and Hector, our two cowboys, through the stream, past the schoolroom and barns and into the corral. That means two more for lunch today. Adriano asks if Diccon and Tiggy can help, which pleases them enormously. No more school till tomorrow! It's quite nice for me too as I can do some work in the garden in the afternoon.

A jeep arrives with some people to see Ben who is in the workshop mending the Land Rover. As all visitors are offered a drink, I go over to the kitchen and bring back a jug of lemonade.

Lunch is a merry meal. We are a little unusual in that we like to eat together: cowboys, cleaning lady, the odd visitor, and us. Everyone clears their place when they have finished. There is a mixed language conversation of Spanish and English so that the children learn both, helpful for choosing 'O' level subjects later. The cowboys remark that another cow has been peeled (killed by poachers who take the meat and leave the entrails, head and skin behind). We have been losing one or two animals a month recently to these illegal butchers, as have other cattle farmers in the area, and we are plotting with a certain macabre humour methods of dealing with the problem. I don't think, though, that Ben would make a good vigilante. When he reaches for his revolver the safest place to be is where he's aiming. I must tell you a really funny example of what he calls his prowess. The other day I noticed an iguana creeping along a branch of my favourite 'hybiscus' bush and knew that all the flowering buds would soon be eaten if something wasn't done pretty quickly. I was really fed up as I've tried so hard to make the garden lovely. Well, Ben went to the bedroom where he keeps his revolver stating that he could accomplish four good things with one shot: please me; save my hybiscus from a predator; provide a supper for our tractor driver's family; and

The children at work herding cattle.

impress the workmen with his marksmanship. Stealthily approaching the iguana who had just bitten off a flower--I could see a petal sticking out of the corner of its mouth--Ben aimed and fired. In passing, the bullet severed the main stem of the bush, and the unscathed iguana scuttled off to climb the nearest tree where it disappeared from view among the foliage. We were all so convulsed with laughter that even Ben managed a sheepish smile.

When lunch is over I wash up and let all the poultry loose for the afternoon. They roam freely devouring small snakes, spiders, and bugs. I've often wondered if that accounts for our chickens laying so many tasty eggs with lovely speckledy shells.

The children have finished their recorder practice, in which Tiggy is showing some promise, and I watch them get on their horses. Diccon gallops off in front and Tiggy, her legs barely long enough to reach the stirrups, urges her horse to catch up. Her determined little voice imitating the cries of cowboys when they're herding cattle--'Hiya ha ha, hup, hup, hup'--fills me with wonder.

I get on with tying up the tomatoes in my vegetable garden. This had to be completely enclosed with a low cement wall topped with a wire netting cage to keep out iguanas, archaic reptiles that otherwise would

The author conducting a pregnancy test on one of the cows.

devour all the runner beans, cucumbers, and the few other vegetables we can grow. I love my garden. It's so rewarding. A cutting of hibiscus may well be a small bush and have flowered within nine months. Trees that were seeds a year ago are now a good metre tall. I'm sure that every day the hedge outside the kitchen grows over an inch! When I'm digging, chickens get in the way around my feet scratching for bugs. Lizards, disturbed in their holes, scamper away to safety leaving nests of white leathery eggs which chickens soon find and gobble up. It's hot work and I'm forever wiping my face on the shoulder of my shirt, which is already wet through, but somehow I don't mind. Odd, for I hated the heat in England.

Kitchen towels have been boiled and must be rinsed out. Taking them to the stream, I sit on the stone and have a rest. Cool water flows around the towels and my knees and little fish dart all around. When Diccon and Tiggy were babies, I bathed them here several times a day.

It's a beautiful shaded spot. Above me I notice weeds collected around the mesh that filters the water for the turbine and, leaving the towels, go to clear them away. Horses from the front field have been wading in the canal, grazing on water plants and pulling them up by the roots. It's a chore to clean the mesh but a blessing that the horses clean

The author with a work crew planting grass seedlings.

the canal. From my vantage point a pink flowering tree partially obscures the view of the house, but my garden looks like a picture from the front of a calendar. Natural sounds surround me, falling water, bird song and the chirping of cicadas. In the mango tree there is a little 'chudding' noise calling my attention to a red squirrel half hidden in the branches. There used to be more of them but I think young boys hunt them for food with their catapults. Returning to the house I hang my towels on the line where they will soon be dry.

People with their firewood and washing begin to return from the river. Young lads proudly hold up the fish they'd caught threaded through their gills on to a stick and shout a friendly greeting. This is a happy place where everybody can enjoy the large river that flows through the farm just a field away from the house. We don't see or hear them when they're there, so their presence never bothers us.

I notice clouds building up for rain, and go to plant a few coconuts before putting on the kettle for a cup of tea. Ben hears my shout to join me and we try and enjoy a few moments of relaxation before remembering other things we want to get done before nightfall. I must make butter, which now with the Kenwood is easy. Some chocolate brownies would be nice, and looking around the kitchen decked with ripening bunches of fruit I think of making some banana ice cream. On the dresser I usually have papayas, pineapples, coconuts, baskets of onions and tomatoes, oranges, and lemons. It's a lovely kitchen where people come in and join us for tea or a drink of lemonade. I can hear the children coming back with the milking cows. Today they had horses, sometimes they go on foot, but when they don't like the bull they catch and ride the donkey, pretending to protect themselves by taking their homemade bows and masses of harmless palm stalk arrows usually fired at the cows to coax them along. The calves are separated from the cows for the night and stay under a roof in the corral. The mothers are turned out to graze in a nearby field.

Daylight will soon fade. All the turkeys are gabbling and parading, like a lot of fussy clergy, up to their run where they wait for me to let them in. The white ducks waddle home from the stream. There are the towels to bring in and fold, more avocados to pick up, and the eggs to be collected.

First the towels. They are all sunny and warm and smell nice. There are two small frogs under one of them, dear little creatures with sucker feet. They often come into the bathroom where they stick to the walls and catch insects attracted by the light at night. One of their favourite places to perch is the shower nozzle where they observe one having a shower. Another is just under the inside lip of the lavatory bowl. More than once I have shot into the air in sudden panic as one has leapt and attached itself to my bare bottom!

Another trip down the platanera *for avocados. In the evening it's different. All the shadows on the trees are a darker green and the soil has been disturbed by hen scratches. There is a bunch of bananas ready to be cut, and a trail of red leaf-cutting ants to be dealt with—a job for Diccon in chore time tomorrow. Parrots, which have been screeching in the mango trees all day where they have been feeding, are quiet. It's a wonder that there are any mangos left.*

Against the lowering sky winging flocks of startlingly white egrets return to their roosting places. The evening chorus of cicadas nearly drowns the sound of a tractor returning with the men from their work in the fields. Chave comes into the kitchen with Hector to buy a pound of cheese which I sell to them at half price. They are good chaps and they chat and joke while I weigh the cheese and give them some mangos and an avocado each to take to their families.

Night is falling and before I turn my attention to making supper I go out for the eggs and shut the poultry house door. It's really nice when we are all sitting around the table, showered, feeling tired and able to enjoy our food in a leisurely manner, talking about the day's doings and what has to be done tomorrow. I enjoy it most when all the other children are home. There is always so much to hear and laugh about. Sometimes during the first couple of weeks of rain after the dry season we have to turn off the inside lights and wait to eat while swarms of beetles and termites on mating flights beat themselves to death on the outside porch light bulb. Their bodies are eagerly snapped up by the darting tongues of enormous toads who contentedly rock back and forth. I'm sure I've observed them burp happily and smile before resuming their feast!

Diccon and Tiggy go to bed. It's a long day for them from six in the morning till eight at night. Either Ben or I read a chapter to them before they fall asleep while the other washes up. Then, if Ben has to do farm accounts, I take out my sewing machine. With everyone working there is an awful pile of clothes to be mended which never seems to get any smaller! I prefer making presents of new clothes for us all.

Much love,

Jill

I had gone to Chiriguana on some errand when I happened to notice a scruffy youngster clutching a plastic bag—which I soon discovered contained all his worldly belongings—climbing down from the cab of a truck. Thanking the driver for the lift, he looked at me uncertainly then, making up his mind, came over and held out his hand. Having embarrassed myself on more than one occasion by treating sons of friends as if they were total strangers, and welcoming unknown children with a hug, I asked him to excuse my bad memory and confessed that I couldn't place him.

"I'm Wilson, Henry's son."

"Wilson," I looked at him appraisingly. "It must be nearly eight years since I last saw you, and you've grown. How are you? And Henry, is he well?"

"No." I saw his jaw trembling. "I've left home."

"Wilson, what's wrong?"

He was on the verge of tears but backed away as I leaned forwards to comfort him.

"Dad's been murdered." He clenched his fist as a spasm shook through him. "Mum thought I could come to you. May I?"

I seated Wilson next to his plastic bag in the Land Rover and, after buying him a sweet roll in a newly opened bakery, started back to the ranch. I pressed him for details in case there was anything urgent that I could do to help, but from what he told me it was too late. His thoughts came out in jumbled sentences making his tale difficult to piece together, but I understood this was not the first time he had left home. Henry had not been one to accept setbacks philosophically, and when a marijuana harvest had failed, he had vented his anger on those around him. Picking up Wilson's youngest sister, who had been crying continuously with pain from some ailment, Henry had swung her to and fro in an effort to calm her. Annoyed that she cried even more he had brusquely tossed her on to the bed. She landed with her neck straddling the headboard and later that evening died. The ensuing strain in the house had been unbearable. Wilson fled in fear to Bucaramanga and joined a group of street children who spent their nights in dark alleyways huddling together for warmth under blankets of newspapers and on beds of discarded cardboard boxes. He spent nearly a year in their company surviving by scrounging food from the plates of the clientele at roadside restaurants and earning tips by carting and carrying in the public market. On his return home he had found Henry engaged in a bitter altercation concerning the disappearance of some sacks of marijuana. Someone waited behind a tree with a shotgun and settled the dispute by shooting Henry in the back as he passed. Fearing further bloodshed, Henry's widow had sent Wilson to me.

Jill's reaction was typical. She adopted him as one of our family and put a second bed in Felix's bedroom for Wilson so he would have a companion of his own age. He remained with us for three months trying to adapt to our foreign customs and joining in the chores and games. But as Jill lacked the fluency to translate classes designed to be taught in English into Spanish, he found the school curriculum uninteligible.

However hard we tried to help Wilson overcome the traumas of facing the world too early, he retained within himself a private reserve to protect his sensibilities from the injuries inflicted by adults. Even when it seemed that he desperately needed to show affection, something inside him switched off and he backed away from making a commitment. Only towards the end of his stay

A Caribbean shoreline in the Guajira.

did we see signs that he was freeing himself from a fear of being hurt. The night his mother sent word that she wanted him back, he held out his arms and gave both Jill and me a hug. Four years later he returned to Poponte as one of the young leaders of the guerrilla group E.L.N.—National Army of Liberation—who were extending their domain.

❦ ❦ ❦ ❦

Jill never allowed us to slip into the rut of seeking commercialised amusements to keep us happy. She had her own ideas about healthy entertainment. If she thought meals needed to be enlivened she'd tell the children to anchor our dining room table in the middle of the river where supper would only be served to those who came wearing a floral headgear fabricated by themselves. Swirling water tried to sweep us downstream as we grabbed the table with one hand and ate with the other. On Sunday mornings, after the chores were done, she might invite Adriano's family to join us for a day's outing at a natural water slide where a stream flowed down slabs of slate to a waist-high pool. There, she'd divide us into two relay teams. Starting at the top of the slide, and taking

The author, Diccon and Tiggy on the beach at Caña Veral.

turns, each member had to reach the pool before the next in line could follow. To avoid being obliged to participate, Adriano's wife would busy herself making a *sancocho* lunch

Jill also enjoyed holidays camping by the sea in the Tairona National Park at the foot of the Sierra Nevada de Santa Marta. The area was renowned for its spectacular coral sand beaches and groves of elephant-footed coconut palms that soared at improbable angles to crowns of interlacing fronds. When stirred by gentle breezes on a sunny day the fronds rustled and swayed with a languid grace giving a welcome tracery of shade but, when whipped by tempestuous winds, they arched like the tattered ribs of an umbrella blown inside out.

The shoreline was a Caribbean paradise. Coconuts littering the ground waited to be split open. Fishermen arriving in sea-going canoes to camp were always glad to sell part of their catch. Wild lemon, avocado and mango trees supplied fruit and numerous streams, whose beds glittered with fool's gold*, ran with pure fresh water. Each stretch of beach ended in a promontory beyond which beckoned other bays of turquoise sea. In coves unrippled by waves we sometimes noticed seahorses swimming beside us.

Indians inhabiting the area before the Spanish conquest had constructed a stone stairway leading to Pueblito, a small village in a cooler climate about a thousand feet above sea level. Blocks of granite, some weighing several tons, had been shaped, smoothed, transported and used as bases for houses, paving for causeways and spans for bridges. To accomplish such works without knowledge of iron, draught animals or the wheel, implied that the Indians had developed a sophisticated society whose members labored in co-ordinated working groups.

Diccon became fascinated by the cultural values that prized such unnecessarily mammoth, but monumentally impressive, works in stone. In the absence of any fortifications, celestial observatories, sacrificial altars or evidence suggesting slave labor, there was nothing to explain the colossal expenditure of man power except Indian pride in his surroundings.

✦ ✦ ✦ ✦

One week, Roger arrived. He was on his way to the mountains of southern Chile where he was to climb with Eric Shipton, but had made a detour to deliver four bicycles of different sizes, sent to the children by their grandfather. Roger had taken them through the Colombian customs without paying duty, declaring that his occupation was a trick cyclist! Wishing to contribute something to the children's education, he offered to give a lesson in field ecology.

"You've all seen bats flying around at night and just before dawn," he began. "Some catch insects, some eat fruit, others are blood sucking vampires. Before you get out your badminton racquet to swat a bat flying around your bedroom, you should learn to distinguish between the beneficial and harmful species. Some bats are very small; others are very big, they…"

"How big?" interrupted Barnaby.

"Well, there are bats with a wing span of a metre."

"Why haven't we seen one then?"

"Probably because a bat of that size wouldn't fit through the ventilation holes in the house walls. There's probably a colony of bats inside the hollow tree in the front field. Shall we go and see if we can identify them?"

Roger sent Marcus and Felix to collect fallen leaves and green weeds and push them through a rotted gap in the tree's base. When he signalled, they were to be burned. Rachel was to stand by with notebook and pencil and he and Barnaby would climb the tree carrying our badminton net and a rope. About fifty feet up they reached a hole yawning into the sky and spread the net over it.

Left: The author on a pathway paved with granite flagstones in the village of Pueblito. *Below:* Large slabs of granite encircling the base of what at one time was an "important" house.

"O.K. we're ready to catch them. Light the leaves and fan the smoke," shouted Roger.

Perhaps I should have sensed the danger, but I didn't like to interfere in a project devised by my guest to make school more interesting. At first the pile of leaves and greenery smouldered according to plan and Roger and Barnaby were lost in a haze of smoke emerging from a dozen cracks and openings in the tree trunk beneath their perch. We expected bats to get caught in the badminton net at any minute and our eyes were focused on the top of the tree. But as Marcus and Felix fanned, the smoldering pile of leaves suddenly burst into flames which ignited the decayed wood lining the hollow trunk. Roger and Barnaby found themselves above a roaring inferno which, had they not rappelled rapidly to earth, would have incinerated them in a double auto-de-fe. The few singed bats managing to flap through the holes in the disintegrating badminton net escaped unidentified.

Notified of an unforeseen delay concerning his trip to Chile, Roger accepted our invitation to accompany us on a tour around Colombia in the Land Rover.

Roger buys a round of drinks.

Our journey started in the barren northern tip of the upper Guajira and ended in the National Park of San Agustín in the southern Department of Huila. The Guajira, now more prosperous due to the development of Serrejón—one of the world's largest open-cast coal mines—was in those days as deprived as any corner of the Sahara. Large reservoirs scooped out by bulldozers and filled during seasonal rains provided the inhabitants with water which they took away for drinking in home-made earthenware pots. Free roaming animals drank around the perimeter and left their droppings in the shallows.

The Guajiran Indians, the Wayuu, were a closed society with strict tribal laws. Traditionally the men wore thigh-length shirts and a colourfully tasselled G-string; the women voluminous ankle-length dresses. Both either went barefoot or wore sandals with decorated canvas tops and truck tire soles. Their livelihood was based on three main activities. The first: bagging salt from depressions on the coast after seawater evaporated. The second: importing contraband from the Dutch Antilles. The third: providing illicit airstrips for the transport of marijuana to the United States.

The Guajira is also a natural habitat for several species of birds, the most conspicuous being the pink flamingos, roseatt spoon-bills and buff colored oven birds. Roger was a store of information on these and many others and gave us a running commentary on their habits. We never knew exactly where we were as dirt roads meandered at random in all directions and none of them appeared on the map. When we thought it was time to stop for the night we drove off whatever uncharted track we happened to be on, through a wilderness denuded of its low vegetation by voracious goats, until we found a grove of tall thorn trees suitable for slinging our hammocks.

One night in an overgrazed area I was awoken in my hammock by a goat which had raised itself on its two rear legs to tentatively nibble my beard! Each

Guajiran Scenes. *Top*: Foraging goats, the cattle of Wayuu Indians. *Middle*: Women of the Wayuu carrying clay flagons to take water from a communal reservoir to their homes. *Bottom*: The author helping himself to a bag of salt from a depression.

A G-string clad Indian dismembering a goat.

morning we took our bearings from the rising sun and followed the first trail that headed in the general direction we wished to travel.

Our Land Rover had a military-green colour and still carried English licence plates. I had left them attached as they made the vehicle look official and helped to deter uneducated soldiers and policemen from making nuisances of themselves at highway check points. When we arrived at Puerto Estrella, one of the contraband ports, the reaction to the vehicle was traumatic. People on the single street disappeared behind doors slammed shut. The only living things in sight were two men with sawn-off shotguns guarding a partly unloaded contraband launch and, watched by his family, a G-string-clad Indian dismembering a goat hanging head downwards from a dead tree.

"Let's see what's in the launch," cried Barnaby excitedly.

I drove towards it and got out never imagining that we had been mistaken for a squad of raiding Custom and Excise agents. The Indian raised his blood splattered knife and started towards me in a decidedly unwelcoming manner. I was probably saved from the fate of the goat by Rachel and Barnaby racing past him to the wharf, followed by Marcus helping Diccon and Felix carrying Antigone. Jill then greeted the Indian in such a gracious manner, holding out her right hand, that he stopped, dumbfounded. Turning, he signalled with his knife to the men in the boat to continue with the unloading. Houses disgorged girls in long flowing dresses and boys in colourful shirts and G-strings. The children were soon smiling at each other and before driving on we had filled our tanks with gasoline and acquired five gallons of water from which the larger impurities had been filtered. No matter what brand one uses, tea in the Guajira always has its own distinctive flavour.

Days later on a road in the south of Colombia we were stopped by an army patrol. A group of guerrillas was thought to be active on the road ahead and we were advised not to continue.

"What would you like to do?" I asked Jill. "Go on or turn back?"

"That chap was rather dithery. If there are guerrillas in the area, why isn't the army doing something about them? I cannot see what possible interest the guerrillas could have in a family of touring civilians. If we had worried about all the possible mishaps that might befall us, we would never have left the ranch and wouldn't be here. Roger, what do you advise?"

"I wouldn't want to take responsibility for what could happen to your children if anybody started firing, but I agree with what you just said. They neither know who we are nor have reason to see us as a threat. If they're interested in their public image, I can't imagine that they'll shoot us out of hand."

"But aren't the guerrillas our enemies?" queried Barnaby.

"Not necessarily," I answered. "Some may be good and some may be bad, but sometimes people seem to be enemies because you allow yourself to think of them as such. Do you remember that Indian skinning the goat? He thought we were his enemies and was preparing to knife us, but Jill diffused his aggression by responding to him positively. He suddenly calmed down because he found there was no threat on which to focus. If we do meet guerrillas, and sooner or later we will, we're probably going to have our differences, but that doesn't mean we have to fight. I think I've told you the tale of the two parsons of differing faiths."

"Is it the one," said Barnaby, "when one parson said to the other, 'Let us allow ourselves to disagree. You will doubtless continue to worship God in your way, but I shall worship Him in His'"?

"Yes, that's the one. Most contentious issues have been debated for centuries by better brains than ours. It's best to keep an open mind on subjects of dispute until one has heard both sides. Then you have the right to an opinion, but don't be dogmatic about what can't be proven objectively."

"Hey, you two," called Marcus, "cut the cackle and let's hit the road."

✐ ✐ ✐ ✐

If there had been any guerrilla activity it didn't disrupt our journey. We drove on and spent several days visiting the enigmatic stone figures found in the archaeological park of San Augustin. Of the society that produced them little is known. Ranging from less than one to seven metres in height the sculptures have monstrous facial masks depicting jaguars, eagles or frogs. Unique in Colombia but similar to carvings found in Guatemala, they indicate a cultural connection between the two countries in prehistoric times.

Our journey had given us all a greater appreciation of Colombia's diversity and the children new projects for investigation in their school work. Roger continued on his travels towards Chile.

I heard later, in a letter from a mutual friend in Peru, that Roger had encountered difficulties in taking photographs in a famous native market. Confronted by Indians, resentful of the persistent clicking of tourist cameras, who either scowled, turned their backs or stood with outstretched hands demanding money, Roger had devised a cunning plan. His frequent trips to wild parts of the tropics had given him a weathered appearance so he thought he would disguise himself as a native. He'd sit against a wall with his knees drawn up, trilby hat pulled down over his ears and canvas-topped sandals peeping out beneath a homespun *ruana* and pretend to be asleep. When he felt he had merged inconspicuously into the market background he would stealthily raise the edge of the *ruana* and snap photographs of the surrounding bustle without the Indians being aware of what he was doing. He had just settled down with bowed head and slowly ruminating jaws, as if enjoying a wad of coca, when his composure was shattered by a flash bulb popping in front of his face and the sound of a braying mid-western American voice.

"Saaay Agnes, c'mon over here. Look at what I found. The cutest little injun' squattin' against this wall."

Roger looked up to find an obese figure, bedecked in a gaudily printed blouse and skin tight shorts, taking a new roll of film out of her knapsack.

"Madam," he growled, "kindly have the courtesy to move along."

Another lady, presumably Agnes, approached un-strapping a camera.

"Gee, Agnes, this cute little injun' speaks English." She leant forward and wheedled, "Where'd' ya learn our lingo, cutie?"

"I and my forefathers spoke English correctly long before your country was discovered," Roger retorted struggling to retain his manners. He was on the verge of telling her other things as well but merely hissed, "Now 'b' off."

"Huh!" puffed Agnes to her companion. "All he's ever likely done is work on a banana boat out of Guyaquil. C'mon honey, I aint gonna waste another photo on trash the likes of him."

♪ ♪ ♪ ♪

Even though Jill and I led low profile lives, we were conscious of a barrier between us and the people. We felt that to settle permanently and reap benefits from Colombia without integrating ourselves was neither socially nor morally acceptable and decided to apply for naturalisation. For an ex-pat such as myself, who enjoyed bolstering his spirit by singing "For he is an Englishman,"* the decision to adopt another nationality was not easy. However, the Queen, in her gracious Majesty, realising that Britons contemplating such an act must be under considerable pressure, allows them to retain their passports and have dual nationality. Two of my friends, the Major General and the Governor who had visited the farm after the flood, sent laudatory testimonials to Bogotá. Valledupar's Mayor requested me to sing Colombia's national anthem in his ante-chamber and, seeing that the family was healthy, granted us Colombian citizenship. While our material life apparently continued much as before, our emotional attitude to the country changed. When exasperated we could no longer shrug our shoulders and think, "What can one do with these people?" because we were now one of them ourselves.

Feeling Colombian allowed us to out-manoeuvre a squatter found planting crops on the ranch without suffering pangs of conscience. While searching for missing cattle, the children came across a Poponte homeowner—whom Marcus code-named "Donger"—fencing off an acre of Curucucú where he had planted maize and yucca as if the land were his. Waiting for the day when a commission I'd asked for was due to assess Donger's claim to ownership of the land on the basis of his sprouting crops, they left the house barefoot at three in the morning and went to the disputed area by the light of the waning moon. Systematically they pulled up every maize and yucca seedling and stuffed them into the sacks that each of them carried. The contents, pitched into the nearest river, disappeared downstream. Tell-tale holes in the ground vanished under the scuffing of bare heels. Later in the morning, hidden at a discreet distance, the children watched with glee the commission's growing impatience with Donger as he nearsightedly pirouetted in futile circles looking for the proof of his squatter's rights. My good friend the doctor, the ranch's representative on the commission, had little difficulty in steering the officials to the shade of a tree where a chicken *sancocho* and a bottle of whisky awaited them.

🖋 🖋 🖋 🖋

Visitors to the ranch often arrived weeks before their letters asking if they could stay. Many were old friends and among these were Brian Moser and Donald Tayler whom I had known at Cambridge. They first came to Colombia

---

*Lyrics from a rousing chorus in Gilbert and Sullivan's operetta, *H.M.S Pinafore*.

in 1959 to film Amazonian tribes and record indigenous music, both of which made significant contributions to the success of the Granada Television "Disappearing World" documentary series. Photographs illustrating their book, *The Cocaine Eaters,* and their ethnographic collections donated to the British Museum belong to an era long vanished.

Persuaded by Brian that a documentary of Curucucú would have popular appeal, in 1980 ITV sent a film crew to record our life on the ranch. The result was an hour-long programme entitled "Ranchers of the Sierra," presented twice on British television. As a reward for our help with the editing, we all had our return passages paid for a holiday in England. It marked a turning point for the family.

Rachel and Marcus stayed in Totnes with Jill's parents to take advanced courses in the local comprehensive school. Felix, to have an equal chance to broaden his outlook, finished his last two years of high school at the newly co-educational Fountain Valley in Colorado where I had been a student twenty-five years earlier. Barnaby went to a Fountain Valley alumnae's eighty-thousand-acre spread in Wyoming to experience American ranching.

Jill and I, Diccon and Tiggy all stayed on at Curucucú. The ranch hadn't shut its door on the older children. They often returned to help for they knew that as long as Jill and I were here they'd find a home with a warm welcome.

ELEVEN

A Chastening Episode

*The breeze was sly with a whisper as if it
had things to tell which it couldn't say openly.*

—Anon

Among the smallholders high in the cordillera behind Poponte lived a
young lad called Camito. He came from an unusual background even by
the local's flexible standards. His father cohabited concurrently with three
common-law wives—two of whom were sisters—in a long, one room cabin
where he sired a total of twenty-seven children. Twelve rested in peace in the
family burial plot in a corner of the garden. The remaining progeny slept on
the dirt floor in a corner of the communal bedroom. None of them were
allowed to cry or fuss for whatever reason and should they be frightened at
night they clung to one another for reassurance and comfort. In each of the
other three corners slept a wife. Camito's father had a hammock slung in the
middle of the room and visited each of them by turn. When a friend reacted
incredulously to the boast that he satisfied all three every night, he was forced
to admit, "Of course I only reach a climax in one of them."

The first wife worked in the bottom of a saw-pit cutting boards which she
later took on mule-back to Poponte for sale. The second was in charge of
domestic chores: cooking, washing, cleaning and mending clothes passed on
from the eldest sibling to the next in line. The third was responsible for tend-
ing the crops and providing food.

When one field lost its fertility, she felled another tract of forest with an
axe. The older children helped to plant, weed and harvest, while younger took

A young girl takes care of her younger sibling.

care of the youngest. Perhaps it was natural that Camito, as soon as he felt the stirrings of manhood in his loins, wished to be independent. One day, during his twelfth year, he tied a machete to the string securing his trousers and trudged up the forested slopes of the cordillera until he came to unclaimed land. There he staked out a section for himself and boarded with his nearest neighbour for two years, exchanging three days of work a week for his food. The other days Camito worked for himself on his homestead. By the age of fourteen he had felled five acres of forest, built himself a palm-thatched cottage near a spring of water and acquired a bride.

In Poponte everybody knew and gossiped about one another. Comments about Camito were invariably favorable. It was difficult not to think well of him, for when he smiled a candid goodness lit his face. Although his features lacked finesse, his nose being knobbly, small children intuitively trusted the gentle kindliness in his eyes and allowed themselves to be picked up and given a ride on his shoulders. Shrieking with delight they clung to his ears as he swooped and danced.

While many *campesinos*, in the hope of impressing their friends and creditors, changed into their newest clothes before entering Poponte, Camito seemed to have only one pair of trousers and a patched shirt suitable for wearing in public. He completed his outfit with sandals made by himself and a battered straw hat he'd exchanged for a dozen cooking bananas. Talk in the village was rife with tales of Communist agitators recruiting peasants in the cordillera. I understood that Camito's independent spirit had kept him free from revolutionary entanglements and I thought it important to keep him that way. When he timidly asked if I would help him get a loan to plant maize and beans, I remembered that I would never have got where I was without a helping hand and accompanied him to the bank to sign as his guarantor.

The season was unusually dry and I was too busy at Curucucú to worry about Camito's crops in the hills. Not a drop of rain had fallen for a month when I chanced to meet him in the street near José Chiquito's bar. I could see he was worried.

"*Hola, amigo*," I greeted him." Got problems?"

"Bad news, Don Ben. If it doesn't rain soon the maize and beans will be too stunted to recover," he said.

"Would a bottle of cold beer cheer you up? Let me get you one."

Camito gratefully accepted my offer and we took two to the shade of a tree and sat down.

"O.K. Tell me what I can do to help you?"

Cutting boards in the hills behind Poponte.

Camito took a swig of beer, wiped his mouth on his sleeve and gave me an embarrassed look.

"Come on, Camito. If you've planted marijuana let's hear about it."

"I did plant maize and beans, I really did, but I've also got about two hectares of marijuana. The trouble is that's dry as well. The maize is lost, the beans will be stunted but the marijuana's where it could be irrigated if there were eight hundred metres of hose pipe."

What a damned nuisance, I thought. It had never been my intention to get mixed up with a crop of marijuana. I was caught in a cleft stick. I didn't want Camito to join the guerrillas because he felt himself abandoned, but if I told him to pull up the marijuana and then paid off the loan to the bank myself, I would be humbugged by the next *campesino* asking me to guarantee a loan. We opened more beer bottles till, after a third round, I agreed to supply the hose pipe and pay the wages of a workman to help him install it and irrigate the crop. I hadn't envisaged what my involvement meant or where it might lead.

It was common knowledge that many *campesinos* planted marijuana. It was the only crop which gave them the hope of significantly adding to the basic income derived from traditional husbandry. With a successful harvest of marijuana the life style of a peasant family changed. A few cows, a mattress, a sewing machine and sheets of galvanised zinc for a new roof were suddenly affordable. Without the slightest doubt, the cultivation of marijuana was an important factor in maintaining the stability of rural society.

Marxist promises to alleviate conditions for the downtrodden poor were no longer of any interest to *campesinos* in reach of middle class living standards. What happened to the marijuana after it was sold was the concern of people elsewhere.

In theory, any marijuana found by the authorities was destroyed. In practice, virtually all anti-narcotic police units would turn a blind eye if their palms were greased with money. As a force they were badly paid, poorly equipped and customarily posted to localities without accommodation for their families. They saw money flowing out of the hills in the form of marijuana and stooped to take their cut. Even among the special police in civilian dress, whose job was to investigate corruption, there were officials who found the opportunity to augment their meagre salaries too tempting to resist.

To protect their crops from authorities eager either to tax or to steal, growers cultivated marijuana in mountain clearings surrounded by densely wooded ridges . When transporting the harvest they developed the cunning of smugglers. At suitable phases of the moon, strings of sure-footed mules were led down mountain trails to rendezvous with buyers. Each mule train was preceded by two wary *campesinos* armed with shotguns.

Smoking marijuana was rare amongst the *campesinos* I knew. Their work ethic was incompatible with taking a drug that diminished their capacity to provide for their families. They relaxed with tobacco and alcohol, the latter being more of a social lubricant than an escape from reality.

I didn't see much of Camito for a couple of months. I understood the irrigation had been successful and that he was about to harvest. Then one day, as I was welding a piece of machinery, a jeep arrived at the farm filled with unsavory looking characters who could only have been gangsters or anti-narcotic agents.

Signalling to me, one of them ordered, "Come here."

"*A sus órdenes, señores,*" I replied mocking Colombian courtesy. Shutting off the arc welder, I went to see what they wanted.

A man got out of the jeep and flashed an official looking identification. He eyed me craftily and said, "We're investigating marijuana cultivations in this area and your *campesino* friend, Camito, has come to our notice."

I tried to sound bored. "Yes, I remember the name."

"We know you have helped him to irrigate. We don't like to molest *campesinos*, so perhaps you would care to collaborate so we don't pull up his crop?"

"Does Camito have marijuana?" I faltered.

"Don Ben, don't waste our time. You gave him hose pipe. Do you expect us to believe that you don't know how he uses it? We're not stupid." He stroked the handle of the .38 revolver sticking out of his low slung holster as if daring me to contradict him.

Well, I thought, he can hardly accuse me of ethical impropriety, but if he imagines I'm going to abandon Camito to his own devices easily he's mistaken.

"The hose pipe was bought so that Camito could conduct water to his house. But I'm not his father and he does his own thing." I threw my open hands into the air in a gesture of my ignorance as to what else he might have done with the pipe.

"Don Ben, my men are becoming impatient. You are a reasonable and intelligent person. Would you prefer to collaborate voluntarily, or for us to search your barns and find hidden drugs?"

His companions grinned unpleasantly. The planting of drugs by narcotic agents on persons they wish to victimise is an old and effective practice. I remembered a piece of Colombian folklore about an unfavourable settlement being preferable to an expensive lawsuit. Clearly these agents weren't going to leave with just a glass of lemonade.

"Well," I replied, "I don't have any money on the farm as it's not pay-day. In any case I shall have to ask Camito what this is all about. Perhaps we could talk again in a couple of weeks?"

The response came with a finality that left no room for stalling. "Either we search your barns with unfortunate consequences for you, or you write a cheque now and go with us to cash it in Chiriguana."

Over the years I had learned that it was convenient to have two bank accounts, the first with sufficient funds to pay for services in Chiriguana and a second with a minimal ballance to show to people who wanted loans. This seemed just the moment to use the latter.

"I don't believe there's much in my account just now as I've had to buy some expensive spare parts, but we can see what there is."

The posse accompanied me into the house where Jill gave them some

Camito (*right*) with armed workman stripping marijuana plants.

lemonade. She looked at me anxiously. "Don't worry," I whispered. "It's OK. Be back soon."

The second account showed a balance of eight thousand five hundred and fifty-four pesos—not a lot of money in those days when the average weekly wage was ten thousand pesos. They wanted all of it but settled for seven thousand. I made out a cheque for that amount; two agents climbed into the Land Rover to accompany me and the rest of them followed in their jeep. Passing the police station at the entrance to Chiriguana, one of my passengers waved to the officer on duty who nodded his head and went inside. Continuing to the bank, I cashed my cheque, handed over the money, and started back to Poponte. For the first time ever, I was stopped at the police station and ordered to wait while they searched the Land Rover. Having in it a light-hearted book I kept there to pass delays pleasurably, I spent the next half hour reading and laughing out loud. From time to time curious friends, seeing the parked Land Rover, stopped to inquire whether I was in trouble. I could only reply that I didn't think so. Finally the police Captain summoned me into his office.

"Don Ben, why did you come to Chiriguana today?"

"To cash a cheque."

"And where is the money?"

"I paid a debt."

"How much?"

"Seven thousand pesos."

"To whom?"

"To some people I have never seen before. I don't even know their names."

"Why did you pay seven thousand pesos to people you don't know?"

"Because they were owed this money by a friend of mine who had asked me to pay them."

"*Paja!*"* the Captain shouted angrily. "You paid that money to the anti-narcotic police in order to protect your friend Camito."

"If you want to believe that story, it's your business," I replied coldly, not liking the turn of the interrogation.

The Captain leaned back in his swivel chair and rubbed a hand over his brow as if pondering how to proceed. "I could protect all of you from the anti-narcotic police. How would you like that?"

As an answer I raised and hunched my shoulders while turning the palms of my hands upwards implying that it was up to him to tell me more. Obviously he needed me for something.

Making up his mind, the Captain leaned forward. "I have a plan I'd like to put to the marijuana growers. Can you arrange a meeting with them next Saturday afternoon? Choose somewhere discreet in the area of Poponte."

"You must be joking! The way the police are treating *campesinos* who grow marijuana at the moment, do you really think they'll appear voluntarily and identify themselves?"

"That's the problem. I have the seniority to curtail anti-narcotic police units who abuse their authority and I wish to avoid conflicts within my jurisdiction. To explain my position, I need to meet a deputation of growers on neutral ground."

From my experience that morning it was easy to imagine a victimised farmer ambushing a police unit and causing dire repercussions in the community. Having just been relieved of some hard earned money, I was not feeling disposed to help any police without further information.

"Give me an outline of your plan. The growers must have a basis for deciding whether or not to meet you."

---

*A colloquial expletive of which one translation is "nonsense."

"*Bueno*! We know that the area behind Poponte is producing a lot of marijuana and we've received instructions to search and destroy. Now, do we make enemies of the campesinos by destroying the plants in the field, or do we confiscate the marijuana from the big dealers after the *campesinos* have been paid? They'd benefit if we took the latter course of action. But to do that, we need information from the growers on shipments. In return we'll keep all anti-narcotic units away from Poponte. Is that a fair deal?"

I nearly laughed out loud at the thought of what Gilbert and Sullivan would have done with such a plot, but managed to keep a straight face. "The idea is intriguing, but it's not for me to pre-judge the growers' decision. You have detained me here longer than necessary. If you really want my help, show your policemen that I'm not being held here under duress and ask them why I wasn't treated to the courtesy of a *tinto* and a glass of cold water. Then I'll be on my way."

A double *tinto* and cold water were quickly produced.

As I drove back to the ranch I wondered what would happen if the police Captain double-crossed the growers. They wouldn't receive much sympathy if they complained to a higher authority. Should this higher authority feel it necessary to investigate the Captain, he would implicate me. Any protestations of innocence on my part would not be convincing if it was disclosed that Camito's crop of maize and beans had failed and I, as guarantor, would be called to pay his bank loan. Earlier I had seen myself as an observer; now I felt myself being pushed on stage as a principal actor without having been shown the script.

The growers in Poponte had a mixed reaction to the tale of my escapade with the police. Some had already been asked to collaborate and were soured by the experience. "*Maldito sea*! Have the police ever been known to help us?" they asked. No one could remember a case of them having done so. Many simply didn't believe that the Captain was acting in good faith. Others argued that it was preferable to have an agreement with a known officer than pay collaboration money to unknown anti-narcotic agents who at any moment might be replaced with others equally greedy. Any business transaction involving marijuana was a risk, but if a meeting with the Captain resulted in a deal where only big dealers were harassed, it made the risk of such a meeting worth taking. I sent a message to the Captain telling him to come.

The meeting took place in a grove of mango trees on a hillock in the middle of a field with unobstructed vistas on all sides. It was an unprecedented occasion: a police Captain discussing marijuana distribution with a deputation of growers. Both parties were wary of committing themselves and by the end of the afternoon nothing had been settled except to continue the dialogue after all other Poponte growers had been briefed.

I was, therefore, somewhat surprised to see the Captain accompanied by a well known Lebanese-Colombian rancher—I shall call him Don Tiberio—at my door the following morning. They dissimulated the real purpose of their visit from Jill—whose remarks strongly condemning drug traffickers were widely known—by shaking hands with effusive smiles of friendliness and asking if I could show them where they might bring their families to picnic by the river. As I suspected, neither of them had the slightest intention of either picnicking or swimming, and as soon as we were out of earshot Don Tiberio proposed a marijuana deal totally different from the Captain's. It was more credible in that altruistic motives had been abandoned in favour of personal gain. Everyone was going to make money!

"There's an airstrip on my ranch that's been there for years," Don Tiberio said. "Fumigation pilots and friends from Barranquilla use it so often that no one pays any attention when a plane lands. Recently my associates extended the runway to accommodate a DC-3 which, conveniently, happens to be the plane they've just bought. They plan to fly top grade marijuana, known in the trade as 'Colombian Gold,' to the United States."

I looked at the Captain to see if there was any reaction, but his face was an inscrutable mask.

"Our friend here," Don Tiberio continued, "estimates that growers in Poponte could supply a plane-load of Colombian Gold. As neither of us want others meddling in our business, he has agreed to escort shipments to my airstrip. You, Don Ben, look after your *campesino* friends, and they trust you. We're agreed that you're the only person who has the connections to organise them into a growers co-operative." The Captain nodded his head in affirmation.

Oh my God, I thought, what have I done to merit all this trust? The idea of becoming a wholesale dealer in marijuana was appalling.

"Look here, Don Tiberio, there are some things I absolutely will not do. Whatever you may have heard about my involvement with Camito, I neither grow nor approve of growing marijuana and share my wife's opinion that marijuana is a stepping stone to the use of hard drugs."

"Are you saying that you'll turn your back on your *campesino* friends and refuse to help them when they could sell their marijuana well?"

"I didn't say I wouldn't help them. *Campesinos* are my friends and their friendship is important to me. I've gone through times of economic hardship myself cutting scrub and planting maize so I understand why traditional husbandry leaves peasants looking for a more profitable crop. International demand has made marijuana a plant worth cultivating. With a few successful sales a peasant family has enough money to enjoy some of the good things of life. If there's an alternate legal crop giving an equivalent income, nobody's told them what it is. Why should peasants be punished for trying to attain the standard of living enjoyed in the countries that buy marijuana? It's grossly unjust for police to confiscate a peasant's crop and sell it for themselves. *Campesinos* abused by authorities join the guerrillas and that's a fact none of us can afford to ignore. Let's reach an agreement. I won't get involved by actively buying or selling, but for the sake of the social stability of the community I'll compromise in the role of an intermediary."

"*Ave María*, you make yourself sound so plausible! If you weren't already involved, I might even imagine you were virtuous." Don Tiberio smirked complacently before adding, "Surely you wish to recoup the money you used to help Camito? Let me tell you something. The morals of everyone in the marijuana business are compromised. We're ordinary human beings, not saints. Suppose we were thirsty and a friend who had just sold his marijuana offered to buy us a drink, do we insult him by refusing because his offer is paid for by tainted money? We would soon be shut off from society if we did. You mentioned just now that friendships were important to you. They are to me, too. Tell the *campesinos* that I'll not just pay ten thousand pesos per hundredweight to those who want their money now, but twenty thousand pesos if they risk waiting until the plane has taken off safely."

"Double or nothing?"

"Yes, but with the protection of the Captain here, the risk of nothing is scarcely worth considering. If there is any slip-up, we'll all lose."

"What sort of slip-up could happen?" I asked, fascinated by his audacity.

"Suppose the army pounced on the airstrip while we're loading and impounded everything. I suppose you know that to repossess a property after it's been confiscated is expensive. One has to pay a fine equal to the land's registered value. The plane and the ranch are worth a great deal more than the *campesinos*' marijuana."

"They probably are, but what do the police get out of this?"

"They'll receive an agreed percentage, paid by my associates, after the plane is safely in the air."

"How do you propose to silence the man whose marijuana is rejected because of its inferior quality? Where does he sell? You can't afford to have a disgruntled *campesino* talking out of turn."

"Everyone knows it's difficult to dispose of second-rate goods. If *campesinos* with low grade marijuana are patient until the plane takes off, I'll see if we can agree on a reduced price. At the moment, the cost of bribes, transport and re-sale commissions makes buying anything less than top quality Colombian Gold impossible."

"That's as may be," I said, "but who's going to be responsible for the safety of the marijuana once it's classified? I wouldn't want to have a lot of irate growers gunning for me because somebody stole it, or if the plane never came, or any one of a hundred possible accidents occurred."

"*Amigo mío*, the reins are in my hands. Neither of us can be expected to guarantee total satisfaction. You have the essential contacts in Poponte and I have an agent of my complete confidence who will introduce himself to you tomorrow morning."

Don Tiberio tore a piece of paper into two with a zigzag rip. Handing me one section, he continued, "He'll bring the piece of paper that fits. Please, take him to the growers and let him work out details. You need to have Camito's crop well sold and I need to have my agent introduced by somebody the growers trust."

Don Tiberio was a wily old bird. If I didn't agree to his last request, he would certainly find another way of achieving his objective and any influence I might have would be lost. He might even reject Camito's crop. I was in a catch-22 situation.

"OK," I sighed. "Send him along."

Even before confirming his identity with the scrap of torn paper, Don Tiberio's man revealed himself by his blazing bravado. Within hours of arriving in Poponte his swashbuckling aura had swept the villagers into a state of euphoria. Anyone counselling caution was dismissed as a wimp. Here was a grower's dream come true: the opportunity to cut out the police and middlemen and sell their marijuana for twice the going rate. They fell over each other in a desire to please. I was feted for having made the introduction and not a single grower was canny enough to demand his ten thousand pesos in cash. Day and night mule trains plied up and down the mountain trails bringing marijuana into Poponte to be classified. Families occupying two or three rooms squeezed into one as the others were filled to the roof with bags of aromatic Colombian Gold.

Ignoring native prudence, growers laughed and boasted about their good fortune and within a week rumours of what was happening had reached the ears of those who pay for such information. One night a six-ton truck carrying fifteen well-armed anti-narcotic police drove into the village. Men and boys were herded into the street at gunpoint and impotently watched their houses being ransacked. The astonished joy of Cortés when he saw the splendours of Montezuma's palace was nothing compared with the delight of these policemen who found enough Colombian Gold to fill their truck several times over. Under the glare of its headlights sacks of marijuana were slit open, checked for purity of content and loaded. Women and children were not idle. Scurrying in and out of back doors they carried bags of marijuana to hide in paddocks, on roofs, down well shafts, anywhere to scatter and save some for themselves. When at last the truck could hold no more it was driven away. Among the epithets hurled at the departing raiders, one curse summed up the collective anger: "You triple bastards, sons of whores back to your syphilitic great-grandmothers! May your testicles shrivel till they drop!"

From there, the conversations went something like this:

"They've been here before pretending to be buyers and now they come back in uniforms and steal. *Ay, Dios mío*, all police units are shit."

"Stuffed into different uniforms."

"Shit stinking thieves."

"They didn't even pretend they were going to burn what they stole."

"No, and they didn't burn what they left behind either. Think they'll come back for it?"

"Quick. Cut a tree down and block the road."

A group of youths ran for their axes, and racing down the road to a tall palm tree, vented their hatred and anger in felling it.

"Where's that stupid son of a bitch, Don Ben? I bet he's behind all this. Let's go and see what he's lost."

"Agh, don't be so silly, There's no marijuana on Curucucú. Camito had some in his father-in-law's house, but they took the best of that."

"I"m going to take what's left of my marijuana out of here before those bastards return," said a Don Vito. "Hey, Alberto, lend me your driver and pickup."

"O.K. compadre, but if anything happens, you're responsible."

"I know, thanks."

Soon Alberto's pickup was loaded and lurched out of the village, through Hacienda Poponte and along a dirt track leading to Don Vito's farm. Dark masses of roiling clouds rumbled among the peaks of the cordillera.

"I bet it's raining up there," the driver said. "*Santa María*! Did you see that lightning!"

Don Vito glanced at the sky. "I don't care what's happening up there, just get on. My marijuana's going into hiding and not coming out before the plane arrives."

Presently the pickup came to a ford where the turbulent current of the river seemed to be rising. "Better loosen the fan belt," suggested the driver and groped under the seat for a spanner. "Damn! Alberto's taken the tools. Want to risk crossing as we are?"

"We must. If it rains here my marijuana will get sodden. If we get stuck you go and tell Don Roland I need to borrow a tractor to pull us through."

The driver cautiously eased the pickup forwards. Without warning the front wheels dipped into a depression and the ventilator fan sprayed water over the distributor cap, leads and spark plugs. The engine coughed, spluttered and stalled. Cursing his bad luck, the driver trudged off to bring back a tractor. As the rising water began to swirl around the door and seep into the cab, Don Vito took off his new shoes and sat sideways on the seat. Suddenly, rain crashed on to the roof of the pickup with a fury that turned the river into a seething torrent. At each crack of thunder he involuntarily crossed himself lest the next probing fork of lightning to zigzag across the sky hunt him down. Wind, tearing leaves and branches off trees as if they were confetti, whistled and roared with maniacal frenzy and blew the rain horizontally. Water rose over the seat. Grabbing his precious shoes, Don Vito opened the door on the lower side of the current and struggled towards the bank.

"*Virgen Santísima, sálvame!*" he implored. "*No más, no más!*"

He was only partially heeded, for although the lightning struck elsewhere, by the time the driver returned with a tractor and chain the force of the rushing floodwater had rolled Alberto's pickup on its side and swept the marijuana downstream.

Sodden, impoverished and dangling a wet shoe in each hand, Don Vito limped barefoot back to his house in the village.

The downpour had also been disastrous for people in Poponte. The sacks of marijuana taken out of the houses by women and children and those left by the raiding police were soaked. To prevent the marijuana from rotting it all had to be thinly spread out, constantly turned and dried in the shade. For days afterwards Poponte smelled and looked like a hippie bazaar. In every available room in the village, on each side of the street where there were trees and under makeshift tarpaulins, ankle deep marijuana was cosseted by villagers who anxiously examined it for signs of mildew. Had the raiders come back looking for more, I believe there would have been bloodshed. The villagers worked overtime hoping that the aeroplane, due any day, would not arrive before their marijuana was ready.

When I called on Don Tiberio for the latest news, he was supervising men hiding fifty-five-gallon drums of aviation gasoline by rolling them into a thicket at the end of his runway. He proudly showed me a baffle he had made to divert sparks from the exhaust pipe of a portable motor pump. He didn't want the highly volatile aviation gasoline fumes to explode while refuelling the plane.

"There're so many people to pay off," he complained. "On the day the plane arrives I have to telephone the General in X [name withheld] and give him its return flight path, so that he can arrange for it not to be intercepted as it leaves Colombian air space. For that he gets a million pesos deposited in his bank account."

"For money like that he should provide a fighter escort," I joked.

"He would, only then there would be all the politicians to pay off if the planes were discovered landing in the United States."

"But surely you have family connections who would help?" I teased.

"Alas, that's no longer possible." Don Tiberio wrung his expressive hands ruefully." Some of the family are playing for the other side.

The following day Don Tiberio's agent reappeared in Poponte and confirmed the plane's arrival in four days' time. As inevitably some marijuana had mildewed after the rain, he had to re-select what was suitable for export. Every *campesino* imagined that he'd been promised top priority. They were all in debt, but having held out for so long for the twenty thousand pesos, not one of them was prepared to sell for less. Don Tiberio, having trouble covering his own expenses, steadfastly refused to advance a peso to anybody.

"This is a co-operative venture," he reminded them. "We all make double, or we all lose."

The only change of plan came in the transportation of marijuana to the airstrip. Having been victimised once too often by the police, nobody trusted the Captain's offer of safeguarding the convoy. Fearing that a rival authority might highjack the marijuana, the growers' families waited till nightfall and then carried their sacks Indian file through rough country to a disused track. There a tractor and trailer, guarded by armed *campesinos*, made a succession of journeys over open savanna to Don Tiberio's airstrip. As no outsiders were involved, the marijuana was transferred without mishap.

During the afternoon of the plane's expected arrival Poponte was deserted. Every man, woman and child had found a reason to gather on the landing strip. Adding to the festive mood, Don Tiberio ordered his cowboys to roast a heifer. *Aguardiente* bottles appeared from hip pockets and people were decidedly merry when at dusk the noise of a low-flying aircraft was heard approaching. Suddenly there it was! It made one fly-over, banked sharply and landed. In the swiftly descending darkness nobody noticed or commented that the plane had seen better days. Flickering flames from the barbecue's fire provided just enough light for loading the marijuana and for Don Tiberio and his cowboys to refuel the wing tanks.

The technique of compressing marijuana into blocks by using hydraulic jacks was not yet common practice and the aroma in the confined body of the plane became intoxicating.

"I hope you don't smoke this stuff while you're flying," someone cautioned the pilot.

"Never. I have a few joints before so I'm not nervous on take-off. Once in the air all I have to do is breath normally and I'm high." Everyone laughed.

Finally the cargo doors were shut on the last sack and the plane was surrounded by boisterous *campesinos* celebrating with the last of the *aguardiente* the money that would be theirs on the following day. The roadway to the airstrip had been barricaded. Should there be any indication of trouble, three rapid shots from a sentry would be the signal for the plane to risk a take-off by starlight. It would be dangerous but preferable to being confiscated on the ground.

Happily the night passed without incident and with an early morning *tinto*, without which few Colombians can function properly, the pilot strapped himself into his seat. Waving a cheerful farewell, he started the engines and taxied to the downwind end of the strip.

There is something wonderfully intriguing in watching an old aircraft prepare itself to take to the air from a dirt runway. Clouds of dust billow behind as the engines rev, the fins on its wings waggle and then the incredible happens. With a mighty roar the first ungainly wobbling movements grow into a confident surge lifting the wheels off the ground.

"It's away! We're rich!" the people shouted exultantly.

They threw their hats in the air and embraced each other with joy. The short-lived exuberance turned to despair as the motors spluttered and the plane instead of gaining altitude crashed into the intertwined branches of two stout trees where it left the wings and motors before nosediving to earth some twenty feet farther on. With a mighty WHOOMPH of exploding gasoline the detached wings and motors burst into flames.

"The marijuana!" somebody screamed. Oblivious to danger, the crowd stampeded towards the wrecked fusilage and tore open the cargo doors. In their frantic desire to empty the hold lest the marijana catch fire, no attention was given to the shaken pilot being bustled into a jeep and driven away by Don Tiberio.

With Don Tiberio gone, there was nobody to control the swarm of opportunists who surged towards the wreckage. Sacks of marijuana evanesced into nearby underbrush and the growers only managed to save for themselves half of what they had loaded.

Very sensibly, the police in Chiriguana stayed away till late afternoon. Their report, confirmed by the judge, was a triumph of local jurisprudence. A crashed aeroplane had been found at the end of Don Tiberio's registered runway. While the pilot was not available for questioning, as he was suffering from concussion and had been transferred for medical treatment, the accident was clearly attributable to failure of the motors which were completely charred. There was no evidence of illicit cargo being transported nor an improper use of the airstrip. Barring some possible investigation from the owners of the aeroplane or their insurance company in the future, they recommended that the file be closed. No one wanted the airstrip condemned.

At first the growers wrath focused on Don Tiberio as the person responsible for the loss of their marijuana. They went to his home to demand a settlement. He wasn't there. Nobody could say where he had gone or when he would return. Don Tiberio's agent had also absented himself. With no one else to blame, all eyes turned on me.

A few days after the crash, I received a message requesting my immediate presence before a tribunal of growers in Poponte. I replied that urgent repair work prevented me from complying. Word came back that out of respect for Jill they would refrain from coming to the ranch if I met them on the road in ten minutes. There was no feasible alternative but to go and have a showdown. I fully expected the growers to be armed and, no longer having the support of Henry, looked around for a couple of stalwart companions to join me. My friend Brian Moser, a veteran survivor of hazardous situations, providentially had been visiting the farm and rallied to my side. Barnaby, on holiday from

Wyoming, said he wouldn't miss it for anything and volunteered his support. We armed ourselves as obtrusively as possible and climbed into the Land Rover. I took the wheel and we set off. Down the road the way was blocked by a group of about fifteen irate growers, mostly wielding machetes.

Pointing a shot gun at me, the leader demanded, "We want our money, Don Ben."

"I don't have it."

"Then send someone to get it. You're responsible for our losses and don't think you're going to drive on till you've settled up. You're going to pay us."

"Hold on a minute. You all knew and accepted Don Tiberio's conditions of payment—'we all win or we all lose.' If you have a claim, make it to him. He arranged for the aeroplane and he was going to re-sell your marijuana. Remember that Camito and I also lost."

"We don't care about your losses; you can't escape with that. You introduced us to the agent who said we'd be paid twenty thousand pesos per hundredweight when the plane took off. It's not our fault it crashed."

"We want our money," chorused the crowd. "We were promised payment when the plane took off and we want our money now!"

"We all want our money," I replied. "Find Don Tiberio and settle accounts with him. I've got to pay Camito's debt in the bank . I never asked you to plant marijuana, nor guaranteed to buy it."

I took my foot off the clutch. The leader had intended to stand his ground but, seeing that he would be run over even if he did fire his shotgun, he leapt to one side and I drove through the gap. Few civilians start a shoot-out when there is a risk of being shot themselves. I held my breath until the jeep rounded the next corner, then sagged in my seat.

"Whew! That was a close call. Well done, chaps. I really thought that guy might shoot me."

"Good job for him he didn't try," declared Barnaby. "I had him covered and was ready to drop him real quick." He grinned at the thought. With a start I realised that the boy who had gone to Wyoming had toughened into a resolute young man.

"What did you make of it, Brian?"

"I wouldn't have believed it if it hadn't happened," he chuckled. "What a way to entertain your house guests!"

"You know what I think?" said Barnaby. "I believe those guys'll soon run out of steam. If we go to José Chiquito's and start buying beer, I'll bet they'll be joining us in half an hour."

"It's certainly worth a try."

A crowd of curious villagers soon gathered in José's bar and showered us with questions. Shattering my image of being miserly over standing drinks for the idle of this world, I ordered beer for everyone. As Barnaby had predicted, the group that had stopped us on the road drifted in, hot and thirsty. I included them in my debt to the bar until the effects of drinking alcohol in the heat of the mid morning sun had mellowed the tension.

"Listen," I said. "I doubt that Don Tiberio is going to show his face for a long time. I'm not apologising for him or giving anybody any more introductions, but the marijuana boom hasn't come to an end just because one aeroplane crashed. We're lucky to have our own farms and our healthy lives. If you still have marijuana and wish to cultivate more, look for your own outlets. As for me, after helping Camito get rid of what's left, I'm quitting."

"You're afraid!"

"Yes, I'm afraid. I nearly lost my sense of proportion, my wife's sympathy and support and, very importantly to me, your friendship. Everybody here who grew marijuana was merely trying to give his family a decent standard of living but at the end of the line marijuana corrupts a society by traffickers making fortunes addicting others to dope. None of them give a damn about Colombians or conditions in Poponte, but that doesn't justify us thinking that it's O.K. to grow and sell marijuana because if we don't somebody else will. That doesn't make it OK for the addict and his family. I don't know if it's true that one reaps what one sows but I feel the fates are telling me to stop. I believe in them, you know."

The following Saturday I met Camito again, looking gloomier than ever. He had been unable to sell the marijuana rejected by Don Tiberio's agent and, taking a screw of paper from the crown of his hat, showed me some dark brown flower heads.

"This is what we've got," he said." Colombian Gold reject, and nobody wants it. The police took the good stuff in their raid on Poponte."

"How many sacks have you got?"

"Twenty. They're hidden under a tarpaulin near the main road, but I doubt if they'd make enough to cover the loan."

A month after I had been obliged to repay the bank, the marijuana was still unsold. We went to inspect it and found, that although Camito had stacked the sacks in rows above crossed logs, mildew had entered the bottom layer. Rodents had chewed holes in the tarpaulin and rainwater had seeped into the top. Breeding mice had burrowed holes through the middle and their distinct odour permeated what was dry.

"Jesus! not even an addict would smoke this stuff now," observed Camito. "If you soaked it in detergent for a week it would still stink. It's all rubbish."

We looked at each other warily, half expecting to find anger and recrimination for this final disaster. Nobody relishes being blamed for the misfortunes of friends. There was only recognition that we had trusted each other, tried and failed.

Camito took off his battered straw hat and tore it in two. "My farm's a mess because I haven't had time to look after it properly and I'm damned if I will ever plant marijuana again." From his honest, troubled face his eyes glanced at me ruefully. "I'll make you a proposition. Let's divide this stuff. I'm going to burn my half. All I've got to show for my efforts is a debt."

"And experience," I added. "But look, you only need one match because we'll burn all of it. The fates obviously never meant me to make money with marijuana."

Camito decided to save the tarpaulin as he could patch the holes and use it when he threshed beans. He took out his machete and slit the sacks allowing the marijuana to burn more easily. As we fanned the flames panicking mice scurried here and there in the smoke.

"Damn little animals," sighed Camito. "If it hadn't been for them I might have had the money to buy a new hat."

TWELVE

Alone

Already I have shed the leaves of youth.
Stripped by the wind of time down to
winter branches linear and alone I stand.

—Anne Morrow Lindberg

E xhilarating escapades of trafficking in marijuana both fired the imaginations and fueled the discontent of peasants seeking alternatives to drudgery. Growing marijuana required months of exhausting work, but for heroic glamour why not join the guerrillas and sweep into oblivion the oligarchy that kept the wealth of the country, political power and lucrative job appointments amongst themselves? That was the valiant option!

During the evening of January 5, 1980, members of the E.L.N.   (the Communist army of national liberation) kidnapped Doña Teleri and her sixteen-year-old son from Hacienda Poponte. Dressed as soldiers—and mistaken for members of the regular army—the abductors had been invited into the house and the seizure had been easy. For most Colombians, however, the act was repugnant. Kidnapping was synonymous with selling human beings and recalled days of the slave trade when African ancestors had been shackled in chains and imported to build the fortifications at Cartagena. The realization that the Marxist guerrilla movement was financed in part by ransoms was for many a brutal, eye opening shock.

Teleri and her husband, Cyril, had been installed as managers of Hacienda Poponte shortly after the General had freed Roland from the Chiriguana jail.

As well as improving the ranch, they had devoted much of their time to promoting village welfare. The Hacienda was considered one of the best employers in the area and provided a livelihood for dozens of *campesino* families. In the absence of any specific wrong doing on Teleri's part which might have justified the abduction, the commonly accepted explanation was shameless opportunism. Teleri's father was rich and she was accessible. However, if the guerrillas imagined they were going to extract a ransom quickly, they soon discovered their error. After their initial demand was rejected, it took seven long and tedious months of bargaining before Teleri and her son were set free.

Any hope that our low profile would leave us untouched was shattered when we, and everyone else in the municipal area of Chiriguana considered wealthy, were "requested to collaborate" with the guerrillas by paying a revolutionary tax known as "*la vacuna.*" The penalty for failing to comply was not in doubt; one was shot. Finding no protection in the law, many ranchers took their families to live in cities. As we had no other home in Colombia where we might shelter, nor reason to be ashamed of our lifestyle at Curucucú, the only way we could continue to tranquilly live on the ranch was to have a civilised meeting with the E.L.N. bosses and come to an agreement guaranteeing our safety. Somehow I had to find a way of doing this

Entering a guerrilla base hoping to find the Commandant sympathetic and good-humoured, was as foolhardy as entering the cage of a lion in a zoo and putting one's head in its mouth to find out if it was hungry. I chose a more circumspect approach. What would happen if I went to one of the clandestine left wing meetings, pretended to be matey with some of the discontents and through them got an introduction to their leaders?

The meeting's catch-phrase, "When the rich enemies of the working classes are overthrown the poor will eat cake and the rich will eat shit," had attracted a crowd from many backgrounds. Some were affluent, others poor. Some had a smattering of education, others were illiterate. From the grumbling remarks around me I gathered that their feelings of discontent were a legacy attributable to the social outrages perpetrated by the brokers of power during "*la violencia,*" and the concerns of a wealthy foreigner were not of the slightest interest to any of them. I soon realized that if a government informer noticed me in their company the General would be told and I would forfeit his good will. I concluded that the family's safety lay in continuing our normal lives as unobtrusively as possible. Sooner or later the guerrilla bosses were bound to contact me.

E.L.N guerillas on parade.

Having successfully cowered Chiriguana ranchers into paying protection money, the guerrillas sought to win the allegiance of ordinarily disinterested *campesino* families by making them feel important. Televised news coverage of peasants camped in front of government buildings without food, shelter or hygienic facilities protesting the lack of public services not only gave them a sense of self esteem for the first time in their lives but pressured politicians to speed rural development. For one planned demonstration I was "requested" to drive a group of *campesino* in my Land Rover to a neighbouring town. On the journey, I asked my passengers what they were going to lobby for. There was an embarrassed silence as not one of them knew. What mattered was their physical presence. Attendance was mandatory. On arrival they would be told whether to clamor for schools, roads, rural electrification, health centers or potable water. They were still unaware that they had become expedient pawns subject to unscrupulous manipulation. It took the execution of a peasant, accused of recalcitrant, anti-revolutionary behavior because he stubbornly insisted that looking after his farrowing sow was more important than attending a public meeting, to convince them of their predicament.

Guerrilla commanders in other areas blatantly disrupted Colombia's economy by blowing up oil pipe lines, dynamiting pylons of the national grid, destroying bridges on main roads and subjecting urban areas to random bomb explosions—curious policies to pursue if they thought to win popular backing.

I asked a university student who spent his vacations with the guerrillas what had led him to become a Marxist. "It's the corruption in the government starting with the electoral system and the quality of candidates," he replied. "Things have got to change. Politicians make life and death decisions and are elected to positions of supreme power without passing a single test of morality, integrity or fiscal responsibility. It's not the quality of the candidate that matters, it's the amount of money behind him*. Electoral contests are financed by the drug cartels or other special interest groups who hire astute campaign managers, crafty speech writers and agents to buy votes. When their stooge is elected, he or she manipulates political appointments for the backer's cronies and shields them from investigation. Campaign expenses are recovered several times over from public funds and auditors employed to fix the accounts. Is it surprising that corruption reigns and that the political arena is controlled by millionaires?"

"Surely there must be some honourable exceptions," I said.

"Damn few. Take 'X' [name withheld] for example. Publicly he's a respected politician, privately he acts like a juvenile delinquent."

"Oh really! He can't be that bad."

"He's a disgrace. Apparently he had been told that the President was going to name him Governor of the Department of Cesar so he invited all his cronies to his house to celebrate the public announcement on the radio. They switched it on and heard that another man had been appointed. O.K. he was upset, but was it necessary to whip out his revolver and fire five shots at a photograph of the President hanging on the wall? That sort of behaviour doesn't win my vote."

While, unfortunately, much of the student's criticisms were valid, I thought his becoming a revolutionary unbalanced. The politician from Valledupar might have shown deplorable immaturity—or emotional instability—but his behaviour was innocuous compared with the tyrannical excesses of many Party leaders in Communist countries. The student should have been grateful

---

*The 1994 electoral campaign of the successful presidential candidate, Ernesto Samper Pizano, is reported to have received SEVENTEEN THOUSAND MILLION PESOS from members of the drug Cartel de Cali. Ref. Juan Carlos Giraldo, *Los Rodrigues Orejuela. El Cartel de Cali y sus amigos*. Ediciones Gato Azul, 2005, Buenos Aires, Argentina, page 62.

that he was in Colombia where citizens are allowed to verbally express dissension without being imprisoned.

✦ ✦ ✦ ✦

Jill and I were greatly heartened when Marcus and his newly wedded bride, Juliet, decided to leave England and help us run the ranch. Jill had missed a woman's companionship and I was happy to let Marcus take charge of the machinery. In appreciation of their support, I helped them buy a second-hand light green Land Rover. Early one morning the guerrillas came to borrow it. The request was phrased in a form that made refusal impossible, and Marcus had no option but to hand over the keys. Sorrowfully, he and Juliet watched their vehicle disappearing down the driveway. At midday the wife of one of the workmen, who always listened to radio bulletins, rushed over to tell us that the Mayor of Chiriguana had been kidnapped and taken away in a light green Land Rover. We were frantic! According to gossip, the army had a compound where they incarcerated guerrilla collaborators in cells overlooking a pen of half-starved savage pigs. Each evening a prisoner was taken to the pen, stripped, knee-capped and left to his fate. While other prisoners might cover their eyes they couldn't help but hear a horrible shriek followed by the shrill squeals of pigs as they tore into their dinner. As my Land Rover was out of service we ran panting all the way to Cyril's farm, borrowed a car and sped to the nearest army base to explain how Marcus's vehicle had come to be used. Fortunately the Major in charge believed us and promised, in the unlikely event of the Land Rover ever being recovered, that it would be returned. As it happened the guerrillas had mistakenly abducted the Mayor's look-a-like brother who, being more of a liability than an asset, was set free two days later. On the following afternoon Marcus and I received instructions to wait until nightfall and then walk unaccompanied down our driveway. We hadn't gone farther than two hundred metres from the house when we were suddenly illuminated by blinding headlights. I shrugged my shoulders.

"If anyone wants to shoot us, this is their moment. But as they haven't, shall we go on?" We'd scarcely turned the palms of our hands upwards to show we were unarmed when guerrillas stepped out of the darkness and surrounded us. Satisfied that we had obeyed their instructions, they thanked Marcus for the loan of his car and returned the keys.

The following week a set of marked tools disappeared from the ranch work-

shop. We placed placards in various Poponte shops offering a reward for information leading to their recovery and, as we had hoped, a *campesino* came to tell
us where they were. He had noticed them in the tool box of a collective taxi
when a spanner had been taken out to loosen the studs on a wheel with a flat
tire. We found the taxi driver, claimed our tools, paid the reward and took down
the notices. For us that was the end of the matter. The guerrillas, however,
demanded to know more. Was the person who had sold the tools to the taxi
owner a man they had cautioned never to steal again? They made their
investigations and, satisfied that indeed he was, used him as an example of
what those that ignored guerrilla warnings could expect. Revolutionary justice decreed that he be publicly executed in the doorway of his home and his
body be left for his wife and sons to bury.

However much Marxist sympathizers like to portray Colombian guerrilla
leaders as contemporary Robin Hoods dedicated to rectifying human right
abuses, evidence of multiple atrocities refute that claim. Official investigation
of young guerrilla conscripts in a communal grave brought to light the reason
for their deaths. They had become disillusioned with their restricted freedom
and had asked permission to return to their civilian homes. To ensure that they
would be unable to inform authorities of the location, type of weaponry and
means of servicing the clandestine encampment, the guerrilla Commander had
ordered their execution.

Frightening though these acts of terrorism were, I was far more concerned
about Jill's health. I had taken her, while on holiday in Seattle, to consult Dr
Joel Baker, a distinguished oncologist. As a medical student Joel had been my
first guest on the ranch and we had kept in touch by exchanging Christmas
cards. He examined the lumps on Jill's breasts which had not responded to the
homeopathic remedies in which she believed. Hoping it was not too late to
save her he performed a double mastectomy operation. Tragically, the cancer
had spread into lymph glands beyond the reach of his scalpel and Jill was told
she had only months, or at best a few years, left to live.

Jill had always tried to fill each waking minute with what Rudyard Kipling
called "sixty seconds worth of distance run." Now, when time had an unfor-
giving urgency, she was heroic in her courage and determination to leave
proud and happy memories for her family. Every second was precious and she
determined that not one of them be wasted. Two weeks after her operation we
flew three thousand miles to the wedding of Barnaby and Barbara in Virginia.
The extension of the family signified a continuation of herself and it was

important to her to show how much she cared that her children were growing into independence. The following day we flew the three thousand miles back to the hospital to begin post-operative treatment.

Radiation therapy caused Jill traumatic unease, she felt it incompatible with whole body harmony and decided her hope for a cure lay elsewhere. While Marcus and Juliet, who had just given birth to her first son, Saphod— looked after the ranch, I took Jill, Diccon and Antigone to spend the winter in Devon, England, well known for the abundance of reputable natural health practitioners. Placing Diccon in the local comprehensive and Tiggy in the primary school—their first exposure to conventional education—Jill had time to continue her quest for an alternative cure. She was strong willed in these matters and to avoid stress, the entire family agreed to support her. By springtime Jill felt ready to return to the ranch, a decision made easier by the newly married Rachael and Matthew choosing to spend a year there.

Friends had mentioned various Colombian healers, but there was one, Alfonso Rubio, who was recommended for his sincerity and gentleness. He lived about seventy miles away on the far side of the Magdalena river in a mountain farm above Morales. In previous years we would have undertaken a cross-country expedition for the fun of new experiences, so, determined not to let that aspect disappear from our lives, we went to consult him.

The communal aluminum river taxi transporting commuters up-river hit a submerged hard wood spike, filled with water and sank. Fortunately this happened in a channel between two island sand banks which allowed us to wade with the other bedraggled passengers to a nearby beach. We emptied our rucksacks and festooned the contents on weeds warmed by the blazing sun to dry. The temperature must have been well over one hundred degrees and the tepid river water failed to quench our thirst. The boatman was unconcerned. "Sit back, relax and enjoy the view," he advised. "There's another water taxi due in two hours. It'll pick us up."

"What if it's full?" Jill whispered. "I'm all for going on in the next thing that passes. It can't be worse than sitting here and at least we'd be moving."

A motorized dugout canoe transporting riverine dwellers to their homes chugged into view and we flagged it down. Progress was leisurely for every time it stopped to set a passenger down, or pick one up, people working nearby crowded around to exchange the latest gossip rather, thought Jill, like families of parakeets in a mango tree.

It was midday before we arrived at Morales. The only people in sight were two nude Indian youths gutting fish in a canoe. Shyly waving to our boatman they modestly leapt into the murky river water which hid all but the whites of their eyes and shining teeth bared in friendly smiles

The rest of the town's inhabitants were apparently taking siestas behind their shuttered bedroom windows. Disembarking at the wharf we set off in search of accommodation. Pigs rose from a mud bath in the middle of the road and snuffled expectantly around our feet. Finding that we had not come to feed them, they wandered off to root for delicacies in a pile of nearby garbage.

"Why, hello there!" called a voice. From a window a nun waved to us. As we drew near, she introduced herself as a native of Kansas and invited us into her spotless home. She'd been stationed in Morales for three years among Spanish speakers and was glad to talk in English. After gratefully consuming several glasses of filtered cold water, we asked if she knew of our next destination, the frontier outpost of Plasitas. She did, and was happy to tell us all about it. Plasitas, she said, had been given the name of *Mico Ahumado*, or Smoked Monkey, by a lumber crew sent to harvest the stands of hardwoods growing there. Stranded without provisions after their access road had been washed away by torrential rains, the lumberjacks had saved themselves from protein starvation by shooting a troop of monkeys which they preserved in the form of smoke-cured jerky. Apart from hiring mules, the only means of transport to Plasitas was a WWII American Army Studebaker truck, which lived up to its reputation of indestructibility by making the journey every other day. Those wishing to travel in it gathered at the hardware store, which was the collecting point, early in the morning. She would undoubtedly have told us a great deal more had we not begun to yawn.

"You're tired and need a siesta," she suggested. "Go two blocks and on the left you'll find a restful hotel."

Thanking the nun for her courtesy and help, we continued up the empty street and came to the hardware store. Across the street, on the left, we saw the expected sign HOTEL and went to investigate. The communal bathroom had the usual primitive amenities but the bedroom not only had a ventilation grill above the window but beds that were comfortable. We stretched out and were soon asleep. Giggles from two little boys clinging on to the bars of the grill woke us. Noticing our open eyes, the older one asked what our names were and where we lived. They would have continued their cross examination at length had our hunger not dictated that we ask them where we could find a restaurant.

"Walk up the street to the embankment and you'll see where a lot of visitors eat."

As we followed the boy's directions, we noticed that the river served Morales in many ways. People carried water from it in five-gallon tins to their homes, and returned with laundry to be washed and rubbish to be thrown away. It was also an outhouse, the provider of fish, and highway to the world. Under the shade of an open sided thatch we noticed lunch being served at a long planked table. There appeared to be only one choice of food but the agreeable sensation of mingling with local customers persuaded us to sit down and wait our turn. The proprietor of the restaurant, his attention centered on the radio news, swatted some flies that had settled on his bare stomach and shouted to his wife to bring two more meals: clear soup flavored with coriander and a gristle covered bone, fried fish accompanied by *patacones** and a tomato and onion salad, followed by coffee. Coffee wouldn't normally have tempted Jill but as it was a drink made with boiled water she accepted two cupfuls. Having eaten we spent the rest of the afternoon idly wandering along the river bank relishing the freedom of having no chores waiting to be done and wishing for no other company than our own.

"I can't imagine a journey in England providing as many comical incidents as the ones we've had today," murmured Jill. "I'm really glad we came. The bizarre times we've shared couldn't have happened anywhere but in Colombia."

"I'll never forget them," I told her.

The truck to Plasitas made an early start. The prettiest nubile girls joined the driver on the padded bench in the cab. We stood in the back with the rest of the passengers. A local wit enlivened the journey by mimicking a well-known politician who, in his electoral campaign, had promised road improvements. As each cavernous gully tilted the truck and threw all the standing passengers into a heap, or when low branches caused us to duck, we kept our good humour by joining him in shouting "*Viva el mentiroso malparido!*" (Long live that lying, ill-born bastard!)

It had been rumoured that in the hills behind Plasitas drug cartels employed a private army to guard laboratories that processed coca leaves into crystalline

*Green cooking bananas, cut into cylindrical sections about two inches long, which are lightly fried, flattened between two boards, fried again, and sprinkled with salt. Delicious!

View of a peasant's homestead.

cocaine. Village shops could sell basic foods to prevent drunken disturbances but the sale of alcohol was forbidden. Anything which might attract the police was banned. Every new arrival was scrutinised. Scarcely had we set foot on the ground before armed scouts accosted us wanting to know who we were and why we were there. With disarming candour Jill told them of her need for a herbal remedy and showed them the scars from her operation. After briefly consulting together, they took us to a hostel whose owner promised to have saddled horses ready at dawn for our journey to Alfonso Rubio's farm.

Dewdrops glistened from spider's webs spun between branches at the side of the trail that zigzagged upwards towards a ridge. Occasionally a simple homestead, like a child-painted picture, came into view beneath us. Behind, in the distance, the Magdalena river seemed no more than a silver thread. In front, rolling hills stretched to the horizon. It was magnificent countryside, both for pioneers looking for a legitimate new life and drug cartels seeking to hide their illicit activities.

Sprays of orchids growing in simple wooden baskets welcomed us to the Rubio's home. At the sound of our horse's hoofs in the yard, the door of what was clearly a kitchen was opened by a woman with merry brown eyes who introduced herself as Alfonso's wife. She informed us that he had gone foraging for fungi with their youngest grandson, but we were welcome to wait his return. Sensing Jill's unease, she put her arm around her shoulder as if she were a trusted friend and invited her to enter the house. From the drinking trough where I unsaddled the horses I could see the white shoelace tying her grey plaits together bob up and down as she made some emphatic remark. A hen, selected from the flock attracted to a handful of scattered maize, was seized and had its neck wrung. It was a peasant's generous way of indicating that we were expected to stay for lunch.

Alfonso returned from his foray, pleased with his finds. He was a tall, spare man with bushy eyebrows who walked slowly, carefully scanning the ground for plants with curative properties. Although still active at seventy years of age, he admitted to tiring easily. His wife ushered us into her parlor and, with the grace of royalty bestowing a favor, served us freshly brewed coffee in a selection of battered tin mugs. As we waited for them to cool, Alfonso spoke about the benefits of natural remedies.

That very morning he had found a puffball fungus used to poultice chronic festering sores. Jill was intensely interested and questioned him about his feelings towards the plants he used.

"There's something wonderful about plants," he said. "It's as if they had souls which respond to love. Have you ever noticed that plants tenderly harvested have greater curative properties than those roughly pulled up?"

"The herbalists who prepare the Bach Flower Remedies I use would agree with you," Jill replied. "They believe that stress affects the physical characteristics of every living thing."

"When I was young priests taught me that transubstantiation was an exclusive feature of Church doctrine. But in nature, when I observe how the healing power of one body can be resurrected in another, it makes me look at all the world's creations with reverence." Alfonso placed a gnarled hand on the head of his grandson sitting cross-legged at his feet. "I'm convinced of a blessed natural unity with power to heal. This child is my companion and I pass my knowledge on to him so it may live to benefit others."

"Don Alfonso, can you help me? I'm ill with cancer," Jill said softly.

Alfonso rose to his feet. Taking Jill gently by the hand he led her past the baskets of orchids to two chairs at the end of the balcony where they could talk privately. After lunch he explained to me what I had to do.

"Capture a mature rattlesnake without bruising it. As you cut its head off, ask forgiveness. Then, if you bury the head with the poison glands, skin, intestines and tail deep in the soil, a vital curative power will be preserved in the flesh of its body. This you must fillet and dry in the sun. The treatment for Jill begins with a thumb-nail sized portion of meat which she must chew slowly eight times a day. In the second week the dose may be reduced to six times a day, and in the third to three. I believe it will help her condition."

Back on the ranch I offered five thousand pesos for a live, un-harmed adult rattlesnake and within days Jill had begun to take Don Alfonso's cure. After a month, even though her doctor in Bucaramanga thought that her condition had improved, she became physically repulsed by the process of chewing meat. It didn't help when I ground and encapsulated the rattlesnake meat so that it could be swallowed. Her whole being opposed absorbing the flesh of a slaughtered animal. It was incompatible with her vegetarian principles and she rejected the argument that the power of the consumed could be resurrected in another body as so much sophistry. After she discontinued Don Alfonso's treatment, we had nothing left to offer her but love.

Possibly the cancer had already spread too far. In August 1987 Jill showed signs of retaining abdominal body fluid. I took her to the best orthodox doctors in Colombia but she found the impersonal clinical tests they wished to perform terrifying and asked if she could to be treated once again by a faith healer in Devon who had cured the continual headaches which had followed her operation.

At her insistence she flew to England alone and went to her parents' house without telling friends she was there. The family respected her wish to meditate and come to terms with what was destroying her without interruptions. In October the swelling in her body became physically unbearable and a doctor drained six gallons of fluid. While she felt more comfortable, her condition rapidly deteriorated and the message to come went out: to Marcus and Juliet, Diccon, Antigone and myself on the ranch; to Rachel and her husband Matthew who had moved to Bogotá; to Barnaby and his wife Barbara in Virginia; and to Felix in California.

Those of us from the ranch arrived on the afternoon before her death. We had all tried to keep alive positive thoughts so that our presence would not be unsettling but when I bent to kiss her I recognized the end was near, and she saw this in my eyes. The others came and sat around her bed. As we talked, hoping we were saying the right things, words choked in our throats in sorrow for what might have been different, and one by one we became silent. A shared love connected us, for death may not be the end but the beginning of a new dimension. That night she gave my hand a last squeeze of recognition and was gone. She died as she had wished, in her own bed, with her family near, and in her parents' house. Whilst the faith healer had failed to cure the cancer, he undoubtedly helped her to relinquish the will that might have clung desperately to a body that no longer served her purpose. She hadn't totally left us. As Diccon sorrowfully sat on the bed in which she had died, he looked up and saw her looking at him through the window. I felt so curiously uplifted by the vision that I could only think that Jill wished Diccon to know that she was free from pain.

We buried Jill in the village cemetery of Staverton, her Devon home, after a church service filled with admirers paying their last respects to a courageous woman. In similar spirit her four sons chose to be the pallbearers. In the evening I and some of her closest friends went to Lannacombe Cove to share memories of Jill in a place where we had all spent camping holidays together. As we walked along the cliff path, one of them told me a secret.

"Before Jill went to Colombia to share your life seventeen years ago, I gave her my promise not to tell you something, but now I think she would forgive me if I broke my silence. In a routine check-up she was told she had a positive Pap smear showing pre-cancerous cells."

The revelation helped to explain Jill's compulsive determination that every day be filled with creative activity. It is possible that conventional treatment could have extended her life, but she chose otherwise in the belief that happiness could cause her body to balance its disorders.

She was a devoted mother and a faithful companion.

I loved her.

THIRTEEN

The Thing It Contemplates

To hope till hope creates
From its own wreck
The thing it contemplates...

—Percy Bysshe Shelley, "Prometheus Unbound"

A note from the E.L.N. demanding four revolvers and three million five hundred thousand pesos in cash (at that time approximately twelve hundred pounds) was waiting for me when I returned to the ranch. It cautioned that my life depended on my silence and ended with the revolutionary slogan "Liberty or Death." If I hadn't already realized that they took themselves seriously I might have thought I'd been threatened by a group of melodramatic juveniles in a Halloween rip off. Revolutionaries were welcome to die for their cause if they thought it did them any good but I hadn't come to Colombia to involve myself in subversive activities. Deciding to opt for liberty, I took the note to the colonel in charge of the Secret Service Operations in the army headquarters in Valledupar. The meeting was brief. Having read the note, he sighed and said "I'm truly sorry but there's no way we can offer you protection. Our forces are already overstretched. You'll have to co-exist with the guerrillas as best you can. Yes, you'll have to give them something but please, try and get them to accept food or clothes instead of guns or money." As I turned to go, confirmed in my fears that the government forces had lost control of the countryside, he added as though it were encouragement, "Keep in touch. Good luck."

My relationship with the E.L.N. wasn't my only problem. Diccon was fifteen, Antigone twelve, and their schooling was now my responsibility. I'd soon be without the help of Marcus and Juliet. With one young son, and another on the way, they had regretfully, but sensibly, decided to live in a safer environment. Marcus had found a job in Bucaramanga and in five day's time was taking his family to live there. Adriano, the ranch foreman, informed me that apart from the E.L.N., an even more dangerous guerrilla group, the F.A.R.C.— The Armed Revolutionary Forces of Colombia—were active in the cordillera behind Poponte. He added, however, that in the nearby Department of Cordoba, the Marxists were not having everything their own way.

"A couple of months ago two brothers, Fidel and Carlos Castaño, got together with their neighbours to form a band of vigilantes. They're known as the Auto Defense Units of Colombia, or A.U.C."

"Sounds interesting. Tell me more, I said.

"Well, it seems they got conned by the guerrillas. Although they had paid regular protection money, the guerrillas kidnapped the Castaño father.* The sons paid the demanded ransom to get him back and were told, "If you want to see your father alive pay another." They did, and were handed his corpse."

"Good God!"

"Fidel was recently killed in a skirmish but the great news is that Carlos and his neighbours are being successful in clearing the countryside of guerrillas and their collaborators. The A.U.C.'s won popular support for doing what the army should have done. I'm told ranchers in the vicinity of Monteria are bringing their families back from the cities to live and work on their lands again."

A firm patriotic response to the Marxist revolutionaries was long overdue. For thirty years the guerrillas had steadily been gaining dominance throughout the Colombian countryside and I was heartened to think that among farmers a leader had emerged with the courage, charisma and organizational skills to combat them. If the A.U.C. ever arrived in Chiriguana, I'd certainly give them my backing.

Any private army combating Marxist guerrillas at a national level must have massive popular support in order to withstand the criticisms from international left wing activists who can be counted on to treat any paramilitary offensive as a breach of human rights. Fortunately, in Colombia responsible rural leaders had traditionally been "allowed" to take the law into their own

---

*For readers interested in Carlos Castaño's account of the activities of the A.U.C., I recommend his book "Mis Confessiones," published and reprinted eight times by Editorial La Oveja Negra, Bogotá.

hands and eliminate small groups of bandits when it seemed in the interest of the common good. A respected nearby rancher, Euclides Cordoba, from the village of Potrerillo, had recently found his family held at gun point by thieves who had kidnapped his daughter and were ransacking his home. Acting with resolve, Euclides formed his neighbors into an impromptu vigilante posse and pursed the thieves on foot across open country for thirty-six hours and only went home when the last had been shot. After resting for a day, Euclides presented himself to the General in the Santa Marta army base—the highest authority in the area—and explained his actions. As the vigilantes had succeeded in eliminating a group of terrorists which army patrols had repeatedly tried but failed to do, instead of putting Euclides behind bars, the General took him to the army club house where they celebrated with a bottle of scotch!

It was widely rumored that many high ranking officers in the army had tried to supply Carlos with ordnance but such action had been thwarted by highly placed Marxist sympathizers in the government. Initially the A.U.C. had been financed by gratefully given contributions from guerrilla-harassed ranchers and businessmen. In a country where taxes were paid grudgingly it was a tribute to Carlos's integrity. In a display of responsible commitment to society he responded by not only supervising the construction of forty-two staffed schools and ten health centers in Magdalena Medio, but by personally interviewing each new recruit to keep his troops free from psychopaths. Nobody else was effectively restoring social security and peace in the countryside.

Inevitably, as the conflict with the guerrillas spread and troops of the A.U.C. grew to an estimated thirty thousand, it became impossible for Carlos Castaño to vet the motivations of all newcomers and the initial crusading spirit which had forged the original recruits into a well disciplined and dedicated band was corrupted by subordinates. The cost of weaponry surpassed the income from private donations and to be able to combat guerrillas on a national scale the A.U.C.—which repudiated the practice of kidnapping—was obliged to find another way of funding its activities. As the F.A.R.C. had already done, they involved themselves in the drug trade. It was the beginning of a moral decline which continued when splinter groups, trained by foreign professionals, offered their services for hire. International corporations and private businessmen employed them as security guards, cartel bosses as assassins to eliminate competitors.

Ironically, much of the success of the billion dollar business of trafficking in cocaine, which earned guerrillas the alternative name of "narco-terrorists," is due to the sophisticated weaponry sold to them by armament factories located in the countries which suffer from drug addiction problems.

Undoubtedly, mercenary life, whether left wing guerrilla or right wing para-military, attracts much of the unsavory and criminally inclined elements of society. In armed confrontations whether it be between the A.U.C. and the guerrillas in Colombia—or in conflicts anywhere else—civilians, thought by one side to have helped the other, perish. Non combatants of any age or sex collaborating with the faction they imagine will be victorious put not only their own lives but those of their relations in danger. If the other side wins, families of those accused of having transmitted information about troop movements, disclosed the whereabouts of prominent citizens, delivered provisions and messages or acted as scouts are considered fifth column sympathizers and are shot.

Carlos was given national television coverage when he offered to disband the A.U.C. if the Marxist guerrillas did likewise. Unfortunately his restraining influence was not accepted by other A.U.C. commanders and he was assassinated for trying to curb their excesses. Although Carlos indisputably operated outside the law, for many Colombians he is remembered as a revered folk hero. (Another flamboyant brigand who was shot by specialised army personnel was Pablo Escobar, king of the Medellin cartel, who secretly met the Colombian President Lopez Michelson in Panama and offered to cancel Colombia's foreign debt with a private cheque in return for being allowed to deal unrestrictedly in marijuana!)

When *Perestroika* deprived the Marxists of political credibility, the guerrillas, instead of returning to a civilian work ethic as offered by a government amnesty, continued their arrogant life style as members of the drug mafia. Strutting down the main streets of a village toting sten guns and taking whatever they fancied was preferable to honorable work.

Nearly every rural area dominated by guerrillas had gone into economic decline. As anyone with an image of moderate affluence was subject to being kidnapped, investment in cattle and cash crops dwindled and ready cash was diverted to dollar shares or spread in urban development projects.

Guerrillas were certainly to blame for the rock bottom real estate prices in Poponte. As I was neither prepared to deprive my children of their inheritance by disposing of the ranch for a pittance to some speculator nor abandon my home, I had only one choice: reply to the guerrilla letter. I re-read it. There was no specific mention of a dialogue but, if I could make the guerrilla leaders think that I was a potential proselyte, they might visit me. It was a gambit worth pursuing. I sent a message welcoming the opportunity to meet their leaders, provided they were introduced by a third party of mutual confidence. Two nights later this confidant came to see if I was alone and could receive two of the guerrilla hierarchy at the ranch within the hour. My guts twitched at the prospect but I replied it would be a pleasure. Placing a bottle of whisky, glasses and ice on the table, I gave serious thought to what would create an image of unity between us. If the topic of guns and money were not to dominate the conversation, I would have to convince them of my genuine concern for social and political reform achieved by peaceful means. Hopefully the meeting would be positive.

A knock at the door announced the arrival of my guests. The intermediary made the introductions and remained outside to act as sentry. My whisky was refused, but I managed to steer the discussion my way by asking the first question.

"Don't you feel that we, as Colombians, should be able to find the talent among ourselves to deal with the country's problems without foreign interference?"

"*Claro que sí.* That is why the E.L.N. is united in the struggle to free our country from the yoke of foreign imperialists. Our heroic leader, Camilo Torres, always maintained that Colombians were capable of formulating solutions for Colombia's problems."

"I totally agree with him. Many of my family were born in England, but we all adopted Colombian citizenship because, after living and working here, we came to admire and respect your way of doing things and wished to join our future with yours. Surely if our patriotic aims are the same, shouldn't we join hands in the task of creating a just and prosperous society?"

"*Muy bien*, but you must prove your commitment by complying with the requests in our message. Anyone refusing to play their part in helping the freedom fighters is an enemy to the cause."

"There I have a problem. Your country accepted me, my wife and our children to become Colombians and we gave our oaths to respect that privilege. We cannot now betray that trust by providing guns to murder the family that received us. Your situation is different. You were born here. You didn't consciously choose to become Colombians. If engaging in fratricide is necessary to achieve your ends, I cannot join you. I am a rancher and you are guerrillas. Just as I do not expect you to stick your arm up the rectum of a cow to perform a pregnancy test, do not expect me to take part in your violence. To my way of thinking, striking somebody dead is a prerogative of God. I'm sorry, but I just don't possess that degree of moral certitude."

"So how are you going to prove your sincerity to the cause?"

"Colombia needs both of us. I'll gladly work with you for the benefit of the community if I think my contribution constructive."

I pointed out that for a social revolution to succeed, geese which lay golden eggs should be made welcome, not frightened away, and that the support of the middle classes is vital. To gain it, revolutionary leaders would have to behave in such a commendable manner that the government officials they wished to overthrow would appear shoddy by comparison.

For nearly two hours we exchanged ideas. In denying that they resembled either gangsters or Russian imperialist puppets pulled by strings from Moscow, my guests were obliged to profess that the criteria which guided their actions was based on patriotic humanitarian principles. We came to a tentative agreement that my reasons for not participating as they had wished would be respected but, as they were leaving, they tested the sincerity of my concern for social improvement by proposing a deal. I could give them a once only payment and never be asked for anything else again. I smiled and asked if they really believed that society could be changed by anything less than a lifetime commitment. Finding my answer satisfactory, they agreed I could supply them with food, clothes and medicines and, when asked to do so, collaborate with ranch equipment in community projects.

For a few days afterwards I felt that the meeting had gone quite well and life might continue as before. Adriano was not so sure. He was a native born Colombian and understood better than I the convolutions of his compatriot's minds. He doubted if a native Communist commander would accept evasive arguments and piddling bags of groceries as alternatives to the guns and money demanded. To teach me a lesson, or to make sure that I complied with their demands, they might kidnap Diccon and Antigone. It was a possibility I couldn't risk. Snap decisions are prone to subsequent regrets but my parental responsibility left only one agonising decision: the children had to leave the farm with Marcus who was about to depart for Bucaramanga.

Tears trickled down by beard as I looked for Diccon and Tiggy to tell them that they had to go. Their roots were embedded in the ranch and with Jill gone the familiar surroundings provided security.

I found them in the corral cutting their horses' manes.

"Diccon, Tiggy, come. I've something painful to say."

"Dad! what's wrong?"

"I didn't give in to guerrilla demands. Adriano's afraid they'll kidnap you to teach me a lesson. All I can think of is to send you with Marcus to Bucaramanga."

"But he's about to leave."

"I know. There isn't time to pack. Just put a few things in your rucksacks. I'll send on the rest later."

"Won't we ever be able to come back?"

"I can't promise. For now, take images of the things you love in your mind's eye and I'll try and keep everything safe."

An hour later I was waving to the blurred figures of my children growing fainter in the departing Land Rover. Jill's death had depleted my emotional resilience and I felt like a gymnast required to vault over a hurdle without a spring board. The sound of my children's tearful voices choking "goodbye, Dad, goodbye horses, goodbye home" reverberated in my head.

I went to their room intending to tidy up but I couldn't begin. The enormity of feeling I had failed them and sent them away overcame me. I fell on to Diccon's bed, clutched his pillow and sobbed.

The catharsis of weeping relieved some tension but didn't solve any problems. I couldn't allow myself to be less brave than I wished my children to be. I had to pull myself together. Splashing water on my face from their washbasin, I went to look for Adriano.

"I feel I've got to do something physically active. If I rode around the ranch, would you come with me?" I asked him.

We took a trail to the top of the valley ridge overlooking land belonging to *campesinos* whom I'd known to be hard working and proudly independent. The torment of giving time, goods and verbal support to guerrillas had also affected them. Fields once carefully tended had reverted to secondary growth and many homesteads appeared to be abandoned. Only a few elderly peasants remained. Having abandoned their lands during "*la violencia*" they were too weary to pack up and move yet again. Smoldering with discontent at a government which had failed in its duty to protect its citizens they were clinging stubbornly to what little they had. I was beginning to understand the depths of despair that drove a man to stick his machete into the guts of a tormentor.

I couldn't accept such a fatalistic option. Curucucú had given me an intensely enjoyable life and it would be impetuous folly to lose everything I had achieved by engaging in a physical battle I had no chance of winning. On top of

that ridge with the wind in my face, I remembered some lines from Shelley's
"Prometheus Unbound," which my aunt, Margaret Isherwood, had encouraged
me to learn by heart:

> *To suffer woes which Hope thinks infinite;*
> *To forgive wrongs darker than death or night;*
> *To defy Power, which seems omnipotent;*
> *To love, and bear; to hope till Hope creates*
> *from its own wreck the thing it contemplates;*
> *Neither to change, nor falter nor repent;*
> *This, like thy glory, Titan, is to be*
> *good, great and joyous, beautiful and free;*
> *This is alone Life, Joy, Empire and Victory.*

I turned my horse's head and, beckoning to Adriano to follow, rode back to
get on with planning a future.

✦ ✦ ✦ ✦

Adriano and his family moved into the house I had shared with Jill and I
moved a few of my basic possessions to the second story guest apartment.
Should the guerrillas take me, I'd suffer less if I'd trained myself to do without
all of my accustomed luxuries. I ate with Adriano and his family and one night
each week took my turn to wash the dishes. It continued a ranch tradition
started by Jill that helping to clear up after a meal was a courtesy to the person
who had prepared the food.

Birdsong still welcomed the beginning of each day and looking across the
front fields to the mountains from my single bed I recalled my daily habit
thirty years earlier of getting up at five-thirty to feed the chickens, the dogs
and myself. I'd have a wash in the stream and be ready for the day's work when
the men arrived at seven. I'd been full of energy then and making improvements to the ranch had been fun. Gazing around my solitary bedroom, I
recognised that the seventeen years spent with Jill had been an amazing privilege. Finding another woman possessing similar qualities who would want to
live on the ranch now that it was in a guerrilla dominated zone seemed
unlikely. The relationship that Jill and I had established with our workmen was
highly unusual if not unique. Some of our employees had been treated—and
had responded—as though they were adopted members of our family. My

loneliness was lessened by the thought that I was blessed to still have three of them whose companionship gave me the confidence I needed to continue.

Adriano had proved himself both loyal and honest. He'd been brought up on an isolated cattle ranch with minimal schooling. Although incapable of keeping proper written accounts he knew enough to realise that we'd soon catch on if he presented us with fictitious ones. His father had taught him how to recognise and distinguish the peculiarities of cattle and, incredibly, he could extract from his memory the genealogy of every animal in the Curucucú herd. His children were Diccon and Antigone's closest friends.

Sofanor had been thirteen when his father was murdered in a Poponte brawl. His mother had brought him to the ranch and asked us to give him part-time employment so he could buy his own school uniform and books. He was a pleasant, well mannered lad and was always grateful for any coaching I could give him. After going to school in the mornings he worked on the ranch in the afternoons. His eagerness to learn when confronted by something he didn't understand, his cheerfulness and willingness to accompany me on my errands in the Land Rover even if I told him we might not be back till dark resulted in my taking a special interest in his future.

Lucho had an ebullient generosity of spirit that made him friends wherever he went. Having more or less mastered the three R's, he had found little else of benefit in the village school. Anxious to succeed in life, he had proposed that I allow him to plant two hectares of the ranch in yucca, maize and watermelons. I would provide the capital outlay and he the manual labour. After deducting our respective costs, profits from sales would be equally shared. At the end of three years he had bought a lot on Poponte's main street and on Sundays took sand from the river with the farm tractor and trailer to make cement bricks for building his house. Having lived with a series of Poponte beauties he had decided to settle down and was seriously wooing Adriano's youngest daughter, Anna Julia. We often worked together on some ranch project and if we paused to rest he would dash off, pick some grapefruit and return with a glass of juice. I was once with Lucho mending the garden gate when a car arrived bearing men who said they belonged to a special police unit authorised to inspect ranches for firearms. They flashed their identity cards and I led them inside. Lucho followed. I only recognized my error when all the farm hands were herded into the sitting room at gun point and I was led away to empty every drawer and cupboard on the homestead. "Hold on," cried Lucho, "Don Ben needs an assistant. He has a faulty knee and I always accompany him." By choosing to be at my side he gave me the assurance of his companionship. I could rely on him in any weather, under any circumstances and at any hour.

With the support of those three, Curucucú became a haven of sanity in a countryside beset by turmoil and violence. The ranch was not just any old place that paid a wage, the ranch was a way of life that meant as much to them as it did to me.

Throughout Colombia, racketeers, often in company with poorly paid government security officers trained in the brutal tactics of counter-insurgency, masqueraded as guerrillas to extort "*la vacuna*" for themselves. Victims seldom dared ask whom they were paying, as it was courting death to demand the identification of an oppressor. The police and the army were reluctant to go to a ranch being pillaged. If a guerrilla, disguised as a peasant, was fatally wounded in the skirmish, an investigation to determine whether there had been a human rights violation invariably followed. The dishonorable discharge with which many a commanding officer was rewarded for having sent his men to maintain order served to deter effective action. Indeed, security forces had been lured into the countryside and ambushed so frequently that during night hours no civilian need could extract them from their bases.

Even traveling on the main roads, either in a private vehicle or in a bus, became hazardous. Guerrillas established what became known as "*la pesca milagrosa*" in which all traffic was stopped and appraised for its value. Owners of expensive cars were detained until someone brought a ransom. One authenticated event describes a bus being attacked three times on a journey from Cartagena to Bogotá. After the second robbery there was nothing visibly worth stealing so the third set of robbers, hoping to find secreted valuables, ordered the passengers to undress inside the bus and then stand naked on the roadway while their clothes were ransacked. When nothing of value was found, the robbers closed the door of the bus and angrily told the chauffer to drive the bus into a grove of tress that dotted the savannah at the edge of the road. There the passengers were ordered to strip and wait outside the bus while their clothes were searched. Furious at finding nothing worth stealing, the robbers left the pasengers in their nakedness and drove on.

I sometimes thought that officials showed more interest in issuing a permit for a butcher to slaughter a cow than they did in burying an unidentified cadaver. On one occasion I received a request from the Police Inspector to see if I could identify a pale colored corpse found on the road entering Poponte.

The first thing I saw on arrival was the Inspector sitting on a stone trying on the dead man's shoes. The corpse was unknown to me but a cursory examination indicated that death was probably caused by a blow to the head. The body was taken to the cemetery where voluntary grave diggers distributed the remaining clothing among themselves.

✖ ✖ ✖

As a treat, Adriano's wife, Mira, always made a special lunch on Sundays. I was about to sit down at the table to enjoy it when I recognized a youth in faded military fatigues and with something slung over his shoulder approaching the house. I went out to greet him.

"Wilson!" I cried. "What a surprise!" He lowered a sack and we gave each other a hug. "My God it's good to see you. Come in. You haven't eaten? I'll tell Mira you're joining us for lunch."

"Thank you. I'd really appreciate that. I haven't had a home cooked meal for ages." As we sat down, Wilson looked around appreciatively. "This is just as I remembered. You haven't changed much."

"You have. You look like a guerrilla scarecrow."

Adriano gave me a warning kick under the table and turning to Wilson asked bluntly, "Are you a guerrilla?"

"I'm the political co-ordinator for the E.L.N. in this area."

There was nothing else for me to do but laugh out loud at my gaffe.

"In my sack you'll find a box of *panela*. Take it as a gift. We just hijacked a truckload of the stuff on the main road."

While Mira plied us with food, Wilson told us what he had done since his visit to the ranch after Henry's murder. Leaning back when his plate was empty, he said, "Thank you. Once again Curucucú has shared its food with me. I'm sorry Jill is no longer alive. When I needed a refuge, she welcomed me into her home and, in memory of her, I'd like to wash up."

We carried our dirty plates to the kitchen and he collected them in the sink, washed, rinsed and placed them in the rack to dry while I made coffee.

With a key positioned guerrilla deciding to be friendly, my future looked considerably brighter.

A few days later the E.L.N. held their first public meeting in the village street. Everybody was ordered to attend. The regional Commander had arrived and wished to reassure himself that we were being adequately indoctrinated. Obediently, we allowed ourselves to be herded into a group before a tractor's trailer from which he harangued us.

"Comrades," he began, "I welcome you."

"*Gracias!*" shrilled a lady standing next to me.

I turned and stared at her in astonishment. It hadn't occurred to me to utter that particular sentiment. Apparently she had been to other meetings of this kind and knew what was expected.

"Our country," he continued, "is being raped by rich foreigners who exploit the working classes and steal the natural resources which are our just inheritance. We must be vigilant in fighting to destroy everything the oligarchy represents and in demanding our rights." He continued in that vein for ten minutes and at one point looked directly at me. I feared he was about to say that to demonstrate revolutionary vigour, the imperialist present amongst them would be shot. He didn't, but it was the first time I'd been made aware of how vulnerable one is when faced by a ranting fanatic holding an automatic weapon. The Commander sat down to scattered applause and the meeting dragged on as a series of stooges stumbled through memorised speeches so badly that it was embarrassing to listen to their remarks. I doubt if anyone in Poponte was the wiser for having attended the event, but the Commander was satisfied that his troops had been able to crowd the villagers together for two hours in the middle of the morning without being disturbed by either the police or the army.

A month later, the F.A.R.C. guerrillas overran the police station in the nearby village of Ricon Hondo. One guerrilla and two policemen died in the siege. After the battle, the locals were "invited" to judge the surviving policemen stretched face downwards on the ground. When the community was gathered, the policemen were prodded into a sitting position one at a time. The question was then put to the villagers.

"Is this policeman good or bad?"

If the community shouted "good" he was told to lie down again. If the community hesitated, he was shot.

Every year in the municipal area of Chiriguana someone was kidnapped and held for ransom. It was seldom obvious to me how the selection was made, but with each abduction the list of eligible victims became shorter. Given my background, my name was sure to be included. To take me would be easy as, apart from Teleri and Cyril, I was the only rancher who slept on his farm. While, of course, I was happy not to have been kidnapped, the omission could be interpreted by the government that I was an undercover guerrilla agent. It was even possible that my name was on an official file labelled "Subversives."

In Poponte, most people had information of interest to the Secret Service, but to pass it on without risking one's life was virtually impossible. The only telephone was in a public exchange where every conversation could be overheard. Anyone noticed by guerrilla informers talking to soldiers was likely to be executed. A civilian wishing to communicate with an Intelligence officer whose discretion could be trusted had to go to an army base, identify himself to a series of sentries and then be escorted to the command post in full view of conscripts doing their national service. If there were guerrilla sympathisers amongst them, the visit would certainly be reported.

Fortunately, foreign aid began to modernise the appearance of the Colombian army. Beforehand the hotchpotch equipment worn by government troops in the countryside made them, from a distance, difficult to distinguish from guerrilla patrols. One was ill-advised to identify oneself before being certain to which side they belonged. A son of a prominent politician discovered this to his regret when on a main highway he mistook a *"pesca milagrosa"* for a routine army check point of personal documents. Thinking himself important, he drove straight to the front, identified himself and demanded to pass. The error cost his father a lot of money.

Although the army and the guerrillas referred to each other as "the enemy," they were fellow countrymen and as such exhibited an understandable reluctance, should they by chance see a relative belonging to the other side, either to shoot or be shot. When the army entered Poponte the guerrillas hid in the undergrowth; when the army left, the guerrillas re-emerged. It might not have been what Kipling had in mind but it was their interpretation of his words, "East is east and west is west, and never the twain shall meet."

♪ ♪ ♪ ♪

A month after I'd sent Diccon and Antigone to Bucaramanga with Marcus, I enrolled them in the Anglo-Colombian School in Bogotá. Among the children of European parents they would be inconspicuous. Rachel and Mathew who had rented a large house welcomed them as lodgers during term time, and for their Christmas holiday I took them to my sister and brother-in-law's house in California. Looking along their book shelves, I saw Bronowski's *The Ascent of Man* and opened it. Two passages caught my attention: "[Man's] imagination, his reason, his emotional stability and toughness make it possible for him not to accept his environment but to change it" and "...real mastery comes from understanding and molding the living environment."* I believed there was a purpose in the coincidence that had brought me to read these passages and, on my return to Poponte, I resolved to instill seeds of a social and cultural evolution in the minds of guerrillas whenever there was a suitable opportunity. Formerly I had passively given in to the guerrillas when they demanded a cow or provisions and had allowed them to be masters of the moment. Now their visits would be a chance for me to encourage them to think about the positive possibilities of being a revolutionary. Even if only one of them would admit that revolutions of mindless brutality, hurts avenged, and vengeance revenged were no more than barren repetitions of blighted social conflicts, my resolve to remain at Curucucú would be justified.

Due to my friendship with Wilson I came to the favorable attention of his newly appointed E.L.N. boss, Francisco. He was an extraordinarily talented leader who had eluded capture as few people could describe his features. Endowed with a histrionic flair he altered his appearance by combing his hair either to one side or to the other or in the middle, using radically different sets of false teeth and having glasses that made him look studious, sporting or blind. By settling *campesino* disputes fairly, firmly and quickly he became more respected than the judiciary in Chiriguana. When, after a few weeks of reclusive guerrilla life camping in the bushes, he needed a change he either went to José Chiquito's bar to carouse or, if needing something more intellectually stimulating, turned up on the ranch. We'd discuss some aspect of Marxist dogma and I always felt pleased if afterwards he'd admit that possibly there were more ways of improving society than those he'd been indoctrinated to believe. Had there been other leaders with his honesty the guerrilla movement might have gained genuine support.

Ignoring the advice of most of my friends and family, I decided that Diccon and Antigone could return to the ranch for their summer holidays. Francisco's willingness to engage in amicable dialogue had significantly reduced the danger of their being abducted and I felt that mixing with guerrillas in the daily contacts between the ranch and Poponte would make the children realize that not all of them were monsters. Some were merely human beings. A few weeks living among them would be a valuable lesson in the art of survival.

Antigone, now sixteen, bubbled with excitement at being home again. She had grown up with Adriano's daughters and within fifteen minutes of her

---

*BBC publication, pages 19 and 69.

arrival they had all changed into swimsuits and gone to the river. During those first days she and Diccon took their horses on day-long rides to places of special importance in their memories and re-established their feelings of harmony with the ranch. The villagers elected Diccon as President of the committee engaged in organizing the annual Poponte fiesta and he found that among the men he was working with, whom had known all his life, some were guerrilla supporters. Putting aside their differences they made the fiesta a success and, with the profits, improved the community centre. Although I felt that Diccon and Antigone were as safe on the ranch as anywhere in Colombia, I enquired where Wilson's mother lived. In the event of either of my children being kidnapped, I was prepared to abduct her and negotiate a swap.

This period of grace ended when Diccon and Antigone returned to their school in Bogotá and Francisco and Wilson were transferred to another guerrilla front. Francisco was shot while transporting explosives into Valledupar and a dispirited Wilson left the guerrillas for civilian life.

In Poponte, they were replaced by a thug bearing the sobriquet of "The Executioner" and a witless, trigger-happy assistant whose eyebrows merged into his hairline. Being the antithesis of Francisco and Wilson and possessing absolute power, they ruthlessly eliminated anyone whom they suspected of being untrustworthy or who dared to criticize guerrilla actions. For reasons they never felt obliged to justify or explain, they came to the conclusion that a paramilitary group threatening their security was being patronized by a wealthy neighbor named Camito Villegas. One afternoon, while returning from one of his farms, The Executioner and his assistant flagged down Villegas's jeep, dragged him into a field and shot him in the face at close range.

A week later they waylaid me. I happened to be with Adriano checking cattle in a field near the entrance to the ranch.

"Get your Land Rover," they ordered. "We want you to drive us to the river."

I whispered furtively to Adriano, "Look for my body if I don't come back," and went to fetch the vehicle. I kept my composure by repeating to myself, "Negative thoughts provoke antagonistic responses, and fear encourages aggression." When guerrillas like The Executioner and his assistant asked someone to take them someplace, that person seldom returned. It was their way of keeping people intimidated.

They climbed into the back of the Land Rover and I heard, "Take the old road. We'll tell you where to stop."

They made no further remarks. Hearing clicking sounds behind me, I looked in the rear-view mirror and saw The Executioner's assistant pushing bullets into a spare clip. He caught my eye and grinned unpleasantly. I was afraid to say anything in case I uttered some inanely inappropriate remark. The fields we drove past were as deserted as those where my passengers, in the name of revolutionary justice, had killed Villegas.

I shuddered at the thought of being murdered. Did these people really believe they were Rambos destined to enter a revolutionary Valhalla as heroes?

My speculation was broken by the assistant's voice. "Turn into the next field."

He stepped down to open a gate. As I drove through, the clarion song of a bird reminded me of my aunt's promise of help and serenity replaced my trembling.

Thwack! The gate banged shut and the assistant climbed back into the Land Rover. Prodding my shoulder with the barrel of his sten-gun, The Executioner demanded, "What did you think of Villegas?"

"I think he was unwise if he thought to cross you."

"I'm told you've been discussing guerrilla policy. Why?"

"How can the revolutionary council make the right decisions if various opinions aren't discussed? My observations were meant constructively."

"Stop here and get out."

We stood by the Land Rover facing each other.

"Look at me." The Executioner glared malevolently, searching my features for signs of guilt. Faith in my aunt's words gave me the confidence to absorb his aggressive vibes calmly and the tension between us faded away.

"Very well, you can go for now," he muttered. Motioning to his assistant to follow, he continued on foot down the path to the river. I desperately wanted to get away in case they decided to come back but my body started shaking so violently that several minutes passed before I was able to climb into my seat in the Land Rover.

The assassination of Villegas caused the guerrillas an unexpected setback. He had given thousands of cattle in partnership to *campesinos* living in the hills behind Poponte and their families were dependent on this income. When Villegas's widow announced that she was cancelling all contracts and was moving with her children to Barranquilla, the news was met with consternation. No other rancher would risk re-stocking the area, and for this, the *campesinos* blamed The Executioner.

The simmering discontent boiled into rebellion when a schoolmaster had his arm shot off at the elbow by a sten-gun fired by a young guerrilla.

Although The Executioner exonerated the lad on the grounds of a mistaken identity, teachers in the catchment area of Poponte closed their schools in protest. Students, unable to complete the academic year, returned to their parents' farms to wield machetes. A week later Poponte awoke to the sounds of exploding bombs and heavy calibre machine gun fire as three helicopter gunships attacked the guerrilla command-post. Enraged students had told the army where to strike and for once they acted with determination. By midday eighteen guerrillas had been killed. Had the politicians, who dictate army strategy, resolutely backed the teachers' revolt and ordered the offensive to continue, the guerrillas would have been driven out of Poponte. Unfortunately the psychological moment to win the students' permanent allegiance, which neither the army nor the police had ever come anywhere near achieving before, was never recognised. The chance withered away as, unopposed, guerrilla replacements filtered back into the area to reassert their control.

✦ ✦ ✦ ✦

As there was no daily newspaper delivery service to Poponte, my source of information concerning current events was the herdsman's wife who apparently never passed out of earshot of a portable radio. In the middle of a meal, when I was a captive audience, she would appear with it clutched in her hand and report at length the latest guerrilla outrage. Worried that at best we would soon only be displaced persons, she urged me to look for a place where Diccon and Tiggy could take refuge.

Ever since vacationing with the family on the Caribbean coast at Caña Veral, Tiggy and I had thought how pleasant it would be to own a small holding by the sea. Looking for affordable beach property, I had even walked with Lucho from the mouth of the Atrato river at Acandi to Sapsuro on the Panamanian border but had found nothing that suited me. The high tide zone of every bay was littered with non-biodegradable rubbish jettisoned by boats entering or leaving the Canal at Balboa. The coast from the Atrato River to Santa Marta was either barren, exorbitantly expensive or, if there were amenities and fresh water, dominated by guerrillas.

Needing to replace the tyres on the Land Rover, I had asked Lucho to accompany me to Maicao, the contraband town on the Venezuelan border, to buy them. As we drove along the Pan American Highway at the foot of the Sierra Nevada of Santa Marta in an area controlled by the A.U.C., he called my attention to a sign nailed to a gateway leading to the sea. It read "Beach lots

for sale." I stopped, Lucho opened the gate and I drove in. The farm's administrator, Lubin Aguirre, led me to the beach and showed me lots thirty metres
wide by two hundred metres deep of which seventy were swamp.

"Is this all there is?" I enquired disappointedly.

"There's somebody along the coast who wants to sell a coconut grove," he
said. "If you've got time, I'll show it to you."

He took us to a mile of beach backed by ten acres of mature coconuts. A
clear running river, rising in the eighteen thousand foot snow-capped peaks
towering in the background, curled around two sides of the boundary and the
underground water from it, he told us, kept the groundcover verdant even in
the dry season. The paved road allowing access to the property belonged to a
power station which as a gesture of good public relations gave free electricity
to the immediate neighbourhood.

I telephoned Tiggy in Bogotá where she was teaching English in the Berlitz
School of Languages. "I've found the property we've dreamed of. It's in the
Guajira. Can you come now?" Taking a leave of absence she came to see it,
liked what she saw and we bought the property. The only building was a ramshackle hut with a leaking palm leaf roof where the daily collected coconuts
were stored and husked. Wishing to give some of my ranch hands a holiday I
invited them to come and help me put up a more permanent structure where
we would be protected from the elements. It was to be open sided, roofed with
sheets of galvanised iron and have a six by fourteen meter concrete floor.

My Poponte born workmen had only heard about the sea and on arrival
they sank to their knees in the waves to taste the water. Everyone drank from
rivers so why should oceans be salty? At night, large blue land crabs scuttled
under our hammocks looking for things to rip apart, but there was never any
need to protect our belongings from humans. The A.U.C. kept the area free of
both guerrillas and thieves. One could safely leave car keys in the ignition
switch overnight, or go away for the day leaving possessions unguarded and
return at night and find everything intact. After the stress of Bogotá, Tiggy
found the tranquillity of the coconut grove enchanting and resolved to build
a guest house there as a home where one day she would raise a family.

At Curucucú I had become resigned to receiving orders from guerrillas
and so was not unduly disturbed when a summons arrived from Feliz, who
had been appointed leader after the transfer of The Executioner. I braced
myself for what I anticipated would be a demand for yet another contribution,
saddled my horse and rode to the designated rendezvous. To my surprise he

didn't want money, at least not mine. I'd been called to see if I'd be the new intermediary between the wife of a neighbouring rancher whose husband they'd kidnapped—referred to here as Juaquín—and themselves. It was an unenviable proposal. The body of the previous go-between had been found just the week before with a bullet hole between his eyes. Feliz, however, thought I would accept not for my ego but in the hope, that should I ever find myself in the position of Juaquín, someone would remember the Colombian adage, "today for thee, tomorrow for me." As an inducement he promised that for the duration of the negotiations I would be exempted from paying the "*vacuna*" tax but, as he made very clear, my involvement must be discreet, honest and helpful. Hard work, luck, and a flair for business had made Juaquín the owner of five ranches and that, in the eyes of guerrillas, was the crime that justified his abduction.

Juaquín and his wife—whom I shall call "Julia"—had divided their family assets in accordance with Colombian custom. The townhouse and furnishings were in her name and the ranches, together with the cattle and machinery, were in his. Banks were willing to lend a sum of money to Julia related to the commercial value of her home. Loans based on Juaquín's assets were more difficult to negotiate. I had known Juaquín for many years. We had started to ranch about the same time and both of us knew the importance of appearances when soliciting credit. On one occasion when his own shoes had worn through the sole, he had gone to the bank wearing a pair of new boots borrowed from his tractor driver. They were nearly the right size and when the mud was knocked off gave an air of nonchalant financial solidity.

"My application was approved," he told me afterwards with a chuckle. "The manager thought I looked prosperous!"

Remembering the laughs it had caused us I suggested to Julia that if she "borrowed' some of Juaquín's cattle and branded them in such a manner that the bank thought they were hers, they would receive them as collateral.

There's a well meaning Colombian law that forbids paying ransom money to kidnappers. Understandably the reluctance of those negotiating for the life of a relation to obey the injunction makes statistics unreliable.

I must remind readers that at this time cellular telephones had not been invented, house telephones could be tapped or listened to by an operator and the only secure contact was by personal envoy. Julia's health made it impracticable for her to ride into the hills to bargain with her husband's captors. The physical strain and emotional stress would put have her at a disadvantage which the guerrillas would certainly have exploited. She gratefully accepted me as the go-between. Having no sentimental ties with her family, I would be able to negotiate with the impersonal, hard-headed detachment necessary to beat down their demands to an acceptable level.

Recalling the plight of what had happened to the Castano brothers who had paid ransoms only to be handed a corpse, Julia wrote a letter for me to pass on to the guerrillas containing questions that only Juaquín would be able to answer. She had to receive the reply in Juaquín's handwriting before discussions could begin.

Adventurers, claiming to know where Juaquín was being held and offering Julia their services for a fee, constantly pestered. Julia resolutely turned them down. She didn't even trust the *"Gaula"*—the government's "Unified Action Group for Personal Liberty"—whose intervention, she feared, would scare the guerrillas into murdering her husband. Worried that conversations from her telephone was taped, she made important calls from a neighbor's flat. If I was to avoid being traced as her agent we agreed to meet in a restaurant, as if by chance, where we were unlikely to be recognised.

The guerrillas opened with a demand for one thousand million pesos which rolled off the tongue easily but was a preposterous amount to ask in a country where at that time a common laborer was lucky if he earned five thousand pesos a day. I countered by suggesting they work one of Juaquín's ranches but without success. They were interested in receiving money, not in earning it.

"Well," I said, "he can't sell them while he's in captivity. All his wife can raise at the moment is one hundred million."

"That's not a serious offer. Tell her if she wants to see Juaquín alive again, she's got to do better than that," replied Feliz angrily.

"Certainly I'll tell her. I'm only acting as the messenger boy between the two of you, but it seems to me that if you've got someone for sale for whom there's only one possible buyer and you value that person for the amount you're asking, you'd better take good care of him. Your superiors are going to be very upset if he dies."

Every month negotiations came to a standstill while Julia waited for Juaquín's hand written answers to her questions and his confirmation of having received the medicines she'd sent. The guerrillas bridled at these delays. The cost of keeping a hostage in the hills was expensive but, as I pointed out, if they hadn't asked an unrealistic amount to begin with, the ransom would already have been paid. Julia had made it obvious that she was not interested in negotiating for her husband's dead body.

The first month of captivity is always the worst. To maintain a tranquility under a twenty-four hour a day surveillance which denies privacy while bathing, defecating or checking body hairs for lice requires tremendous composure. Dwelling on happy moments of a previous existence may help to pass sleepless hours of the night but facing reality at daybreak can be shattering. Only over a period of months do accustomed niceties diminish in importance.

After six months of haggling the asking price had dropped to half the originally demanded ransom and the offer was up to three hundred million. I took the attitude that were I Juaquín and he was negotiating for me, I would console myself with the thought that during my months of abduction I'd been saved spending five hundred million pesos. Neither of us made a profit anywhere near that amount from our ranches in the corresponding time.

My participation in the negotiation came to an abrupt halt when a note was left on my doorstep by a *campesino* whose wife I had once taken to the hospital in the middle of the night. He had joined the A.U.C. and felt he owed me a favor. My regular trips into the hills for meetings with the guerrillas had been reported to his bosses and my name had been put on the hit list for liquidation. The only hope of rescinding the order was for Julia to explain my actions to his Commander-in-Chief. I telephoned her emergency contact telephone number. Would they please fetch Julia to the phone immediately.

"Julia, I've run into trouble and need some high-powered assistance." I explained my predicament and stressed the urgency by reminding her of the fate of the previous go-between.

"I'll do what I can," she said. "Ring me back in fifteen minutes."

The news was alarming. The Commander-in-Chief was unavailable and a counter-order sent by his deputy would, regrettably, be unlikely to reach the death squad in time to save me. Julia's advice was to get out of the country immediately.

I caught the next plane to California where I stayed with my sister until Julia sent a message that Juaquín was free and it was safe for me to return.

Everybody had wanted a speedy agreement. Juaquín had been held for ten months, forced to travel from one hide-out to another and treated inhumanely. Once when travelling on mule-back down a steep ravine he had suffered such pain from an injury to his spine that he had begged to be shot rather than forced to continue. At one farm he had been so repulsed by being obliged to sleep amongst flea-infested dogs and a pig with suppurating castration sores full of maggots that he had become physically sick.

Arriving at a compromise with the guerrillas between the money demanded and the amount offered, my successor had packed four hundred million pesos of used bank notes into a specially constructed water tight compartment welded inside a fifty-five-gallon fuel barrel. An old lorry making regular deliveries of diesel oil from Barranquilla to outlying farms had passed the barrel to the guerrillas. With the ransom paid, Juaquín returned to manage his ranches.

✦ ✦ ✦ ✦

I was pleased when Diccon, having completed his national service in the Colombian army base of Tolimida, with the distinction of being decorated "the best cadet" of his year, was offered work as a bilingual supervisor in the Drummond* open cast coal mine at La Loma, about ten miles from Poponte. It was comforting to know he was safely nearby. When Jill and I were married we had hoped that one day a son would want to take over the management of Curucucú but the lack of resolve shown by a series of governments to combat guerrillas had made taking on a cattle ranch for a young person an unattractive long term prospect. Coal mines, even open cast pits, have limited long term appeal and moving to Panama to work, as many harassed ranchers were doing, became more and more appealing. The country's dollar currency, based on the income from the Canal and the pledge of United States Government to send in the Army if freedom of passage was ever threatened, favored economic and social stability. Buying land there wouldn't necessarily deprive Diccon of a future on Curucucú. If the situation in Colombia improved, it would be feasible to commute and run both enterprises with managers.

Panama is a small country, small enough to survey from the air in a few hours if all one wants to do is locate well watered and fertile areas with good road access. Diccon and I chartered a small private aeroplane and left Panama City at daybreak. We told the pilot to fly along the Caribbean flank of the central mountain ridge and circle any areas which caught our interest. Near the Costa Rican border we crossed to the Pacific side and re-fueled at the David airstrip. Zigzagging back to Panama City we had a bird's eye view of the Canal and landed where we had started in time for a late lunch. With clear ideas of where to look, Diccon continued his search in a hired car. By the end of a month he had found a farmer willing to sell his cattle and three hundred hectares of undulating pasture watered by two rivers at a pleasant temperature two thousand feet above sea level. It was within our budget and I told him he

---

*An American coal company with world-wide contracts.

could buy it. With Tiggy starting a new life in a niche of her choice, I was happy for Diccon to have a place of his own where he could confidently work in peace. As the seller wanted two months in which to arrange his affairs before handing over the property, there was time for Diccon to keep an eye on the ranch while I took a short holiday in England.

Five days before I was scheduled to leave, a patrol of six guerrilla recruits arrived at Curucucú. They had walked from the valley boundary and were hot, thirsty and exhausted. The possibility of having informal and friendly dialogue while they rested seemed too good to be missed so I made a jug of lemonade and invited them into the dining room where there was a ceiling fan. Seated around the table with their sten-guns balanced on their knees, they started discussing the disparity of wealth in Colombia and the reforms they would like to see made.

I had been told that Marxist conscripts were discouraged from expressing individual points of view but the comments around me were those of young men anywhere searching for ways to establish identities for themselves against the world's indifference. I knew it was hazardous to apply my resolve inspired by Bronowski's book but years of dissembling my feelings or fear of repercussions had to end sometime. Placing the lemonade and glasses on the table I said, "You may decide that I'm a doddering old fool, but I think your conversation is extraordinarily interesting. Not many people take the time to analyze what's wrong with society and think how they can improve it. May I join you?"

Two guerrillas made room for me on the bench and I squeezed between them.

"So you think individuals are important?" I was asked.

"Look at the evidence. Doctors develop medical techniques to transplant organs from a corpse to a living body; computer technicians develop communication technology with fax machines and the e-mail; scientists perfect space crafts which land on other planets, collect rock samples and send back information about them. Composers make marks on paper which are then interpreted by musicians to make profoundly moving sounds. Such individuals do more to vitalise society and are more important to its advancement than men who blindly rely on force to achieve their ends."

"Pah! You're just saying that to protect your privileged life style. Advancing society demands unity and sacrifice."

"Not all unities endure and not all sacrifices are worthwhile. Russian revolutionaries sacrificed their very lives for Communism believing it would lead to an egalitarian society but their dreams turned to dust when the government was discredited by *Peristroika*."

"What are you getting at?"

"That the only political parties which thrive are those which are periodically voted out of office. The aspirations of society change. When Carl Marx incited the world with his revolutionary theory workers were virtually serfs, now they're middle class citizens. Most people today own a wrist watch, have a television set, send their children to school neatly dressed and have access to a heath clinic. Political theorists who fail to adapt dogmas formulated a hundred years ago cannot hope to win the backing of men and women experiencing the benefits of a technological revolution."

"You're somebody who should be shot," retorted one of the guerrillas.

"You could do that but would shooting me do your cause any good? It's easy to kill men but impossible to kill ideas. Ideas pass imperceptibly from one mind to another and, when found to be beneficial, spread to all mankind."

"You may have benefited, but what've we got?"

"Look above you and appreciate the ceiling fan. Somebody had the idea of probing the forces of electricity, another used that knowledge to devise an electric motor and someone else attached blades and here we are enjoying the fruits of their inspiration. Nobody should just accept the work of others. We should all try to leave society something of value to be remembered by."

"You don't think our revolution admirable?"

"Not in the way it's practised. Colombians aren't benefited by dynamited bridges, toppled power pylons, highjacked banks, random kidnapping and mined paths that blow the legs off children. Most civilised people consider such things barbarous."

"But if we don't obey orders what do we do?"

"Be creative in a worthwhile occupation. History is full of the follies, conceits and cruelties of mankind. As we judge past generations by their actions; future generations will judge us by ours. I believe that responsibility for what one does cannot be evaded by claiming that one did what one did under orders."

One of the guerrillas raised a hesitant finger and I nodded to him to speak.

"You seem to be telling us that it's not so much what our organisation tells us to do, but what we do as individuals that's important. We're told that revolutionary victory can only be won if we are all united behind our leader. Are you suggesting that he's wrong, or that the class struggle should be abandoned?"

"I suggest that attempting to alter society by force perpetuates violence. Before you try to change society examine the methods you use. Compassion, kindness and tolerance are contagious and constructively influence the way people react to one another."

The jug was empty but, as I rose to refill it, I was stopped by the tone of a request. "I'm told to fight, but now I'm confused. How should I fight and what for?"

"Be an example of the sane and just society you wish to create, a society where people smile at each other and are glad to be alive. It's human nature to disagree but where people like us discuss opinions peacefully fighting will no longer be necessary."

Late that afternoon they climbed on to a trailer and I drove them with the tractor to the ranch boundary. They were debating the pros and cons of revolutionary tactics as they walked off into the dusk.

Two days later I rode into the hills and informed the guerrilla commander that I was going to England for a holiday and would like to pay my "*vacuna*'" before leaving. We agreed on a list of supplies and I had them delivered.

FOURTEEN

A Fresh Journey

*Creation is a continuous process and the process itself is the actuality
since no sooner do you arrive than you start on a fresh journey.*

—Professor A.N. Whitehead, "Dialogues"

On the eleventh of August, 1999, a week after my arrival in Devon, Diccon telephoned to tell me that guerrillas had arrived at Curucucú, saddled our horses and used them to drive away four hundred head of cattle. He didn't know if a cocaine laboratory had been blown up and they had been ordered to recoup their losses by seizing whatever was easily available or whether taking the ranch cattle was a reprisal for my trying to subvert recruits. As other Colombian-born ranchers had been being similarly treated, the reason was not due to my English background.

Diccon rang again on the following day with a message from the F.A.R.C. commander: "Send me forty million pesos and I'll return the cattle. If I don't receive the money within fifteen days, your ranch buildings will be dynamited."

"What are we going to do Dad? There's no way we can raise a sum like that in two weeks. Even if we could, they'd come back for more. Guerrilla demands never stop."

I had a deep love for the homestead's aura of harmony which had sustained me for forty-two years and could think of only one desperately risky course of action which might save it from being destroyed by blasts of dynamite. If, by doing nothing I lost everything I'd be haunted by a sense of betrayal for the rest of my life. The F.A.R.C. clearly intended to squeeze us until we were bankrupt and it was time for us to go but if all they found were gutted buildings, surely they'd be satisfied with their dominance. Blowing them up would then be an expensive and pointless caprice. I gritted my teeth and gave the order.

"Son, the buildings have got to be completely emptied and the ranch abandoned. Save what you can. Get trusted ranch hands to help you. Start quietly and immediately. If the F.A.R.C. get wind of what you're doing, we'll lose everything."

Adriano took charge of bringing the best of the remaining cattle to the corral as if for a routine vaccination while Diccon arranged with known lorry drivers to be ready at a designated rendezvous to transport them to hired pasture beyond the F.A.R.C.'s grasp where they could be sold. Lucho hired a low loader lorry from a contractor in Chiriguana and on the trailer he stacked the four-wheel-drive tractor with its implements, the light plant, tools, roof sheeting, furniture, doors I'd made, seasoned wood from the store room and anything else that would fit. Diccon found the responsibility of sorting personal possessions—which to save and which to burn—emotionally searing. There were no storage facilities in Chiriguana. He didn't dare give things away to friends in the village for fear of of alerting guerrilla agents. To destroy family items of sentimental value seemed a sacrilege. To leave them for scavengers to ransack, as soon as it was known that the ranch had been abandoned, irresponsible. He marked keepsakes for special friends and hoped his wishes would be respected.

In one coordinated afternoon, Adriano, Diccon, Lucho and Sofanor risked their lives by removing everything portable of value from Curucucú. Had they been apprehended by a guerrilla patrol they would probably have been shot. Adriano and his loyal cowboys herded the cattle and horses down the riverbed—where their hoof prints would be washed away—and loaded them up an earth ramp into the waiting lorries. Lucho, accompanied by Sofanor, drove the low loader and Diccon the ranch's laden pickup truck to Tiggy's coconut grove on the Caribbean coast two hundred miles away. Fortunately, years of counting on Curucucú's compliance had lulled the guerrillas into carelessness and the escape, at the time, passed unnoticed.

✦ ✦ ✦ ✦

I had never joined a private pension scheme. It had seemed perfectly obvious to me that a better income could be derived by investing money in cows that produced calves. In time their sale would ensure my comfortable retirement.

My failure to include F.A.R.C. incursions in my calculations caused a reappraisal of my retirement plans. Living in Devon was now beyond my means and I decided to add a kitchen, bedroom, and bathroom to the open sided construction in Tiggy's coconut grove near where she and her partner Lubin were opening a guest-house. My Poponte companions were settling nearby and would be neighbours. Adriano, with the help of his family, opened a saloon bar where locals found they could play *tejo*, billiards and dominos while drinking beer to background music of recorded Vallenato songs. Lucho, with the percentage he earned from contracting the equipment brought from the ranch married Anna Julia and purchased a three bedroom residence. Using the seasoned hard wood brought from Curucucú, a local boat builder made me a fishing launch and Sofanor, having apprenticed himself for three months to a local fisherman, captained the boat as my associate. Accompanied by two experienced locals and guided by a solar navigator he goes to sea at two o'clock every morning to catch red snapper.

I found the Caribbean shoreline delightful and for miles on either side of my new home I met honest people working in peace under the watchful eye of the A.U.C. Although the government officially described me as a "displaced person," when I compared my living conditions to refugee camps in other countries I considered myself extremely fortunate.

A flexible outlook on life helps in adjusting to the uncertainties of the Guajira. When the outboard motor needed an overhaul I took Sofanor to the distributor's workshop in Santa Marta so that he could learn how to change spare parts. Spending a couple of days there was an agreeable prospect. Thanks to the A. U. C., the town's petty thieves had either reformed, been shot or gone elsewhere. People left their cars unattended in front of their houses— an unthinkable risk in Bogotá—and we parked the pick-up over-night in the street near the hotel without mishap. At some early hour of the morning guerrilla forces attacked the A.U.C. command centre in the hills above the road between Santa Marta and Tiggy's coconut grove. Unaware of the raging battle, we started back midday with Sofanor driving. A muscle in my neck had been bothersome and having made a scarf out of a piece of red flannel from the tool box I had gone to sleep with my head resting on the window frame. No one had told me that battling guerrillas identify themselves with red kerchiefs so as not to be shot by their own side. The noise of a car tearing past the pick-up woke me. It screeched to a halt a few yards down the road disgorging what looked to me like a bunch of hoodlums brandishing revolvers and making signs for us to stop.

"Sofa, step on the gas. NOW!" I yelled.

He changed gear, trod on the accelerator and with a mighty roar from the V8 engine, the pick-up leapt towards the startled men. Bullets shattered the windscreen and ricocheted off the bodywork, but miraculously we passed through the fusillade unwounded. Looking in the rear view mirror I could see our would-be assassins scrambling into their car and starting after us. We tore down the road towards the next town where, to our joy, we spied an army check point.

"There're gangsters following us" I shouted as we screeched to a stop. "Look at the bullet marks."

At that moment our pursuers came into view. Seeing us talking to the army, they executed a professionally skidded U-turn and raced back the way they'd come.

"Chasing you were they?" tut-tutted the soldier who asked to see our identity cards. "You're lucky we're here." Looking at my scarf he added, "That car is used by paramilitaries. They probably mistook you for escaping guerrillas. If I were you I'd get rid of that rag. You'll live longer if you do."

I took the soldier's advice and we drove on sobered by how nearly we had become two more statistics in Colombia's complicated and bloody civil war. When Lubin relayed apologies from the A.U.C. for the fright they'd given us, I meekly accepted them. No compensation for damages was offered. Sofanor and I were lucky to be alive and should be grateful that the roads were kept free from roving guerrillas!

No one, of course, is ever completely safe wherever they live. Months after I had been accepted as a harmless—albeit somewhat eccentric—newcomer, I was roused from a deep sleep by an insistent tapping on my bedroom door.

"Don Ben, Don Ben, wake up. We must talk to you."

During my years on Curucucú, *campesinos* needing my help to take a sick relation to the hospital in Chiriguana had often sought my assistance in the middle of the night. Imagining that I was being woken with a similar request I got out of bed, slid back the bolt, and rubbing the sleep from my eyes stepped into the starlight.

"How can I help you?"

An arm slid around my neck and I felt the barrel of a gun rammed under my chin.

"*Quieto*—stay still," a man growled.

I had, on occasion, thought what I'd do in such circumstances and reacted with premeditated resolve. My right hand jerked the barrel to one side and my left elbow rammed into the midriff of my assailant causing him to gasp for breath. As I reached down to grab his testicles, his buddy thwacked a heavy stick across my ribs. I roared in pain and fell to the ground. Fortunately for me my attackers lacked professionalism. Fearing that Tiggy or Lubin, whose bedroom was in another building about fifty yards away, might have heard my scream and come to investigate, they fled into the night. I crawled painfully back into my bedroom, bolted the door and spent the next few hours writhing in agony.

The following morning, after Tiggy had bandaged my rib cage, I sent word of what had happened to the A.U.C. with satisfactory results. They learned from their village contacts that the culprits had planned to capture and take me to the nearest F.A.R.C. base in the hope of making a quick sale. The guerrillas would have had the means to keep me hidden until a ransom was paid.

$$\text{\it ✄ ✄ ✄ ✄}$$

Forty-seven years of living in Colombia had taught me to accept most ups and downs philosophically but Lucho's violent death shook me. Our initial respect for each other had grown into a friendship where we were always pleased when we met, always ready to help and always happy when the other prospered. I saw him for the last time on the beach. Heavy surf had prevented the boat from going to sea for a week and to relieve my crew's boredom we were roasting pieces of goat skewered on green saplings around a drift-wood bonfire.

"*Hola*, Lucho. It's good to see you. Everything under control?"

"No, not really. I need your advice. Can we talk alone?" he said.

"Of course."

We walked to an isolated dune beyond the reach of the crashing wave's spume flecked eddies that surged along the shore and sat down.

"This is as private a place to talk as any. What's troubling you?" I asked.

"My job. I accepted a contract to service the light plant in the cocaine lab up in the hills."

"Why?"

"Because I'd run out of money and they pay well. Clients asking for the tractor to prepare land wanted to pay with the harvest. You know I'm not a coward but for the first time in my life I'm afraid. If the lab was attacked for its cocaine I could be stupidly murdered."

"Oh Lucho, Lucho, Lucho." I shook my head not knowing what to answer nor seeing an easy way out. "If I lend you some money can you quit?"

"If I didn't show up and the generator failed, I'd be shot by the guys who hired me. There's too much money involved for them to forgive anyone letting them down."

"O.K. Say you've got to go because your mother's dying. That way you can leave without giving notice."

Lucho shook his head. "They'd soon find out I was lying. Oh shit!" Lucho's features crumpled as if possessed by a dreadful premonition. "Ben, if anything happens to me, will you keep an eye on Anna Julia and my children?"

"Buck up, Lucho. Anything I could do for them would be a pleasure."

A week later seven bodies, massacred by the E.L.N. in a brutal attack to steal crystalline cocaine from the laboratory, were brought down from the hills. Lucho's head was so disfigured by machine gun bullets that his skull had to be filled out with balls of crumpled newspaper for his face to be recognized.

Ninety people attended his funeral and their donations paid to render the walls of his house with cement and lay tiles on the floor. With my help Anna Julia converted a front room into a general store and became self supporting.

✦ ✦ ✦ ✦

In August, 2005, The A.U.C. invited Diccon and myself to join the Poponte annual three-day fiesta. We accepted apprehensively for while we understood that the A.U.C. controlled the village we knew that the F.A.R.C. controlled the surrounding countryside. However, it was a chance to see Curucucú again and Adriano and Sofanor, who had relations in the village they wanted to visit, said they'd accompany us. The fiesta would have been more fun had the pall of apprehension caused by F.A.R.C.'s presence in the neighbourhood not cast a spell over the villager's efforts to celebrate. In the mornings, mothers carried on the tradition of bringing babies born in the previous year to the church to be baptised and when the midday heat subsided villagers gathered around a corral for the traditional bullfight. In the evening they danced in the street to amplified music. When old acquaintances asked if we'd come back to stay, we had to reply, "Not yet." The risk of stepping on one of the F.A.R.C. anti-personnel mines buried on trails leading into the hills and along river beds, the fate of a fisherman and his boy who had bled to death after their legs had been blown off and the report of finding the two sons on the farm of a prominent backer of the A.U.C. with their hands tied behind their backs and their throats slit, made any other answer impossible.

We were allowed to go to Curucucú twice, but only after scouts sent by the A.U.C. had reported that no F.A.R.C. patrols were in the area. Although accompanied by a heavily armed escort I was eager to see the homestead again. Happily the buildings were still standing but on that first visit I was overcome by the impression of desolation. Weeds grew in empty doorways, screen mesh once covering window frames hung in shreds and termite trails ascended to nests in the roof. Walls were in need of repair, the garden neglected and the fields unkempt. The hour allotted to us for our visit didn't give time to even begin tackling the most urgent tasks. Among the debris left by scavengers in the barn were two broken rocking chairs made by Crisanto.

"Those at least can be mended," said Diccon, and put them in the back of the pick-up.

Our silence as we drove back to the village was unnoticed by the body guards chatting eagerly about their return to the fiesta.

I didn't sleep well that night and it was not until the sunrise that I perked up with the realization that empty doorways, tattered window mesh and termite trails had probably helped to dissuade the guerrillas from using their precious dynamite to blow up the buildings. The titles to the ranch were still held by the family and if what I'd built crumbled it would clear the way for someone to start afresh without disturbing the homestead's special aura. To wallow in self pity and recriminations would negate the years of immense satisfaction that Curucucú had given me. Life on the ranch hadn't been an escape from reality, life there had taught me what reality is. I felt privileged to have lived in Poponte at a time before technical gadgetry lessened the satisfaction achieved by personal endeavour.

Hoping to rediscover the sense of harmony that I'd missed on the previous day, as the dawn broke I left my bodyguard sleeping and returned through my fields to the homestead. As I sat on the stone in the stream where I had so often philosophised, the ranch as I'd known it five years previously appeared in my mind's eye and I knew that my life at Curucucú had not been wasted. With the help of friends and the loyal support of Jill and the children something beautiful had been created that hadn't been there before. A feeling of serenity engulfed me, a serenity unaffected by the state of bricks and mortar, but emanating from the sound of running water and the familiar earth, trees, rocks and wild animals surrounding me

Sometime in the future Diccon or a grandson might plough the overgrown fields and plant African Oil Palms. The guerrillas might have found taking cattle away easy. They'll have their work cut out to take away trees.

Unbidden, two lines from one of Dag Hammarskjöld's haikus came to mind:

> *For all that has been, thanks*
> *For all that will be, "Yes"*

And I smiled.

Postscript

Since the A.U.C. disbanded several years ago, Diccon and I have fleetingly returned to Curucucú to oversee the planting of oil palms—trips made possible due to the improved social security in Colombia for which we credit President Alvaro Uribe's "Plan Colombia" financed by the United States. However. the continued presence of small bands of roving guerrillas in the hills behind Poponte, who, when chased by the Colombian army, cross over the nearby border into Venezuela for protection with Hugo Chaves and return when it's safe to do so, make visiting the ranch for longer periods an unacceptable risk. The prospect of being kidnapped and forced to give a lifetime of savings in ransom money to an organization undermining the country that allowed us to become citizens causes us to tread warily. Nevertheless, the abandoned buildings are being slowly restored and friends have rented pasture for their cattle.

I'm grateful for having followed *The road less travelled by*. The adventures experienced along the way were "right" at the time and have given me a life that still, I wouldn't change for anyone's.

Ben Curry
June 2010

Author's Note

C ritics have asked how, after a lapse of some forty odd years, I could possibly remember, verbatim, the technical remarks of Professor Schultes found in Chapter Five. If I couldn't, did I make them up? My answer is that I kept a diary where I jotted down things of interest. The fact is that spoken words faithfully transcribed onto a printed page seldom encourage the discerning reader to read on. To keep the reader's interest while relaying the essence of remarks made in my presence, I took the liberty, whenever necessary, of both rephrasing comments and editing verbiage. Events and words which I neither personally witnessed or heard in Chapter Eleven have been confirmed by friends in Poponte as being, in essence, accurate.

CPSIA information can be obtained at www.ICGtesting.com
Printed in the USA
BVOW011001140612

292672BV00007B/37/P